Lecture Notes in Computer Science

Lecture Notes in Artificial Intelligence 16227

Founding Editor

Jörg Siekmann

Series Editors

Randy Goebel, *University of Alberta, Edmonton, Canada*
Wolfgang Wahlster, *DFKI, Berlin, Germany*
Zhi-Hua Zhou, *Nanjing University, Nanjing, China*

The series Lecture Notes in Artificial Intelligence (LNAI) was established in 1988 as a topical subseries of LNCS devoted to artificial intelligence.

The series publishes state-of-the-art research results at a high level. As with the LNCS mother series, the mission of the series is to serve the international R & D community by providing an invaluable service, mainly focused on the publication of conference and workshop proceedings and postproceedings.

Alicia Vidler · Samarth Swarup
Editors

Multi-Agent-Based Simulation XXVI

26th International Workshop, MABS 2025
Detroit, MI, USA, May 19, 2025
Revised Selected Papers

 Springer

Editors
Alicia Vidler
Bar-Ilan University
Ramat-Gan, Israel

Samarth Swarup
University of Virginia
Charlottesville, VA, USA

ISSN 0302-9743   ISSN 1611-3349 (electronic)
Lecture Notes in Artificial Intelligence
ISBN 978-3-032-16327-1   ISBN 978-3-032-16328-8 (eBook)
https://doi.org/10.1007/978-3-032-16328-8

LNCS Sublibrary: SL7 – Artificial Intelligence

This Springer imprint is published by the registered company Springer Nature Switzerland AG
The registered company address is: Gewerbestrasse 11, 6330 Cham, Switzerland

Preface

Multi-Agent-Based Simulation (MABS) is a framework for using simulation to support policy and decision-making across domains. It brings together multi-agent systems engineers, simulation researchers, and scholars in the social, economic, and organizational sciences. The MABS workshop series convenes communities that build multi-agent systems and those that model social, socio-ecological, and socio-technical processes. In this setting, agent-based theories, metaphors, models, analyses, experiments, studies, and methodological principles meet in simulation to explain and predict, test hypotheses, and improve designs and systems.

This book constitutes the refereed post-workshop proceedings of the 26th International Workshop on Multi-Agent-Based Simulation (MABS 2025), which took place in Detroit, USA on May 19th, 2025, in conjunction with the 24th International Conference on Autonomous Agents and Multi-Agent Systems (AAMAS). This year's workshop focused on the advances that multi-agent systems can make in real-world problem domains. The papers collected here reflect current advances in modeling methodologies and domain applications, showing how agent-based simulation supports clear reasoning about complex systems and practical questions faced by decision-makers. The papers went through a rigorous double-blind review process, with each paper receiving at least two independent reviews.

The papers in this volume are gathered into four themes. First, conceptual and AI-assisted modeling: biological metaphors are used to frame robust coordination, and two studies employ language models to approximate strategic reasoning and to turn simulation traces into narratives that aid interpretation. Second, public policy and institutions: models of social service allocation, organ-donation design, administrative corruption, and crisis-cell decision-making in flash floods use ABM as a testbed for rules, incentives, and operational choices. Third, markets and engineered systems: a bond-market study analyses shifting power and aversion in bilateral exchange, and an end-to-end UAV multi-agent simulator shows how ABM links control mission-level behavior. Fourth, methods and foundations: work on multilayer-network simulation, synthetic-population construction, and cooperation via tags and group selection advances scalability, realism, and explanatory mechanisms.

The workshop could not have taken place without the contribution of numerous individuals. We extend our gratitude to the authors for their high-quality submissions, to the Program Committee and external reviewers for their careful and constructive evaluations, to the AAMAS organizers for hosting the workshop, and to all participants for the engaged discussions that strengthened the final versions of the papers included here.

October 2025

Alicia Vidler
Samarth Swarup

Organization

General and Program Chairs

Alicia Vidler   University of New South Wales, Australia
Samarth Swarup   University of Virginia, USA

Steering Committee

Frédéric Amblard   University of Toulouse, France
Luis Antunes   University of Lisbon, Portugal
Paul Davidsson   Malmö University, Sweden
Emma Norling   University of Sheffield, UK
Mario Paolucci   National Research Council, Italy
Jaime Simão Sichman   University of São Paulo, Brazil
Samarth Swarup   University of Virginia, USA
Takao Terano   Tokyo Institute of Technology, Japan
Harko Verhagen   Stockholm University, Sweden

Program Committee

Liu Yang   Southeast University, China
Fabian Lorig   Malmö University, Sweden
Benoit Gaudou   Université de Toulouse, France
Nicolas Verstaevel   Université Toulouse 1 Capitole, France
Neil Yorke-Smith   Delft University of Technology, Netherlands
Emma Norling   University of Sheffield, UK
Harko Verhagen   Stockholm University, Sweden
Klaus Troitzsch   University of Koblenz-Landau, Germany
Rajith Vidanaarachchi   University of Melbourne, Australia
Fred Amblard   IRIT - University Toulouse 1 Capitole, France
Jean-Pierre Muller   CIRAD, France
Shah Jamal Alam   Habib University, Pakistan
Loïs Vanhée   Umeå University, Sweden
Bruce Edmonds   Manchester Metropolitan University Business School, UK
Marco Janssen   Arizona State University, USA

Samarth Swarup	University of Virginia, USA
Alicia Vidler	University of New South Wales, Australia
Fjalar de Haan	University of Melbourne, Australia
Bill Kennedy	George Mason University, USA
Paulo Novais	University of Minho, Portugal
Sung-Bae Chao	Yonsei University, South Korea
Jason Thompson	University of Melbourne, Australia
Gustavo Giménez-Lugo	Federal University of Technology-Paraná, Brazil
Ruth Meyer	Ernst Mach Institut, Germany
Nick Gotts	.
Natalie Van Der Wal	Delft University of Technology, The Netherlands
Elizabeth Sklar	University of Lincoln, UK

Contents

Conceptual and AI-assisted Modeling

Insects and Agents: Extending the Metaphor 3
  H. Van Dyke Parunak

Approximating Human Strategic Reasoning with LLM-Enhanced
Recursive Reasoners Leveraging Multi-agent Hypergames 15
  Vince Trencsenyi, Agnieszka Mensfelt, and Kostas Stathis

Automatic Generation of ABM Narratives Using Simulation Traces
and LLM 28
  Zenith Arnejo, Benoit Gaudou, Mehdi Saqalli, and Nathaniel Bantayan

Public Policy and Institutions

Agent-Based Modelling for Public Social Service Distribution 45
  Petra Ahrweiler, Nigel Gilbert, Martha Bicket, Albert Sabater Coll,
  Elisabeth Spaeth, Hassan Bashiri, Ebin Deni Raj,
  and Blanca Luque Capellas

Using Agent-Based Social Simulations to Inform Organ Donation
Policymaking: Adopting the Spanish Approach in Sweden 59
  Bertilla Fabris, Jason Tucker, and Fabian Lorig

An Agent-Based Model of Administrative Corruption in Hierarchical
Organisations 77
  Bertold B. Kovács and Neil Yorke-Smith

Assessing the Impact of Crisis Cell Decisions During Flash Flood 89
  Elisa Cueille, Déborah Bodini, Benoit Gaudou, Delphine Grancher,
  Pierre Nicolle, Olivier Payrastre, Manon Prédhumeau, Isabelle Ruin,
  Galateia Terti, and Nicolas Verstaevel

Markets and Engineered Systems

Shifting Power: Leveraging LLMs to Simulate Human Aversion in ABMs
of Bilateral Financial Exchanges, A Bond Market Study 107
  Alicia Vidler and Toby Walsh

MODIFLY: A Scalable End-to-End Multi-agent Simulation for Unmanned
Aerial Vehicles 128
   Jeremy Cofield, Umer Siddique, and Yongcan Cao

Methods and Foundations

MultiRepast4py: A Framework for Agent-Based Simulations on Multilayer
Networks 143
   Keng-Lien Lin and Parinaz Naghizadeh

Adjustable Attribute Matching in Digital Similars of Populations 158
   Kazi Ashik Islam, S. S. Ravi, Henning S. Mortveit, and Samarth Swarup

Use of Tags and Group Selection to Engender Cooperation in n-Player
Snowdrift Game 170
   William Pittenger, Ethan Beaird, and Sandip Sen

Author Index 183

Conceptual and AI-assisted Modeling

Insects and Agents: Extending the Metaphor

H. Van Dyke Parunak[(✉)]

ABC Research, Ann Arbor, MI 48104, USA
`van.parunak@gmail.com`

Abstract. Social insects were an early inspiration for work on multi-agent systems, and continue to provide parsimonious design patterns for models of decentralized coordination. But the original stigmergic pattern has limitations in accommodating intelligent environments and learning agents, including such socially relevant problems as opinion dynamics. This paper describes an insect example, long-range migration, that goes beyond these limitations. We present a simple formalization of the original stigmergic schema, and inspired by migratory insects, show how it can be extended to accommodate systems that the original stigmergic schema could not handle.

Keywords: Stigmergy · Biomimetics · Learning · Evolution · Modeling Technologies

1 Introduction

In 1959, the French biologist Pierre-Paul Grassé coined the term "stigmergy" to describe how social insects (originally, termites) coordinate their actions by leaving and responding to signs in a shared environment [15].[1] Fig. 1 [23] illustrates the basic schema, which is adequate to explain the emergence of the complex architecture of termite hills, as well as path planning and nest sorting by ants: agents coordinate their behavior by making and sensing changes in a shared environment. The canonical example of these changes is the deposit of pheromones (marker-based stigmergy) [29], though changes in the physical structure of the task itself (sematectonic stigmergy [25,36], as in construction of a honeycomb) is also documented. In this schema, while the agent's actions can change the state

---

[1] The term "environment" in a stigmergic system has a different meaning than in multiagent systems engineering [35]. In the agents community in the early 2000's, the awareness of the importance of something other than the agents in implementing an MAS was partly inspired by awareness of stigmergic environments. However, an agent environment as developed in [35] is middleware that mediates the access of agents to resources, such as communications. In terms of the classic OSI reference model [39], such an environment is at a lower layer than the agents. In a stigmergic architecture, both agents and environment are generally at the top, or application, layer.

© The Author(s), under exclusive license to Springer Nature Switzerland AG 2026
A. Vidler and S. Swarup (Eds.): MABS 2025, LNAI 16227, pp. 3–14, 2026.
https://doi.org/10.1007/978-3-032-16328-8_1

of the environment, the agent's state (for example, whether it is carrying something) changes only by actions of the agent, and is not affected by the dynamics
of the environment.

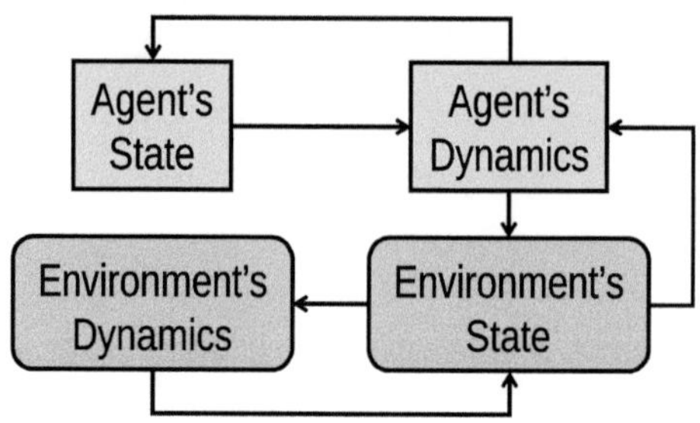

Fig. 1. The classic stigmergic schema.

Early AI researchers observed that coordinated insect behavior had many
parallels with human behavior. Herb Simon was not controversial when he wrote
[31],

> An ant, viewed as a behaving system, is quite simple. The apparent com-
> plexity of its behavior over time is largely a reflection of the complexity of
> the environment in which it finds itself.

But many would pause over his comment a few pages later,

> Human beings, viewed as behaving systems, are quite simple. The appar-
> ent complexity of our behavior over time is largely a reflection of the
> complexity of the environment in which we find ourselves.

Stigmergy has been identified in human coordination [3,19,38] and imitated
in agent-based software, not only to model insect behavior [6,29] and control
robots [4,28,30], but also (drawing more directly on Simon's insight) to generate
psychologically realistic human behaviors in a social model, represented as a
causal graph that agents stigmergically explore [22]. It also finds application in
telecommunications [34] and logistics [12], among other areas.

Previous applications of stigmergy are distinctly asymmetric. Agents change
the state of their local environment, but the local environment does not change
the state of the agents. The asymmetry of classic stigmergy makes it inappro-
priate for modeling important phenomena. For example, in classic stigmergy,

- The environment learns from the agents (that is, agents can change the environment's state), but agents do not learn from the environment.
- Information can propagate in the environment (e.g., pheromone propagation),
  but information propagation among agents (as in social influence models [13])
  is not supported.

Closer attention to some interesting insect behaviors (such as long-distance migration) suggests that even insect systems may require modeling the effect of the environment on agent state. Our agenda in this paper is to use these systems to define a symmetric version of stigmergy that can further inspire computational multi-agent architectures, as classic stigmergy did an earlier generation of agent researchers.

Section 2 presents an insect behavior that requires symmetric stigmergy. Then Sect. 3 sketches formal models of both classic (asymmetric) and symmetric stigmergy, pointing out how the extended model is a useful abstraction not only of migrating insects, but of behaviors of higher-level agents as well. Section 4 outlines directions for further research that build on and extend the concept.

2   The Inspiration: Insect Migration

In the study of social insects, the concept of stigmergy has been a powerful tool in explaining how complex behavior can arise among agents with limited computational resources. Grassé's original application was to cooperative nest building by termites, but simulations have shown that the process can also explain path formation in foraging [14] and inter-nest travel [2], nest sorting [5,10], and task allocation [7,32,33]. Classic stigmergy also offers one of the best known heuristics for the traveling salesperson problem [12]. In spite of these successes, the classic stigmergic schema cannot model some impressive insect behaviors.

Some insect species conduct annual migrations that span thousands of km. Two of the best-known and most studied are the desert locust (*Schistocerca gregaria*), in which as many as 10^{11} insects [27] traverse distances on the order of 5000 km [1] between Africa and the Middle East, and the Monarch butterfly (*Danaus plexippus*), with swarms of 10^8 insects [27] traveling 3800 km [1] between summer grounds in Canada and wintering quarters in Mexico. While path formation is a common stigmergic task, no one imagines that these insects, flying tens or hundreds of meters above the ground, deposit and sense pheromones on the terrain they cross, or that such deposits could reliably persist from one year's migration to the next.

Reviewing this behavior suggests that an extended, symmetric version of the stigmergic schema can in fact explain it. We organize our review around three questions that such migrations present:

1. How can such small creatures find their way and resource their travel over such vast distances?
2. In both of these species (and some other migratory animals as well), no single individual completes the entire journey. Members of the swarm reproduce as they move. How is the navigational knowledge required to make the journey communicated between generations?
3. How does a species develop the navigational knowledge that leads to successful migrations?

Navigational mechanisms (question 1) have been extensively studied, and though many questions remain [18], several mechanisms have been identified.

The overall trajectory of the migration tends to maintain a consistent compass bearing, suggesting that the insects orient themselves, either magnetically or by sensing the azimuth of the sun (with temporal correction depending on the time of day). Evidence exists for both mechanisms, including neuronal circuits for combining circadian rhythms with vision to provide time-of-day corrected solar information [26], and evidence that the animals (at least Monarchs) carry biologically-synthesized magnetic particles [17].

Two additional factors come into play, at least with some species [8]. First, preference for avoiding mountain ranges (e.g., in the case of Monarch butterflies, the Appalachians) can direct different populations of the same species to different destinations. Second, insect flight differs dramatically below and above the Flight Boundary Layer (FBL). Below this altitude, wind speeds are generally lower than flying speed, so that insects can actively choose their own direction. Above this layer, the insects are carried by the prevailing winds, which can vary by altitude and season. Thus, if an insect knows what direction it wants to go, it can change altitude until it finds winds in the right direction. Studies of swarms with radar show that they do indeed preferentially choose wind streams conducive to their itinerary.

In species such as locusts that require food sources as they travel, we can imagine that terrain features other than mountains (e.g., availability of green plants) may also shape the direction of travel.

In homing in on the final destination, it has been speculated [18] that visual terrain cues, or even olfactory signals left in favorite trees by the previous year's occupants, may play a role.

Except in the last proposal for homing in on favorite trees, classic stigmergy cannot explain these behaviors. We know of no mechanism by which insects can mark the terrain over which they fly or the altitude that they prefer in a way that would be accessible to other individuals. The fact that a single journey may span multiple generations (question 2) suggests that the agents carry a simple genetic recipe for combining local environmental features to guide their behavior. The fully sequenced genome of the Monarch shows DNA sequences that can be clearly associated with migratory mechanisms [37].

With our attention focused on the agents' genomes, the answer to question 3 seems obvious: a given species *evolves* a successful genome for completing the journey. Numerous studies explore the evolutionary drivers for migratory behavior [1,16]. That is, the agents learn from the environment, through evolution, which combinations of clues lead to a completed journey, and which do not.

In the case of locusts or butterflies, the learning mechanism is binary. If the local environment supports the needs of the organism at that phase of the journey (for forage, reproduction, and shelter, both along the journey and at the final destination), the agent and its genome survive. If the local environment is not supportive, the insect dies. Thus the local environment, through evolutionary dynamics, changes the state of the insect (in this case, of the genome that guides the insect's behavior). Put crudely, the local environment either kills the insect (depleting its genome in the population) or supports its continued movement toward the goal (thus contributing to the propagation of the successful genome).

More complex organisms support more sophisticated and nuanced mechanisms for learning from experience, and these would also be supported by symmetric stigmergy. For instance, task specialization in leaf-cutter ants can be explained by stigmergy extended with evolutionary learning from the environment [11]. Our point is that it is natural for agents to learn from their interactions with the environment, and that this learning constitutes modification of the agent's state by the environment, an extension beyond the classic asymmetric stigmergic schema. The example of insect migration shows that even without access to sophisticated learning mechanisms, any organism whose behavior is governed by its DNA can learn from its interactions with the local environment, and analyses of behavior that ignore this impact of the environment on the agent are less powerful than they could be.

Figure 2 illustrates the resulting schema, which differs from that in Fig. 1 in having an additional arrow from environmental dynamics to agent state. In the classic model, environmental dynamics are restricted to things such as pheromone evaporation and dispersion, but the example of migrating butterflies suggests that it is meaningful to think of the environment as acting directly on agents (by killing them, and thus removing their genomes from the population, or by supporting them, allowing them to survive and pass on their genomes). Of course, more sophisticated learning mechanisms may also alter the agent state in response to environmental dynamics. Whatever the mechanism, it is both reasonable and useful to view learning as a change in agent state stimulated by what happens in the environment.

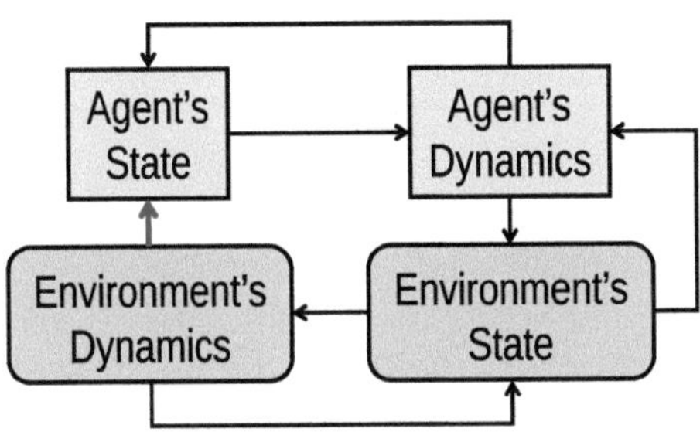

Fig. 2. The symmetric stigmergic schema.

3   Architectural Models

A simple formalism may make these ideas more precise.

3.1 Conventional Stigmergy

Classic stigmergy (e.g., ant path planning using pheromones) can be summarized with the following model:

- A set $A : a_0, a_1, \ldots, a_n$ of agents, each with state as_i and location al_i
- A set $E : e_0, e_1, \ldots, e_m$ of environmental locations, each with state es_i
- An agent location function $AL(t) : A \to E$
- An agent movement function $AM : AL(t) \to AL(t+1)$
- An environmental adjacency relation $ea \subseteq E \times E$
- An environmental neighborhood function $N_E : E \to E' \subseteq E$
- An environment state update function $ESU : as_i \to es_j$, where j indexes the environmental cell where a_i currently resides (e.g., pheromone deposit)
- An environment state dynamics function $ESD : es(t) \to es(t+1)$, typically evaporation
- An environment state propagation function $ESP : es_i \to N(es_j)$, where $N(es_j)$ is the neighborhood of es_j (e.g., diffusion of pheromone to adjacent cells)

In geospatial stigmergy (e.g., ant or robotic path planning), the elements of E tile a manifold, and ea is symmetric, each tile being adjacent to the tiles in its Moore or von Neumann neighborhood. But other adjacency relations are possible

- Ref. [24] applies stigmergy to reasoning over a hierarchical task network, in which ea is asymmetric.
- Ref. [23] applies it to a novel causal graph formalism whose nodes are event types rather than variables. A edge from e_i to e_j indicates temporal succession, and so is asymmetric.[2]

As anticipated, this model exhibits several asymmetries.

- While agents can change the state of environmental locations that they visit, these locations cannot change the state of the agents. The examples of migratory insects show that in fact the environment can change the state of even very simple agents, imposing evolutionary pressure on their genomes, and classic learning techniques with more complex agents are central to modern ABS.
- There is no agent adjacency relation or agent state propagation. But social influence models recognize the critical importance of the influence of agents on one another (agent state propagation), drawing on an underlying social network. Even insect level societies exhibit role specialization in which different classes of agents interact differentially with one another [9,32].

---

[2] Actually, it is antisymmetric. Since the nodes are event *types* that may be instantiated at different points in time, this formalism, unlike a hierarchy, does admit cyclical paths, and an agent can repeat an event type several times in a row, following an edge (e_i, e_i). But $(i \neq j) \wedge ((e_i, e_j) \in ea) \implies (e_j, e_i) \notin ea$.

- There are no agent state dynamics. But if agents can learn, they can also forget.

In addition to its asymmetry, the conventional model is static. No provision is made for the addition or removal of agents or environmental locations.

3.2 Symmetric Stigmergy

It is straightforward to extend the classic model to make it symmetric (and dynamic).

We retain the elements already defined, and extend A, E, and ea to functions of time, $A(t)$, $E(t)$, and $ea(t)$. (Some applications may require the update, dynamics, and propagation functions to be functions of time as well, but we do not dwell on this natural extension.)

Then we add

- An agent adjacency relation $aa(t) \subseteq A \times A$, analogous to the environment adjacency relation $ea(t)$, allowing the modeling of social relations
- An agent neighbor function $N_A : A \to A' \subseteq A$, analogous to the environment neighbor function
- An agent state update function $ASU : es_i \to as_j$, where i indexes the environmental cell where a_j currently resides, analogous to the environmental state update function ESU
- An agent state dynamics function $ASD : as(t) \to as(t + 1)$, which might model forgetting, or more complex integrative reasoning over learned information, analogous to the environmental state dynamics function ESD
- An agent state propagation function $ASP : as_i \to N(as_j)$, where $N(as_j)$ is the neighborhood of as_j (e.g., spread of opinion over a social network), analogous to the environmental state propagation function ESP

This model supports the evolution of migrating insects in the following way:

- The agent's state is its genome.
- ASU includes mutation, a random change in the genome over time, and health, driven by the environment and possibly resulting in death.
- A changes as agents become isolated from the swarm and die, and as new agents are born.
- aa includes the relation of agents to their offspring.
- ASP passes on the genomes of successful agents from parents to children.

The distinction between agents and environment is justified in many applications by two contrasts. (1) Agents are mobile and the environmental locations are stationary. (2) Many agent behaviors of interest require coordination among agents, but we do not usually think of locations as coordinating with one another. But a large class of interesting social systems are appropriately defined by allowing the same sets of entities to serve both for E and A. How would this work? An agent *qua* agent is located at itself *qua* environment. ASU is null, but ASP allows propagation of information among agents. This approach supports not only models of opinion dynamics [20], but also the task specialization mechanisms mentioned earlier [9, 32].

4 Directions for Future Research

Insect behaviors provided the initial inspiration for stigmergic mechanisms, in which agents coordinate by causing and sensing changes in the state of their local environment. Close examination of insect migration, a behavior that cannot be explained by this asymmetric mechanism, suggests that it is useful to recognize an analogous process, in which the agent learns from locations with which it interacts (or in other words, the local environment modulates the state of the agent). Recognition that stigmergy can be symmetric expands the domain of applicability of this simple but powerful mechanism. Here are some examples.

Symmetric Diffusion: One environmental dynamic sometimes modeled in classic stigmergy is the diffusion of pheromone from the point of deposit to nearby locations, generating a gradient that agents can use to find or avoid locations of interest. In social models, agents who encounter one another tend to align their preferences with one another in a process called "social influence" [13]. When agent preferences are modulated by their local environment, the effect is a diffusion of preferences throughout the agent network that strongly resembles the diffusion of presence pheromones through the environment.

The insect analog to *es* is a chemical pheromone deposited by agents on the locations they visit. Many insects use multiple pheromones, yielding a vector-based deposit on each location, and thus establishing a *field* over the entire environment. Artificial stigmergic architectures mimic this behavior with variables on each location that are augmented when agents visit them. Ref. [21] shows that this pheromone field allows a stigmergic system to be viewed as intermediary between a classic agent-based model and an equation-based "mean field" model, and the position of a stigmergic model on this continuum can be adjusted by pheromone parameters .

Our symmetric model establishes a similar field over the set of agents. One implementation that has proven useful is a vector of preferences over the same vector space that defines the field over the environment, so that an agent's choice among alternative environmental options is a simple comparison between its preference vector and the pheromone (or feature) vector of each accessible location. The parallel between the environmental *feature* field and the *preference* field over the agents extends our conceptual resources for exploring the relative benefits of equation-based and agent-based models and developing new designs that combine the strengths of each.

Modeling Environmental Action: Recent advances in social modeling [23] demonstrate how stigmergy can function in an environment made up of dynamic events rather than only geospatial locations. Events are intrinsically active, and it seems natural, even necessary, to consider their impact on agents. A conceptual framework that recognizes the symmetry of agents and locations can enable us to model and explore such active environments, which are likely to be increasingly important in capturing important social dynamics for analysis and planning.

Between Ants and Actors: We noted above that the presence of a field allows us to explore the design space between agents and equations. Symmetric stigmergy extends the design space in another direction. At one extreme, classic stigmergy offers an elegant account of very simple agents interacting through a shared environment. In some cases, the most important environment that an agent needs to consider consists of other, peer agents, and in this case BDI architectures have historically been preferred.

Recognizing the potential activity of local regions of the environment (such as event types in an event graph [23]) gives us an intermediate point between these extremes. Consider the two asymmetries we identified at the end of the previous section: unlike agents, environmental locations do not move, and do not coordinate with each other. But as our notion of what constitutes an environmental location shifts from a geospatial tile to an event type, these asymmetries tend to disappear.

1. In an environment made up of event types, an event emerges when one or more agents are concurrently participating in the event type. Each of these agents has a geospatial location. As the system operates, instances of events thus can pop up at different locations. Movement of event types through space emerges from the execution of the system.
2. We do not usually think of environmental locations as coordinating with one another. But as a set of event types modulates the preferences of their participating agents, we would expect to see some correlation across the time and places at which specific events emerge. Discovering this kind of unexpected correlation across events is of great interest to social scientists, and symmetric stigmergy facilitates its study.

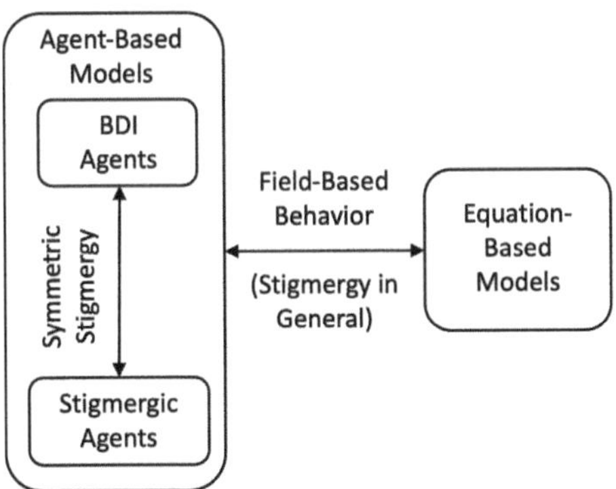

Fig. 3. Stigmergy spans different modeling modalities.

The emerging landscape of modeling options is thus changing. Currently, modelers tend to form disparate and incompatible tribes (using, for example, equations, digital ants, or BDI agents). Symmetric stigmergy provides a common abstract model that can support a continuum of modeling techniques (Fig. 3), offering the modeler a far richer and better nuanced set of choices. Thinking of agent interactions in terms of fields generated by stigmergy (whether symmetric or asymmetric) helps bridge the gap between equations and agents [21], while symmetric stigmergy helps bridge the gap between ant-like agents and BDI agents. The concept of symmetric stigmergy thus points the way to a Grand Unified Theory of modeling, which can help us derive hybrid techniques that combine the strengths of alternative formalisms.

References

1. Alerstam, T., Hedenström, A., Åkesson, S.: Long-distance migration: evolution and determinants. Oikos **103**(2), 247–260 (2003). https://doi.org/10.1034/j.1600-0706.2003.12559.x
2. Aron, S., Deneubourg, J.L., Goss, S., Pasteels, J.M.: Functional Self-Organisation Illustrated by Inter-Nest Traffic in Ants: The Case of the Argentine Ant, pp. 533–547. Springer, Heidelberg (1990)
3. Bassanetti, T., et al.: Cooperation and deception through stigmergic interactions in human groups. Proc. Natl. Acad. Sci. **120**(42), e2307880120 (2023). https://doi.org/10.1073/pnas.2307880120
4. Boldini, A., Martina, C., Maurizio, P.: Stigmergy: from mathematical modelling to control. R. Soc. Open Sci. **11** (2024)
5. Bonabeau, E., Theraulaz, G., Fourcassié, V., Deneubourg, J.L.: The phase-ordering kinetics of cemetery organization in ants. Phys. Rev. E **4**, 4568–4571 (1998). http://www.santafe.edu/research/publications/workingpapers/98-01-008.ps
6. Camazine, S., Deneubourg, J.L., Franks, N.R., Sneyd, J., Theraulaz, G., Bonabeau, E.: Self-Organization in Biological Systems. Princeton Studies in Complexity, Princeton University Press, Princeton (2001)
7. Campos, M., Bonabeau, E., Théraulaz, G., Deneubourg, J.L.: Dynamic scheduling and division of labor in social insects. Adapt. Behav. **8**(2), 83–92 (2001). http://www.ulb.ac.be/sciences/use/publications/JLD/161.pdf
8. Chapman, J.W., Reynolds, D.R., Wilson, K.: Long-range seasonal migration in insects: mechanisms, evolutionary drivers and ecological consequences. Ecol. Lett. **18**(3), 287–302 (2015). https://doi.org/10.1111/ele.12407
9. Chittka, L., Muller, H.: Learning, specialization, efficiency and task allocation in social insects. Commun. Integr. Biol. **2**(2), 151–154 (2009)
10. Deneubourg, J.L., Goss, S., Franks, N., Sendova-Franks, A., Detrain, C., Chretien, L.: The Dynamics of Collective Sorting: Robot-Like Ants and Ant-Like Robots, pp. 356–365. MIT Press, Cambridge (1991)
11. Di Pietro, V., Govoni, P., Chan, K., Oliveira, R., Wenseleers, T., van den Berg, P.: Evolution of self-organised division of labour driven by stigmergy in leaf-cutter ants. Sci. Rep. **12**, 21971 (2022)
12. Dorigo, M., Gambardella, L.M.: Ant colonies for the traveling salesman problem. Biosystems **43**(2), 73–81 (1997). http://www.idsia.ch/~luca/acs-bio97.pdf
13. Friedkin, N.E., Johnsen, E.C.: Social Influence Network Theory: A Sociological Examination of Small Group Dynamics. Structural Analysis in the Social Sciences, Cambridge University Press, Cambridge (2011)
14. Goss, S., Aron, S., Deneubourg, J.L., Pasteels, J.M.: Self-organized shortcuts in the argentine ant. Naturwissenschaften **76**, 579–581 (1989)

15. Grassé, P.P.: La reconstruction du nid et les coordinations inter-individuelles chez bellicositermes natalensis et cubitermes sp. la théorie de la stigmergie: Essai d'interprétation du comportement des termites constructeurs. Insectes Sociaux **6**, 41–84 (1959)

16. Holland, R.A., Wikelski, M., Wilcove, D.S.: How and why do insects migrate? Science 313(5788), 794–796 (2006). https://doi.org/10.1126/science.1127272

17. Jungreis, S.A.: Biomagnetism: an orientation mechanism in migrating insects? Fla. Entomol. **70**(2), 277–283 (1987)

18. Mouritsen, H.: Long-distance navigation and magnetoreception in migratory animals. Nature 558(7708), 50–59 (2018). https://doi.org/10.1038/s41586-018-0176-1

19. Parunak, H.V.D: A survey of environments and mechanisms for human-human stigmergy. In: Weyns, D., Van Dyke Parunak, H., Michel, F. (eds.) E4MAS 2005. LNCS (LNAI), vol. 3830, pp. 163–186. Springer, Heidelberg (2006). https://doi.org/10.1007/11678809_10

20. Parunak, H.V.D.: A mathematical analysis of collective cognitive convergence. In: Decker, K., Sichman, J., Sierra, C., Castelfranchi, C. (eds.) the Eighth International Conference on Autonomous Agents and Multi-Agent Systems (AAMAS 2009), pp. 473–480 (2009)

21. Parunak, H.V.D: Between agents and mean fields. In: Villatoro, D., Sabater-Mir, J., Sichman, J.S. (eds.) MABS 2011. LNCS (LNAI), vol. 7124, pp. 113–126. Springer, Heidelberg (2012). https://doi.org/10.1007/978-3-642-28400-7_9

22. Parunak, H.V.D.: Psychology from stigmergy. In: Computational Social Science (CSS 2020), vol. (forthcoming). CSSSA (2020)

23. Parunak, H.V.D.: How to turn an MAS into a graphical causal model. J. Auton. Agents Multi-Agent Syst. (2022). https://doi.org/10.1007/s10458-022-09560-y

24. Parunak, H.V.D, et al.: Stigmergic modeling of hierarchical task networks. In: Di Tosto, G., Van Dyke Parunak, H. (eds.) MABS 2009. LNCS (LNAI), vol. 5683, pp. 98–109. Springer, Heidelberg (2010). https://doi.org/10.1007/978-3-642-13553-8_9

25. Phan, T.A., Russell, R.A.: An effective collaboration algorithm for swarm robots communicating by sematectonic stigmergy. In: 2010 11th International Conference on Control Automation Robotics & Vision, pp. 390–397 (2010)

26. Reppert, S.M., Gegear, R., Merlin, C.: Navigational mechanisms of migrating monarch butterflies. Trends Neurosci. **33**(9), 399–406 (2010). https://doi.org/10.1016/j.tins.2010.04.004

27. Roffey, J., Magor, J.: Desert locust population dynamics parameters. Report AGP/DL/TS/30, Food and Agriculture Organization, United Nations (2003). https://www.fao.org/ag/locusts/oldsite/PDFs/TS30.pdf

28. Salman, M.: Automatic design of pheromone-based stigmergy in robot swarms, Ph.D. Université libre de Bruxelles (2024)

29. Saund, E., Ari Friedman, D.: A single-pheromone model accounts for empirical patterns of ant colony foraging previously modeled using two pheromones. Cogn. Syst. Res. **80**, 81–89 (2023). https://doi.org/10.1016/j.cogsys.2023.02.005. https://www.sciencedirect.com/science/article/pii/S1389041723000020

30. Sauter, J.A., Matthews, R.S., Robinson, J.S., Moody, J., Riddle, S.P.: Swarming unmanned air and ground systems for surveillance and base protection. In: AIAA Infotech@Aerospace 2009 Conference. AIAA (2009). https://www.abcresearch.org/abc/papers/AIAA2009AirGround.pdf

31. Simon, H.: The Sciences of the Artificial. MIT Press, Cambridge (1969)

32. Theraulaz, G., Goss, S., Gervet, J., Deneubourg, J.L.: Task differentiation in polistes wasp colonies: a model for self-organizing groups of robots. In: Meyer, J.A., Wilson, S.W. (eds.) First International Conference on Simulation of Adaptive Behavior, pp. 346–355. MIT Press (1991)
33. Théraulaz, G., Bonabeau, E., Deneubourg, J.L.: Threshold reinforcement and the regulation of division of labour in insect societies. Proc. Roy. Soc. London B **265**, 327–335 (1998)
34. Umlauft, M., Elmenreich, W.: Ant algorithms for routing in wireless multi-hop networks. In: Soofastaei, A. (ed.) The Application of Ant Colony Optimization, chap. 4. IntechOpen, Rijeka (2021). https://doi.org/10.5772/intechopen.99682
35. Weyns, D., et al.: Agent Environments for Multi-Agent Systems – A Research Roadmap. Springer, Berlin (2015)
36. Wilson, E.O.: Sociobiology: The New Synthesis. Harvard University Press, Cambridge (1975)
37. Zhan, S., Merlin, C., Boore, J., Reppert, S.: The monarch butterfly genome yields insights into long-distance migration. Cell **147**(5), 1171–1185 (2011). https://doi.org/10.1016/j.cell.2011.09.052
38. Zheng, L., Mai, F., Yan, B., Nickerson, J.V.: Stigmergy in open collaboration: an empirical investigation based on wikipedia. J. Manage. Inf. Syst. **40**(3), 983–1008 (2023). (Nico) https://doi.org/10.1080/07421222.2023.2229119
39. Zimmermann, H.: OSI reference model – the ISO model of architecture for open systems interconnection. IEEE Trans. Commun. **28**(4), 425–432 (1980)

Approximating Human Strategic Reasoning with LLM-Enhanced Recursive Reasoners Leveraging Multi-agent Hypergames

Vince Trencsenyi$^{(\boxtimes)}$ [iD], Agnieszka Mensfelt [iD], and Kostas Stathis [iD]

Royal Holloway University of London, Egham, Surrey, UK
`{vince.trencsenyi,agnieszka.mensfelt,kostas.stathis}@rhul.ac.uk`

Abstract. LLM-driven multi-agent-based simulations have been gaining traction with applications in game-theoretic and social simulations. While most implementations seek to exploit or evaluate LLM-agentic reasoning, they often do so with a weak notion of agency and simplified architectures. We implement a role-based multi-agent strategic interaction framework tailored to sophisticated recursive reasoners, providing the means for systematic in-depth development and evaluation of strategic reasoning. Our game environment is governed by the umpire responsible for facilitating games, from matchmaking through move validation to environment management. Players incorporate state-of-the-art LLMs in their decision mechanism, relying on a formal hypergame-based model of hierarchical beliefs. We use one-shot, 2-player beauty contests to evaluate the recursive reasoning capabilities of the latest LLMs, providing a comparison to an established baseline model from economics and data from human experiments. Furthermore, we introduce the foundations of an alternative semantic measure of reasoning to the k-level theory. Our experiments show that artificial reasoners can outperform the baseline model in terms of both approximating human behaviour and reaching the optimal solution.

Keywords: Multi-agent Systems · Social Simulations · Strategic Reasoning

1 Introduction

Multi-agent systems provide environments for individual-based modelling and simulations [28]. Game theory and multi-agent-based simulation (MABS) have established a mutually beneficial relationship: MAS leverages game-theoretic interaction models and strategic tools [31], and game theory relies on multi-agent-based social simulations to investigate strategic decision-making [36]. Large language models (LLMs) have received particular interest in their potential to simulate human-like reasoning and decision-making, and MABS frameworks are used to evaluate LLM capabilities in game-theoretic environments [17]. Traditional approaches often rely on simplified agent frameworks implemented with

A. Vidler and S. Swarup (Eds.): MABS 2025, LNAI 16227, pp. 15–27, 2026.
https://doi.org/10.1007/978-3-032-16328-8_2

a weaker concept of agency [45], which may impose limitations on the system's adaptability and the agent's reasoning sophistication. In contrast, our approach involves a stronger, modular agent concept enabling a decoupled investigation of reasoning processes. Our agents are hosted in a role-based multi-agent framework governed by an umpire who manages game environments and facilitates agent interactions.

We focus on beauty contest games, a well-established concept for studying recursive reasoning [10]. We evaluate the reasoning capabilities of LLM-enhanced agents, integrating recursive reasoning via a formal hypergame representation. Our experiments compare the performance of LLM-enhanced agents against both a baseline economic model and human data, providing insights into the models' ability to approximate human strategic behaviour. Furthermore, we introduce a self-evaluation method κ, a revised measure of reasoning depth that complements traditional k-level theory, offering a more nuanced understanding of reasoning sophistication.

Our key contributions include:

- A flexible multi-agent-based simulation platform capable of hosting a wide array of reasoners, offering a detailed view of reasoning processes;
- LLM-enhanced agents that leverage a hypergame-based model for recursive reasoning;
- Introduction of κ, a complementary measure to k-level reasoning;
- Experiments comparing our LLM-based reasoners to the baseline model and human data.

Our results suggest that artificial reasoners can benefit from the expanded architectural complexity and can not only match but potentially outperform baseline models in both approximating human behaviour and achieving optimal solutions in strategic settings.

2   Background

2.1   Game Theory

Game theory provides a mathematical framework for analyzing decision-making in multi-agent – human or artificial – strategic interactions [30]. A game is formally defined by its players, their available strategies, and utility functions that evaluate the players' outcomes [33]. Beauty contest games (BCGs) provide an experimental testbed for iterative reasoning, where players have to guess a number which they believe will be the closest to the mean of all guesses weighted by a parameter p [10]. BCGs are a popular choice for studies concerning the k-level theory, as optimal play requires thinking about others' thoughts: given the range $[0, 100]$ and $p = \frac{2}{3}$, 0-level players pick 50 and level-k thinkers choose $50\frac{2}{3}^k$. Experimental evidence consistently shows that most human players exhibit 1st or 2nd-level reasoning, with few advancing beyond level 3 [7,14,29].

Hypergames extend standard game theory by modelling individual player perspectives, allowing hypergame models to capture misaligned perceptions [4].

Multi-level hypergames provide a formalized model of hierarchical games representing nested beliefs [40]. A third-level hypergame between players i, j, is a composite structure of lower-level hypergames representing individual players' perspectives: $H^3 = \{H_i^2, H_j^2\}$, where $H_i^2 = \{H_{ii}^1, H_{ji}^1\}$ and $H_{ji}^1 = \{H_{iji}^0, H_{jji}^0\}$. Finally, $H_{iji}^0 = G_{iji}$ is i's perceptual game defining player i's belief of j's belief of i's perspective of G. This theoretical framework provides the foundation for studying how agents engage in recursive strategic reasoning and form hierarchical beliefs about others' decision-making processes.

2.2 Language Models

Large language models (LLMs) are sophisticated neural networks – usually based on the transformers architecture [15] and a pre-trained model on a vast amount of data [32] – that target natural language processing applications [48]. Chain-of-thought (CoT) prompting is a technique that improves LLMs reasoning capabilities by having LLMs decompose complex tasks into smaller problems [42]. Such prompts can be demonstrative examples showcasing what the expected response may pertain to and/or descriptive instructions that guide the model on reaching the expected response [46].

Claude 3.5. Claude 3.5 is a family of state-of-the-art LLM models from Anthropic, supporting multimodal applications [3]. In this work, we evaluate two Claude models: Sonnet offers large context windows and advanced analytical capabilities, suitable for complex tasks and process automation; Haiku is a smaller, cost-efficient, fast model targeting interactive and sub-agent tasks.

GPT-4. GPT-4 is OpenAI's SOTA system supporting multimodal input and output and a long context window arming models with a broad general knowledge and advanced problem-solving abilities [1]. We implement two models: GPT-4o possesses a generally high reasoning performance across various benchmarks; 4o-mini is a lightweight variant for resource-constrained environments.

2.3 Recursive Reasoning

We describe recursive reasoning as an agent's ability to reason about each other's physical and cognitive states [44]. The cognitive hierarchy model introduced the concept of k-level thinkers, proposing that players engage in different levels of strategic thinking, where players on level k best respond to $k-1$ level strategies, assuming every other player must be at most at level $k - 1$ [10]. Epistemic game theory is a branch of game theory which provides a formal mathematical framework for representing and operating with belief hierarchies [11]. Hypergame theory aims to analyse conflict under asymmetric information and misaligned perceptions [5], providing a game-oriented representation of sequential beliefs.

3   Multi-agent Simulation via Centralized Hypergames

Our simulations are materialized in game environments composed of and hosting an umpire, a set of players, and a set of hypergames. We revise hierarchical hypergames from [40] to integrate 2-player BCGs as individual perceptual games capturing the agent's beliefs and reasoning level.

3.1   Perceptual Beauty Contest Games

In our framework, we define BCGs formally as $G = (N, A, U, \Psi)$, where $N = i, j$ is the set of two players, $A = A_i \times A_j$ is the action space, where $A_i, A_j \subseteq \mathbb{Z}$ represent the available actions for players i and j respectively, $U : A \to \mathbb{R}^2$ is the utility function, where for each player: $U_i(a_i, a_j) = -|a_i - p \cdot \mu|$, with $\mu = \frac{a_i + a_j}{2}$ and p as the BCG's scalar parameter and $\Psi = (\psi_1 = \sigma, \psi_2, \ldots, \psi_\kappa)$ is an ordered sequence of κ number of perspectives, where the first component ψ_1 denotes the interpreter (creator) of the game perspective, σ. To help position player beliefs in our BCGs in the context of belief hierarchies, we suggest simplifying assumptions as follows. Given a $\kappa = 2$ level reasoner i, $\beta_i(\beta_j(\beta_k))$ [11] corresponds to i's beliefs about player j's beliefs about player k's reasoning. Then we assume $\beta_i(\beta_j(\beta_k)) \cong G_{ijk}$, where G_{ijk} is the perceptual game capturing the same beliefs, with subscripts denoting the sequential order of perspectives: i's reconstruction of G based on his beliefs about j's beliefs of k's perspective. However, the rigorous analysis of the proposed relationship is beyond the scope of this work. Finally, the set of individual perceptual games invokes the hypergame H^κ, capturing both players' beliefs, where at least one of the players exhibits the highest level of reasoning κ.

3.2   Recursive Reasoners

Agents in our framework are implemented following the standard intelligent agent architecture [34] and inspired by the Observe-Orient-Decide-Act decision-making model [8,38] – as shown on Fig. 1a. An iteration of the game environment comprises the umpire's matchmaking activities and the players' reasoning processes. Given the space of natural language game descriptions X, the umpire v sends game requests to each pair of players to participate in $G^* = (\{i, j\}, \{A_i, A_j\}, U, (v))$. In the facilitated games, the umpire is a passive participant – a pseudoplayer [33].

Each player's reasoning processes are then decoupled and defined as follows:

– The player's revision module – Fig. 1b – processes the game description, reasons about what the opponent's move could be, and constructs a perceptual game. These steps are integrated into an interpretation function $I : G \times N \to G'$, that creates an instance of G reflecting the player's beliefs:
   • $\rho : X \to \Xi, \mathbb{R}$ is the reasoning function: $\rho(x) = \xi_i, \hat{a}_j$ where $\xi_i \in \Xi$ is i's natural language reasoning based on game description $x \in X$ on what the opponent j's guess $\hat{a}_j$ is expected to be;

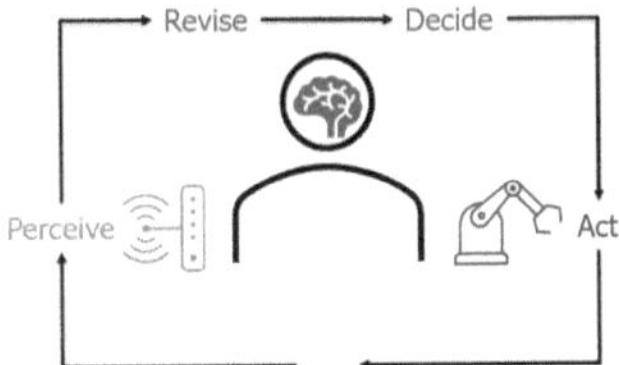

(a) The modular agent relies on its sensor (green) to perceive its environment, uses its mind (purple) to revise the perception and decide which action to take, and acts upon the environment via its effector (red).

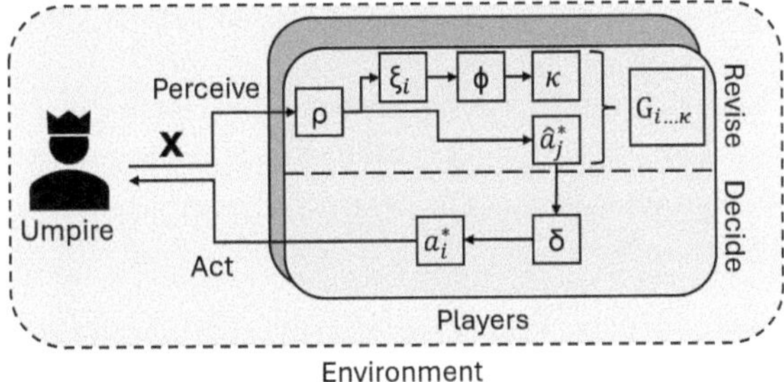

(b) Upon perception of a game request with textual description x, the player revises x, generating a reasoning ξ_i and producing an expected opponent choice $\hat{a}_j$. After $\phi(\xi_i)$ derives κ, the perceptual game $G_{i...\kappa}$ is established. $\delta(\hat{a}_j) = a_i^*$ is what i decides and acts on.

Fig. 1. Overview of centralised MAS framework.

- $\phi : \Xi \to \mathbb{N}$ is the reasoning analysis function: $\phi(\xi_i) = \kappa$, where κ is the player's estimated reasoning level based on the number of nested beliefs present in the reasoning ξ_i;
- i's perceptual game is then: $G_{i...\kappa} = (\{i, j\}, A, U, \Psi = (\psi_i, \ldots, \psi_\kappa))$.
- The decision module selects an action based on the revised expectation:
  - $\delta : \mathbb{R} \to A_i$ is the decision function selecting i's preferred action a_i^* based on the expected opponent guess: $\delta(\hat{a}_j) = a_i^*$;

While k-levels are derived from players' numerical choices, κ provides an alternative measure based on the explicit reasoning steps we observe in players' natural language explanations. These reasoning steps are represented as perspectives ψ in the perceptual game G, allowing us to analyze the depth of strategic thinking through players' own articulation of their decision process.

3.3   Model Prompting Design

We integrate CoT prompting into our multi-step reasoning process across the agent's *revise* and *decide* phases. During *revise*, the LLM mind processes information through sequential steps: first reasoning about the situation to predict opponent guesses, then analyzing the reasoning depth to determine κ, resulting in the κth order perceptual game. The mind's decision function then interprets this processed information to derive the final guess, completing the multi-step reasoning process. LLM prompts follow a modular structure: (1) optional agent profile for context-specific reasoning [25], (2) role and task definition, (3) game/task specific request, and (4) implementation-specific requirements (e.g., *"surround the chosen number in curly brackets: {n}"*).

3.4   Baseline Model

The self-tuning experience weighted attraction model (EWA) is a benchmark model for reproducing human-like strategic interaction in game-theoretic experiments [18].

$$A_i^j(t) = \frac{\phi \cdot N(t-1) \cdot A_i^j(t-1) + [\delta + (1-\delta) \cdot I(s_i^j, s_i(t))] \cdot \pi_i(s_i^j, s_{-i}(t))}{N(t-1) \cdot \phi \cdot (1-\kappa)} \tag{1}$$

Equation 1 defines player i's associated attention to strategy j at time (or round) t, where

- $\pi_i(s_i^j, s_{-i}(t))$ denotes $i's$ payoff for choosing strategy j against s_{-i} at time t;
- N is the experience weight $N(t) = (1-\kappa) \cdot \phi \cdot N(t-1) + 1$ [9];
- ϕ is the change detector function $\phi(t) = 1 - \frac{1}{2}S_i(t)$;
- the surprise index is denoted by $S_i(t) = \sum_{k=1}^{m_{-i}} (h_i^k(t) - r_i^k(t))^2$ with
  $r_i^k(t) = I(s_{-i}^k, s_{-i}(t))$ and $h_i^k(t) = \frac{\sum_{\tau=1}^{t} I(s_{-i}^k, s_{-i}(\tau))}{t}$;
- δ is the weight to foregone payoffs: $\delta_{ij}(t) = \begin{cases} 1 & \text{if } \pi_i(s_i^j, s_{-i}(t)) \geq \pi_i(t), \\ 0 & \text{otherwise.} \end{cases}$;
- and $I(x, y)$ is an index function returning 0 if $x = y$ and 1 otherwise.

Let $t = 0$ denote the agent's initial state. We then define the initial attraction $A_i^j(0)$ according to the cognitive hierarchy model and the Poission distribution function $P(k) = \frac{e^{-\tau}\tau^k}{k!}$ [10] and set $N(0) = 1$. The self-tuning EWA model was trained and tested on a 7-player beauty contest with $p = 0.7$ and $p = 0.9$ [19], for which Ho et al. determined $\lambda = 2.39$ for the sensitivity of the response function and $\tau = 1.5$ for deriving the first-period plays via the CHM-derived Poisson distribution. We adopt these parameters in our experiments without further tuning. Finally, agents choose an action according to $P_i^j(t+1) = \frac{e^{\lambda \cdot A_i^j(t)}}{\sum_{k=1}^{m_i} e^{\lambda \cdot A_i^k(t)}}$.

4   Experiments

We use beauty contest games as the test bench for evaluating our agents' recursive reasoning capabilities, as guessing games are closely associated with k-level reasoning [10]. In this context, k level reasoners best respond to the $k - 1$ level players' choices and at $k = 0$ players choose randomly. In order to classify players by their reasoning, we adopt the guess-based conversion approach presented in [29]. We assume level 0 reasoners choose 50; then we set each kth reasoning level at $50p^k$. More specifically, we use 2-player BCGs to conduct our evaluation. In n-player BCGs, reasoners eliminate weakly dominated strategies iteratively – which process can be extended to infinity – until the theoretical solution of everyone choosing 0 is reached [10]. The two-player game provides a simpler solution concept, where the smaller number wins [16]. Zero is a weakly dominated strategy that always wins, which, in theory, significantly simplifies the iterative reasoning process.

We evaluate our agents on the experiment from [16], involving 132 student participants, pooled from first-year students with no prior game-theoretic training nor existing familiarity with beauty contests and 130 professionals with extensive game-theoretic domain knowledge.

In the first instance, we replayed the 2-player beauty contests using the original experiment design, simulating 25 independent rounds with each LLM. Additionally, we conducted 60 rounds with pairs of agents using the EWA model as the benchmark. Artificial agents were provided with a description worded similarly to what human participants would be given – however, obfuscated to mitigate reliance on game-theoretic analyses in the models' training data –, without any explicit instructions on their reasoning and decision-making. Providing a persona description as context pushes the LLM to behave in the desired way by guiding the reasoning process according to the profile specification [25]. Similarly, in the second set of experiments, we expand our prompting mechanism with an agent profile, allowing us to specify the level of domain knowledge the agent should use for its reasoning. Following the original group descriptions from [16], we ran 15–15 games with the specifications of "first years students with no game-theoretic knowledge" and "professors with expert domain knowledge in game theory" with Claude 3.5 Haiku and GPT-4o – chosen based on their proximity to the human performance and the optimal strategy, 0.

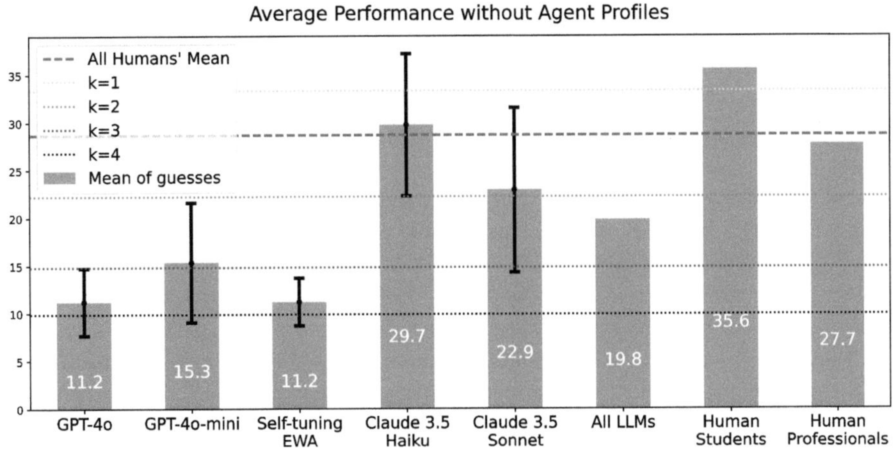

Fig. 2. Per model means, standard deviations and estimated k-levels. Human data for standard deviation was unavailable.

All models outperformed human participants significantly, except for Claude 3.5 Haiku, which approximates the results of the professionals and the joint human player population – Fig. 2. On the other hand, Fig. 3 depicts the results of the second experiment, where player profiles are successfully integrated into

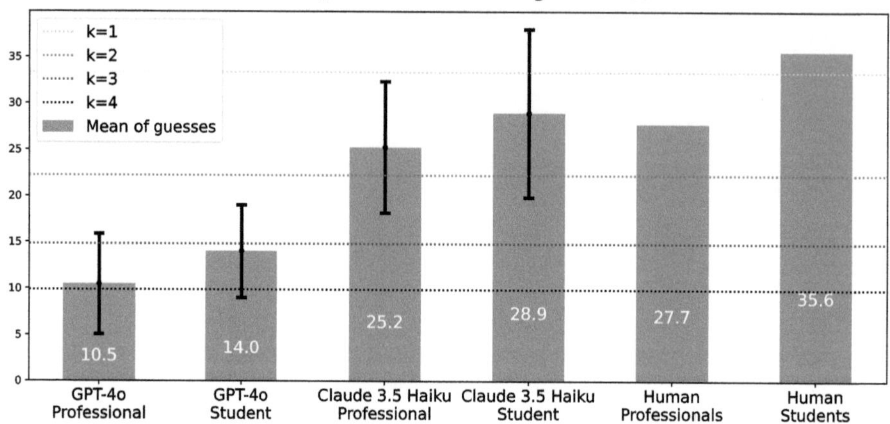

Fig. 3. Per model means (LLMs with profiles), standard deviations and estimated k-levels. Human data for standard deviation was unavailable.

both agents' reasoning processes. Similar to the human groups with different levels of domain expertise, the models acting as students performed noticeably poorer than the models that were described as professionals. However, while 9.85% of human students and 36.02% of human professionals managed to reach 0, none of the artificial reasoners – nor the baseline model – chose the optimal strategy in either experiment. Most studies concentrate on BCGs involving more than 2 players, where 0 is not an obvious solution to the game. This bias is likely inherently present in the LLMs training data, potentially tainting the information used to generate reasoning in the 2-player BCG.

K-level reasoning provides another metric for comparing human and artificial agents' thought processes. Table 1 reinterprets the mean results through k-level classifications, showing that while humans exhibit 1st-level reasoning, only Claude 3.5 Haiku produced comparable results. Other models performed at the 2nd and 3rd levels, with EWA and GPT-4o approaching level 4 reasoning. Additionally, the "Mean κ" and "Median κ" columns report the LLM agents' reasoning steps involved, corresponding to perspectives in their perceptual games.

The second experiment revealed that the estimated k and κ levels are aligned with the expectation that reasoners with domain expertise would outperform and exhibit a higher order of reasoning than non-professionals. While κ can provide a semantics-backed estimate of the reasoning steps involved in the process, it does not yet tell us much about the quality of the agent's reasoning. The results suggest that a semantic qualitative reasoning classification may complement the current numerically defined measures.

Table 1. Mean k-levels are estimated from mean guesses, while mean and median κ levels correspond to LLM agents' self-reported reasoning steps.

Model/Group	Mean Guess	Mean k-level	Mean κ	Median κ
Human Students	35.57	0.84	N.A.	N.A.
Human Professionals	27.73	1.45	N.A.	N.A.
Claude 3.5 Haiku	29.7	1.28	2.17	2
Claude 3.5 Sonnet	22.9	1.92	2.17	2
GPT-4o-mini	15.3	2.92	2.57	3
GPT-4o	11.2	3.69	2.27	2
Self-tuning EWA	11.2	3.69	N.A.	N.A.
Claude 3.5 Haiku Student	28.9	1.35	1.97	2
Claude 3.5 Haiku Professional	25.2	1.69	2.5	2.5
GPT-4o Student	14	3.14	1.8	2
GPT-4o Professional	10.5	3.85	2.4	3

5   Related Work

The recent emergence of LLM agents [39] and LLM-MAS [22] has influenced social simulations. Multi-agent strategic interactions are used to evaluate LLM reasoning [13,27], and LLM-based simulations are leveraged for empirical investigations on strategic behaviours [25,26]. Recent work on LLM-driven reasoning in BCGs focuses on studying agent rationality and reasoning levels [17,24,47]. Centralized role-based architectures rely on an umpire [35] or a game manager [21] to coordinate game-based interactions – such as artificial trading [43] or utility markets [23,49]. Hypergame theory, while effective for analyzing complex conflicts post-hoc [5], has seen limited practical application [6] due to challenges in automation. Most agent-based implementations only borrow conceptually [2,12], with few examples of full integration [20,37].

While prior approaches typically implement a looser agentic concept – a weaker notion of agency [45] – potentially constraining the system's flexibility and bounding LLMs' reasoning [41], our framework offers enhanced flexibility and depth. Our conceptually elaborate multi-agent architecture enables a more nuanced evaluation process, facilitating a systematic review of LLM reasoning and automating the generation of hypergames. This approach provides valuable insights into LLMs' capabilities for recursive reasoning, particularly their ability to form beliefs about beliefs and develop a theory of mind.

6   Conclusions and Future Work

We present a MABS framework integrating hypergames for multi-level reasoning in BCGs. Our contributions are threefold. First, we introduce a flexible multi-agent simulation platform capable of hosting both simple models like the self-tuning EWA and sophisticated multi-step reasoners powered by state-of-the-art LLMs. The platform's architecture emphasizes a strong notion of agency, allowing for systematic development and evaluation of strategic reasoning capabilities. In contrast, existing approaches often employ simplified architectures with weaker notions of agency, which can limit both applicability and evaluation depth. Second, we introduce κ as a complementary measure to the k-level theory for evaluating reasoning. While k-levels are solely derived from players' numerical choices, κ represents the sequential perspectives in an agent's reasoning process, providing an alternative measure of reasoning depth that could offer valuable insights alongside numerical k-level analysis. Third, our 2-player BCG experiments demonstrate that our proposed approach can match and outperform the baseline model in approximating human results and reaching the optimal solution. Additionally, our profile-enhanced agents successfully mirrored the performance gap observed between student and professional human players.

The presented system and experiments highlight the potential for extensions. Integrating semantic analysis techniques for evaluating the quality and coherence of agent reasoning processes would allow us to develop κ into a deeper qualitative measure of reasoning sophistication. Recreating the BCG experiment with human reasoning data would allow us to investigate (dis)similarities in how humans and LLM agents approach recursive strategic thinking, both in terms of k and κ levels. Implementing multi-round and n-player games would enable studying learning processes in artificial and human agents. These extensions would contribute to a more comprehensive understanding of recursive reasoning in artificial – and potentially human – agents while advancing the practical applications of LLM-driven multi-agent systems in strategic decision-making scenarios.

Acknowledgments. The first author would like to express his gratitude to David Levine for his valuable insights on the EWA model.

This work was supported by a Leverhulme Trust International Professorship Grant (LIP-2022-001).

Disclosure of Interests. The authors have no competing interests to declare that are relevant to the content of this article.

References

1. Achiam, J., et al.: GPT-4 technical report. arXiv preprint arXiv:2303.08774 (2023)
2. Aitchison, M., Benke, L., Sweetser, P.: Learning to deceive in multi-agent hidden role games. In: Sarkadi, S., Wright, B., Masters, P., McBurney, P. (eds.) Deceptive AI, pp. 55–75. Springer, Cham (2021)

3. Anthropic: Claude 3.5 (2024). https://www.anthropic.com/claude
4. Bennett, P.: Toward a theory of hypergames. Omega **5**(6), 749–751 (1977)
5. Bennett, P.: Hypergames: developing a model of conflict. Futures **12**(6), 489–507 (1980)
6. Bennett, P., Huxham, C., Dando, M.: Shipping in crisis: a trial run for 'live' application of the hypergame approach. Omega **9**(6), 579–594 (1981)
7. Bosch-Domenech, A., Montalvo, J.G., Nagel, R., Satorra, A.: One, two,(three), infinity,…: newspaper and lab beauty-contest experiments. Am. Econ. Rev. **92**(5), 1687–1701 (2002)
8. Bryant, D.J.: Rethinking OODA: toward a modern cognitive framework of command decision making. Mil. Psychol. **18**(3), 183–206 (2006)
9. Camerer, C.F., Ho, T.H., Chong, J.K.: Sophisticated experience-weighted attraction learning and strategic teaching in repeated games. J. Econ. Theory **104**(1), 137–188 (2002)
10. Camerer, C.F., Ho, T.H., Chong, J.K.: A cognitive hierarchy model of games. Q. J. Econ. **119**(3), 861–898 (2004)
11. Dekel, E., Siniscalchi, M.: Epistemic game theory. In: Handbook of Game Theory with Economic Applications, vol. 4, pp. 619–702. Elsevier (2015)
12. Dharmadhikari, M., Deshpande, H., Dang, T., Alexis, K.: Hypergame-based adaptive behavior path planning for combined exploration and visual search. In: 2021 IEEE International Conference on Robotics and Automation (ICRA), pp. 269–275 (2021)
13. Duan, J., et al.: GTBench: uncovering the strategic reasoning capabilities of LLMs via game-theoretic evaluations. Adv. Neural. Inf. Process. Syst. **37**, 28219–28253 (2024)
14. Duffy, J., Nagel, R.: On the robustness of behaviour in experimental 'beauty contest' games. Econ. J. **107**(445), 1684–1700 (1997)
15. Gillioz, A., Casas, J., Mugellini, E., Abou Khaled, O.: Overview of the transformer-based models for NLP tasks. In: 2020 15th Conference on Computer Science and Information Systems (FedCSIS), pp. 179–183. IEEE (2020)
16. Grosskopf, B., Nagel, R.: The two-person beauty contest. Games Econom. Behav. **62**(1), 93–99 (2008)
17. Guo, S., et al.: Economics arena for large language models. In: Language Gamification-NeurIPS 2024 Workshop (2024)
18. Ho, T.H., Camerer, C.F., Chong, J.K.: Self-tuning experience weighted attraction learning in games. J. Econ. Theory **133**(1), 177–198 (2007)
19. Ho, T.H., Camerer, C., Weigelt, K.: Iterated dominance and iterated best response in experimental "p-beauty contests". Am. Econ. Rev. **88**(4), 947–969 (1998)
20. Kahn, M.: Dynamic-occlusion-aware risk identification for autonomous vehicles using hypergames. Master's thesis, UWSpace (2021)
21. Kobti, Z., Sharma, S.: A multi-agent architecture for game playing. In: 2007 IEEE Symposium on Computational Intelligence and Games, pp. 276–281 (2007)
22. Li, X., Wang, S., Zeng, S., Wu, Y., Yang, Y.: A survey on LLM-based multi-agent systems: workflow, infrastructure, and challenges. Vicinagearth **1**(1), 9 (2024)
23. Liu, N., He, L., Yu, X., Ma, L.: Multiparty energy management for grid-connected microgrids with heat- and electricity-coupled demand response. IEEE Trans. Industr. Inf. **14**(5), 1887–1897 (2018)
24. Lu, S.E.: Strategic interactions between large language models-based agents in beauty contests. arXiv preprint arXiv:2404.08492 (2024)
25. Mao, S., et al.: Alympics: LLM agents meet game theory–exploring strategic decision-making with AI agents. arXiv preprint arXiv:2311.03220 (2023)

26. Mensfelt, A., Stathis, K., Trencsenyi, V.: Autoformalizing and simulating game-theoretic scenarios using LLM-augmented agents. arXiv preprint arXiv:2412.08805 (2024)
27. Mensfelt, A., Stathis, K., Trencsenyi, V.: Logic-enhanced language model agents for trustworthy social simulations. arXiv preprint arXiv:2408.16081 (2024)
28. Michel, F., Ferber, J., Drogoul, A.: Multi-agent systems and simulation: a survey from the agent community's perspective. In: Multi-Agent Systems, pp. 17–66. CRC Press (2018)
29. Nagel, R.: Unraveling in guessing games: an experimental study. Am. Econ. Rev. **85**(5), 1313–1326 (1995)
30. Osborne, M.: Introduction to Game Theory. Oxford University Press (2004)
31. Parsons, S., Wooldridge, M.: Game theory and decision theory in multi-agent systems. Auton. Agent. Multi-Agent Syst. **5**, 243–254 (2002)
32. Qiu, X.P., Sun, T.X., Xu, Y.G., Shao, Y.F., Dai, N., Huang, X.J.: Pre-trained models for natural language processing: a survey. SCIENCE CHINA Technol. Sci. **63**(10), 1872–1897 (2020). https://doi.org/10.1007/s11431-020-1647-3
33. Rasmusen, E.: Games and Information an Introduction to Game Theory. Blackwell (2006)
34. Russell, S., Norvig, P.: Intelligent agents. Artif. Intell. Modern Appr. **74**, 46–47 (1995)
35. Stathis, K., Sergot, M.: An abstract framework for globalising interactive systems. Interact. Comput. **9**(4), 401–416 (1998). Shared Values and Shared Interfaces: The Role of Culture in the Globalisation of Human-Computer Systems
36. Sun, R.: Cognition and Multi-agent Interaction: From Cognitive Modeling to Social Simulation. Cambridge University Press (2006)
37. Tang, Y., Sun, J., Wang, H., Deng, J., et al.: A method of network attack-defense game and collaborative defense decision-making based on hierarchical multi-agent reinforcement learning. Comput. Secur. **142**, 103871 (2024)
38. Tweedale, J., Ichalkaranje, N., Sioutis, C., Jarvis, B., Consoli, A., Phillips-Wren, G.: Innovations in multi-agent systems. J. Netw. Comput. Appl. **30**(3), 1089–1115 (2007)
39. Wang, L., Ma, C., Feng, X., Zhang, Z., et al.: A survey on large language model based autonomous agents. Front. Comp. Sci. **18**(6), 186345 (2024)
40. Wang, M., Hipel, K.W., Fraser, N.M.: Modeling misperceptions in games. Behav. Sci. **33**(3), 207–223 (1988)
41. Wang, Q., et al.: What limits LLM-based human simulation: LLMs or our design? CoRR (2025)
42. Wei, J., et al.: Chain-of-thought prompting elicits reasoning in large language models. Adv. Neural. Inf. Process. Syst. **35**, 24824–24837 (2022)
43. Wellman, M., Wurman, P., O'Malley, K., Bangera, R., et al.: Designing the market game for a trading agent competition. IEEE Internet Comput. **5**(2), 43–51 (2001)
44. Wen, Y., Yang, Y., Luo, R., Wang, J., Pan, W.: Probabilistic recursive reasoning for multi-agent reinforcement learning. In: 7th International Conference on Learning Representations, ICLR 2019 (2019)
45. Wooldridge, M., Jennings, N.R.: Intelligent agents: theory and practice. Knowl. Eng. Rev. **10**(2), 115–152 (1995)
46. Yu, Z., He, L., Wu, Z., Dai, X., Chen, J.: Towards better chain-of-thought prompting strategies: a survey. arXiv preprint arXiv:2310.04959 (2023)
47. Zhang, Y., et al.: K-level reasoning: establishing higher order beliefs in large language models for strategic reasoning. In: Proceedings of the 2025 Conference of the

Nations of the Americas Chapter of the Association for Computational Linguistics: Human Language Technologies (Volume 1: Long Papers), pp. 7212–7234 (2025)
48. Zhao, W.X., Zhou, K., Li, J., Tang, T., et al.: A survey of large language models. arXiv preprint arXiv:2303.18223 (2023)
49. Zhu, B., Wang, D.: Master–slave game optimal scheduling for multi-agent integrated energy system based on uncertainty and demand response. Sustainability **16**(8) (2024)

Automatic Generation of ABM Narratives Using Simulation Traces and LLM

Zenith Arnejo[1,2]([✉])[iD], Benoit Gaudou[1][iD], Mehdi Saqalli[3][iD],
and Nathaniel Bantayan[4][iD]

[1] UMR 5055, IRIT, Université Toulouse Capitole, Toulouse 31000, France
[2] Institute of Computer Science, University of the Philippines Los Baños,
Laguna 4030, Philippines
zenith.arnejo@ut-capitole.fr
[3] UMR 5602, GEODES, CNRS, Université Toulouse Jean Jaures, Toulouse 31000,
France
[4] Institute of Renewable Natural Resources, University of the Philippines Los Baños,
Laguna 4030, Philippines

Abstract. Effective communication of agent-based models is essential for ensuring their usability and transparency. However, conventional documentation approaches often struggle to capture the dynamic execution details of simulations, making it challenging to convey complex processes clearly and accessibly. Moreover, ABMs frequently exhibit emergent and unexpected behaviors resulting from multiple agent interactions – dynamics that static model descriptions does not fully capture. This paper presents a novel methodology for generating execution-based narratives for ABMs using simulation logs and large language models. By integrating process mining, Business Process Modeling Notation, and automated narrative generation, the approach transforms raw simulation data into coherent visual and textual artifacts that faithfully reflect the model's dynamic execution. Unlike conventional documentation – which often relies on subjective assessments and demands significant effort from modelers – this methodology minimizes subjectivity and reduces the effort required from modelers while promoting a more accessible approach to model communication. To demonstrate its expressivity, we applied the methodology to the Luneray Flu Model and successfully produced artifacts such as process maps, business process diagrams, and narrative explanations. This work offers a step toward improving transparency and accessibility in ABM verification and communication.

Keywords: ABM Narratives · Communication Support · LLM

1 Introduction

Effective communication among model developers and stakeholders is essential in modeling and simulation [11]. This is particularly true for agent-based models (ABMs), where a model's value depends on the clarity with which its design and

A. Vidler and S. Swarup (Eds.): MABS 2025, LNAI 16227, pp. 28–42, 2026.
https://doi.org/10.1007/978-3-032-16328-8_3"

results are described to stakeholders [14]. Clear communication fosters better understanding, supports validation efforts, and enhances model reproducibility [10]. However, the diverse and inconsistent methods used to describe models – and the lack of assurance that the implementation, simulation, and results align with the description – hinder stakeholder understanding and raise concerns about model transparency [10]. Importantly, ABMs are characterized by complex interactions among agents that often give rise to emergent behaviors and unexpected outcomes [5]. These dynamic phenomena can remain hidden or only partially described in traditional static documentation frameworks, such as the Overview-Design concepts-Details (ODD) framework, which relies exclusively on exhaustive textual descriptions [9]. Consequently, static descriptions may overlook critical aspects of a model's capabilities that only become apparent during execution.

Given these challenges, there is a need for innovative methods that align model descriptions with the dynamic nature of model execution while minimizing modelers' subjective bias. This paper presents a novel methodology for generating execution-based narratives for ABMs using simulation logs and large language models (LLMs). The approach combines process mining to discover agent workflows, visualization through Business Process Modeling Notation (BPMN), and automated narrative generation with LLMs. This integration transforms raw simulation data into coherent visual and textual artifacts that closely mirror the model's execution dynamics. By capturing the behaviors intrinsic to ABMs, our methodology not only improves transparency but also supports model verification and stakeholder engagement by providing accessible and accurate representations of simulation processes. The remainder of the paper is structured as follows: the Related Work section reviews existing contributions to model descriptions in the context of model communication; the Methodology section outlines the pipeline for automatically generating model descriptions using simulation traces and LLMs; the Application section demonstrates the methodology with a toy model; and the Discussion section analyzes the findings, identifies limitations, and summarizes the contributions.

2 Related Work

Model descriptions are vital artifacts in any modeling project, serving multiple purposes: they facilitate communication, deepen comprehension, enable replication, and allow comparisons with other models [17]. The quality of these descriptions is critical to the success of a project and the usability of its outputs. However, one persistent challenge is balancing detail with readability. Comprehensive descriptions necessary for replication can be overwhelming for complex models, while overly general descriptions risk omitting critical information or creating inconsistencies with real-world systems. This balancing act remains one of the key challenges in developing effective model descriptions for ABMs.

One approach to address this issue is the use of narrative explanations. In the work of [16], narrative explanations were employed to clarify the results of generative simulation models, providing detailed accounts of key events and processes during simulations. These narratives act as intermediaries between high-level summaries of system-level patterns and formal descriptions of model structures, making them particularly useful for participatory modeling projects. Similarly, [3] demonstrated the effectiveness of narrative explanations (or scientific storytelling) in communicating complex human-environment interactions within a transdisciplinary ABM. While these approaches show promise, current methods rely heavily on manual generation of narratives, which are time-consuming and prone to bias and inconsistencies.

A persistent criticism of ABMs is the perception that they function as "black box" systems, leading to hesitancy among researchers and stakeholders to adopt them [6,22]. While model documentations and narrative explanations are crucial in addressing this issue, they often fall short due to the time-intensive nature of documentation and the risk of oversimplifying complex dynamics. This underscores the need for automated approaches to create descriptions that are transparent, accessible to non-experts, and faithful to the model's complexity, while minimizing the effort required for their production.

3 Methodology

In this work, we present a three-part methodology for the automatic generation of model narratives for any given discrete-time simulation.

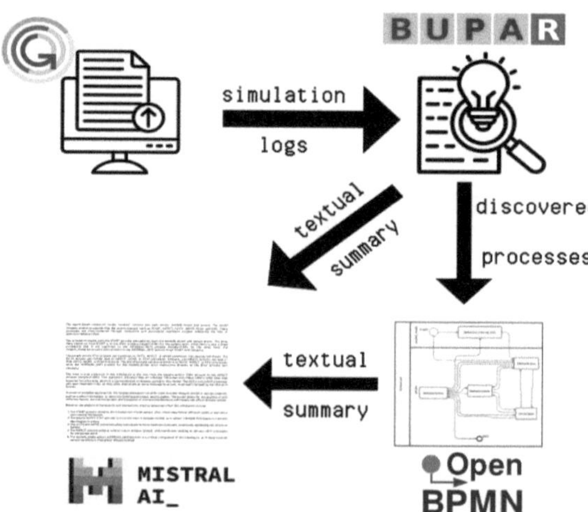

Fig. 1. Methodology for automatically generating ABM narratives.

Figure 1 illustrates the proposed methodology. To communicate the inner workings of the model without relying on its documentation, we focused on extracting information directly from simulation traces or logs using "process mining" [2]. We employed automated process discovery, a key technique in process mining, to derive processes directly from these logs and present them in the form of a process map. The discovered workflow is then further visualized using BPMN to organize the process according to the agents that perform it. Subsequently, a textual summary of the diagrams is generated and used as input for querying the selected LLM. The methodology produces two key artifacts: (1) process diagrams, including process maps (PM) and business process diagrams (BPD), and (2) a simulation narrative.

3.1 Simulation Logging

The methodology begins by capturing simulation logs at each simulation step during model execution, focusing on two types of information: (1) variables whose values change during execution and (2) methods that are executed. Logging the variables whose values change provides insights into which properties of the agent evolve throughout the simulation, while capturing executed methods reveals the agent's actions during the process. These elements were chosen for logging because they directly reflect the simulation's dynamic state transitions and decision points, providing a comprehensive view of agent behavior. This approach is not limited to a specific simulation platform; it can be applied to any platform that supports discrete-time simulation. Since discrete-time simulations inherently progress through distinct time steps, the logging of variable changes and method executions can be consistently implemented, regardless of the underlying architecture. In this study, we utilized the GAMA platform [23] to maximize the use of readily available models and then integrated logging capabilities within the platform.

case_id	activity	time_stamp	value	resource
2	[action]description.segregation_model	01/01/1970 01:00	nil	nil
2	nil	01/01/1970 01:00	27846	[Variable]rng_usage.segregation_model
2	nil	01/01/1970 01:00	1601	[Variable]all_places.segregation_model
2	nil	01/01/1970 01:00	1601	[Variable]free_places.segregation_model
2	[action]initialize_places.segregation_model	01/01/1970 01:00	nil	nil
2	nil	01/01/1970 01:00	1120	[Variable]number_of_people.segregation_model
2	[behavior]_internal_init49.people	01/01/1970 01:00	nil	nil

Fig. 2. Example simulation log.

Figure 2 presents sample entries from the simulation log. The column details are as follows: (1) "case_id" field indicates the execution cycle for a single experiment or the simulation replication for a batch experiment.; (2) "activity" specifies the executed method in the format [<type>]<method name>.<agent type>; (3) "time_stamp" records the simulation clock; (4) "value" represents the current value of the variable; and (5) "resource" provides information on the variable that changed, formatted as [Variable]<variable name>.<agent type>. For the activity type, in the context of the GAMA Modeling Language (GAML), this

can be either a behavior (referred to as a "reflex" in GAML) or an action. Moreover, for log entries corresponding to methods, the 'value' and 'resource' fields
are assigned 'nil', whereas for log entries corresponding to variables, the 'activity' field is assigned 'nil'. The organization of the simulation log is based on the
minimum information required to describe an 'event', which, according to [2],
includes a case identifier, an activity name, and a timestamp. This information
is necessary to proceed to the next step of the methodology.

3.2 Process Visualization

The subsequent step in the methodology focuses on generating process visualizations. This step begins with applying process discovery techniques to simulation
logs to derive a process model that accurately represents the observed process
behavior [1]. By treating simulation logs as event logs, the underlying simulation processes are visualized as process maps (PM). These PMs are constructed
using the Directly-Follows Graph (DFG) algorithm, a widely supported process
discovery approach in process mining tools [1]. DFG represents processes as a
directed graph, where each node denotes an activity, and each directed edge
captures the sequence in which activities occur based on the order of entries in
the event log. Additional information captured includes transition likelihoods on
edges, computed based on the frequency of transitions, and node proportions,
which indicate the occurrence frequency of specific activities relative to the total
log entries.

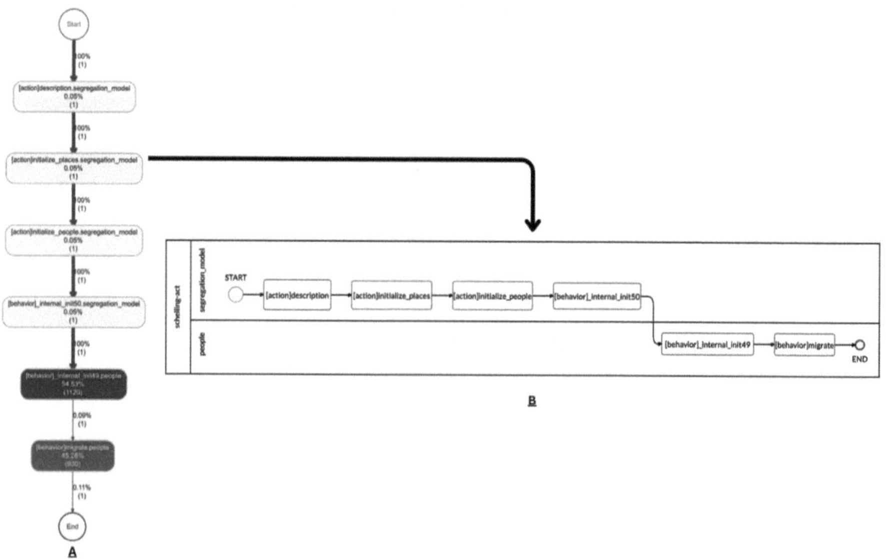

Fig. 3. Example PM (A) and its corresponding BPD (B).

Separate process maps (PMs) for methods and variables were obtained by filtering the logs and then applying process discovery analyses on each. For the methods map, we retained only log entries where the activity field was not `nil`. Conversely, for the variables map, we retained only entries where the resource field was not `nil`. Using the DFG algorithm, the filtered logs were processed sequentially: for each pair of consecutive, distinct log entries, an edge was created, while consecutive identical entries resulted in an incremented edge weight. For example, as shown in Fig. 2, after filtering out `nil` entries for the methods map, the log entry [action]description.segregation_model is followed by [action]initialize_places.segregation_model. Accordingly, Fig. 3A displays an edge connecting the nodes corresponding to these log entries. Additionally, because the log file begins with [action]description.segregation_model, an edge from the START node to this entry was also created. Lastly, to enhance the readability of the generated process map, we filtered out loops and retained only edges with a weight of at least 0.05%. As a result, the final map captures only the processes that play a significant role in the model, either by their frequency of execution or by their relative influence.

In addition to the PM, we visualized the extracted process using BPMN – the de facto standard for representing business processes in a highly expressive graphical format [7]. The use of BPMN for communicating ABMs to business users has also been explored in [19,20]. BPMN provides elements such as pools and lanes to organize processes according to the agents that perform them. Using this notation, the resulting diagram features a pool that captures all logged aspects of the simulation, with its contents organized into lanes corresponding to each involved agent type. For example, Fig. 3B shows a business process diagram (BPD) in which the pool, named "schelling-act", contains all discovered processes from the action logs. The diagram includes two lanes: the "people" lane, representing the sole agent type, and the "segregation_model" lane, which corresponds to the simulation environment.

To achieve these transformations, we utilized tools from the bupaR ecosystem [12], a business process analysis toolkit for R, for process discovery and visualization. The PM was generated using the BPMN 2.0 metamodel available in OpenBPMN [21], while Cardanit [8] was used to automatically generate the BPD layout.

3.3 Narrative Generation

The final step in the methodology is narrative generation. The creation of this artifact is motivated by the widely held notion that narratives enhance human understanding by structuring events into narratives [4]. According to [16], a narrative is defined as a means of explaining the sequences of events and interactions within a system, integrating them into a coherent account to illustrate how patterns emerge from those sequences. In our case, since the focus of our work is on exposing the processes of a given ABM, we limit our definition of narrative to textual descriptions that present the sequences of events and interactions in a simulation model, describing its most important processes and variables.

To achieve this, we begin by automatically generating textual summaries of the diagrams created in the previous step. These summaries serve as the basis for the narrative explanation and are produced with the context length limit in mind – the maximum number of tokens that a large language model (LLM) can process at one time. Then, we used LLM to generate narrative explanations given these summaries. A key requirement for producing a coherent narrative is that the method and variable names in the ABM's implementation code align with real-world terms that accurately reflect what each represents, as this information is captured in the simulation log and, in turn, reflected in the textual summaries. In this study, we employed the 7-billion-parameter language model developed by Mistral AI [13] to generate the narrative explanation for the ABM.

Prompt Engineering. With textual summaries prepared, the next step was to identify how they could be most effectively integrated into the prompt structure for narrative generation. Initial attempts involved a sequence of three consecutive user prompts. The first prompt instructed the LLM to generate narratives based on descriptions of variables and processes derived from the agent-based model. The second prompt then supplied a summary of the simulation derived from a directed weighted graph, and the third prompt added the corresponding summary extracted from the business process diagram. This stepwise prompting approach ensured that the model received all relevant contextual information while still respecting input length limitations. Testing, however, revealed that the LLM struggled to retain previously provided information, underscoring the current limitations of LLMs in maintaining long-term coherence [4].

Table 1. Combinations of textual summaries with corresponding narrative emphasis

Action Log		Variable Log		Emphasis
PM	BPD	PM	BPD	
x	x			Actions executed in the simulation and the connections between agent actions
		x	x	Agent variables that changed during the simulation and interactions between agents' attributes
x		x		Transitions in the executed methods and agent variables
	x		x	Structure of the simulation based on agent attributes and behavior

To address these constraints, the prompt type was changed from a user prompt to a system prompt, with the textual summaries appended to provide complete context. Shifting from multiple user prompts to a single system prompt was necessary because system prompts provide persistent, overarching instructions that ensure all contextual information is integrated and retained across the interaction, overcoming the limitations of user prompts, which apply only to immediate turns and often fail to preserve coherence over extended sequences [18]. The resulting combinations of summaries and their corresponding narrative emphases are presented in Table 1, which illustrates how different pairings of inputs emphasize distinct aspects of the simulation. In principle, all four representations – action log PM, action log BPD, variable log PM, and variable log BPD – could be integrated into a single prompt to produce a unified narrative. However, this option was not adopted in the present implementation. Combining all four inputs simultaneously would result in excessively long prompts, which not only increase computational costs but also risk output degradation: LLMs tend to lose focus, and misinterpret details when the input context becomes too large [15]. To balance comprehensiveness with interpretability, ABM-VISTA adopts a modular strategy, integrating two complementary inputs at a time. This pairwise approach keeps queries tractable, highlights the contribution of each representation, and remains flexible enough to be extended in future work. A promising direction is the use of advanced prompt-engineering or hierarchical summarization techniques that may eventually enable all four inputs to be combined without overwhelming the model.

Based on these design choices, the final system prompt used to query the selected LLM was formulated as follows:

"You are provided with detailed descriptions of a complete simulation execution for an agent-based model. Your task is to: (1) Analyze interactions through careful examination of the interactions between processes and agents within the model; (2) Identify key transitions by highlighting crucial transitions and important paths within the simulation; and (3) Develop a comprehensive narrative that explains the overall purpose and mechanism of the agent-based model, the probable applications of the model in real-world or theoretical contexts, and the key insights and takeaways derived from the analysis of interactions and transitions. Below are the descriptions:"

4   Application

To demonstrate the methodology, we applied it to a pedagogical toy model available on the GAMA platform: a simple Susceptible-Infected (SI) model that simulates the spread of flu in the city of Luneray, Normandy, France [23]. In this model, people agents move between buildings via the road network, and infected individuals can transmit the flu to neighboring agents. The model's implementation is guided by five key assumptions: (1) people move along roads from building to building; (2) they use the shortest path for their travel; (3) all individuals move at a constant speed; (4) upon arriving at a building, individuals remain there for a specified period; and (5) infected individuals are never cured. Figure 4 shows a screenshot of the model in execution.

Fig. 4. Screenshot of the Luneray Flu model during execution. Green dots represent susceptible (healthy) agents, red dots indicate infected agents, grey polygons correspond to buildings, and black lines denote roads. Agents navigate the environment following a pedestrian mobility process, which drives their movement through the spatial landscape. (Color figure online)

4.1   Results

Simulation logs were collected through a batch simulation consisting of six runs, each with 600 cycles. Each run included 2,147 people agents and was executed using identical parameter settings, with log files recorded at every cycle. Logging during batch execution was chosen to obtain a simulation log that provides a representative overview of agent behavior, rather than reflecting the outcome of a single simulation instance. This approach was feasible for the toy model, as it is relatively simple and includes a manageable number of agents. In total, six log files were generated, each averaging 150 MB in size. Following automated process discovery, a PM was created from the action log files, as illustrated in Fig. 5A. The corresponding BPD is shown in Fig. 5B.

Since there is only one main agent type in the simulation – the people agent – the generated BPD nevertheless contains two lanes (see Fig. 5B). The first lane, labeled model6_model, represents the simulation environment. In GAMA, the environment is conventionally treated as an agent named after the simulation (here, 'model6') with the suffix "model". Although this world agent functions primarily as the environment rather than as an active decision-making entity, it is formally defined as an agent and thus appears as a distinct lane in the BPD. The second lane, labeled people, represents the only main agent type present in the simulation. In Fig. 5B, the START node connects to the `[behavior]_internal_init31` method in the model6_model lane, which is

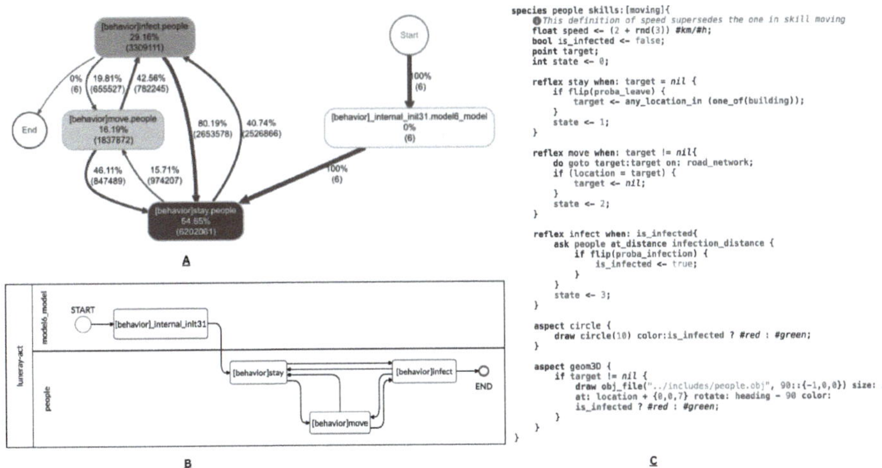

Fig. 5. (A) PM derived from simulation action logs; (B) Corresponding BPD of A; and (C) Actual implementation code for the "people" agent type.

responsible for instantiating the agents. Following instantiation, the next method is [behavior]stay, indicating that the first action executed by the agents is 'stay'. Moreover, the infect method is directly connected to the END node, as the log file shows that the final recorded event before termination is an infect method. To further clarify the interconnections depicted in the diagram, Fig. 5C presents the implementation code for the people agent type.

The system then generated textual summaries of the diagrams and incorporated them into the prompt used to query the language model for narrative generation. As discussed in the previous section, the textual summaries can support multiple narrative variants. Figure 6 is the narrative constructed from the summaries based on the BPD and PM of the action logs.

4.2 Verification

To ensure the accuracy, reliability, and interpretive value of the artifacts produced by the framework, the evaluation followed a three-pronged verification strategy. Each component of this strategy addressed a distinct aspect of the framework's outputs: structural fidelity, narrative quality, and behavioral alignment. Specifically, the evaluation assessed (1) the consistency between simulation logs and the generated visualizations, (2) the quality of the language modelâĂŞgenerated narratives, and (3) the alignment between the narratives and the actual simulation dynamics.

Log-Diagram Consistency. This step served to verify the structural integrity of the visual artifacts generated from the simulation logs. Given that the framework relies on process mining to extract workflows from raw logs, it was necessary to

Comprehensive Narrative
Overall Purpose and Mechanism
The agent-based model appears to simulate the behavior of individuals (people) in response to an infectious process. The simulation begins with the START event, which triggers the _internal_init31 task executed by model6_model. This initialization leads directly to the stay state for the people actor.

From the stay state, individuals can transition to either the infect or move states. The infect state represents a scenario where an individual becomes infected and has a high likelihood (0.8013) of staying in that state. However, there is also a low likelihood (0.1987) of moving from the infect state to the move state.

The move state indicates that individuals are mobile and can transition back to the infect state with a moderate likelihood (0.4369) or stay in the stay state with a similar likelihood (0.4517). The stay state allows for transitions back to either the infect or move states, with moderate and low likelihoods respectively.

Probable Applications
This model can be applied in various real-world and theoretical contexts:

- Epidemiology : Simulating the spread of infectious diseases within a population.
- Urban Planning : Understanding how mobility patterns affect disease transmission.
- Public Health Policy : Evaluating the effectiveness of interventions that encourage staying at home versus moving around.

Key Insights and Takeaways
1. Initialization Phase : The model starts with an initialization phase (_internal_init31) that sets individuals to a stay state, suggesting a controlled or quarantined starting condition.
2. Infection Dynamics : The high likelihood of staying in the infect state indicates that once infected, individuals are likely to remain so for some time.
3. Mobility Impact : The moderate transition probabilities between move, stay, and infect states highlight the complex interplay between mobility and infection risk.
4. End State : The absence of a direct transition from infect to END (weight = 0.0) suggests that the model does not account for recovery or removal from the infectious state, which could be a limitation.

Overall, this agent-based model provides a framework for understanding how individual behaviors and transitions between states can influence the spread of an infection within a population. The insights gained can inform strategies to mitigate disease transmission by adjusting mobility patterns and intervention measures.

Fig. 6. Generated narrative for the Luneray Flu model.

confirm that the resulting PMs and BPMN diagrams accurately represented the underlying simulation behavior.

To conduct this verification, the analysis involved a detailed side-by-side comparison of the information recorded in the logs and the details captured in the diagrams. The comparison revealed full alignment between the following details: methods, variables, and agent types. The only exception is the lack of loops in the diagrams which was because those loops were intentionally removed to highlight core execution paths and improve the clarity of the resultant diagrams. Excluding these intentional simplifications, the one-to-one correspondence confirmed that the process mining outputs remained reliable and structurally faithful to the original simulation dynamics.

Evaluation of LLM-Generated Narratives. Narratives represent a key output of the framework, designed to enhance the interpretability of simulation behavior – particularly for non-expert stakeholders. To evaluate narrative quality, the assessment employed the "LLM-as-a-judge" approach, in which a high-performing language model is used to evaluate the outputs of peer models. This method provides a scalable, consistent, and empirically validated alternative to human evaluation, with previous research demonstrating high agreement between language model assessments and expert judgments [24].

The evaluation used GPT-4 Turbo as the judging model and compared narrative outputs from three candidate models: Mistral 24B, Gemini 2.0 Flash, and Claude 3.7 Sonnet. Each model's narrative was rated across six dimensions: precision, coverage, faithfulness, interpretive depth, novelty of insight, and clarity.

As shown in Fig. 7, Gemini 2.0 Flash consistently ranked highest in overall performance, particularly in interpretive depth and clarity. Mistral 24B, however, remained highly competitive, and its open-source nature, strong accuracy, and

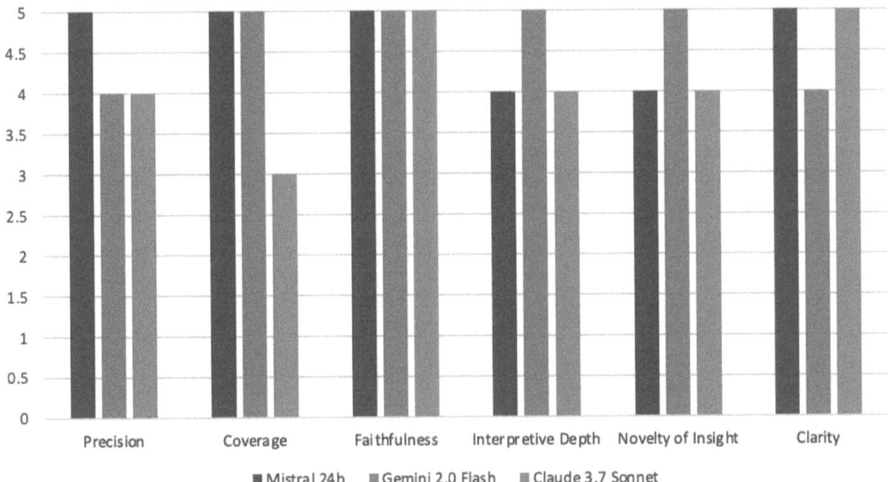

Fig. 7. Comparative evaluation of LLM-generated narratives using GPT-4 Turbo as an automated judge, with scores averaged over three independent assessment rounds to assess the overall performance of Mistral 24B, Gemini 2.0 Flash, and Claude 3.7 Sonnet.

privacy-friendly deployment make it a compelling alternative, particularly in sensitive or constrained environments.

This evaluation step confirmed that the framework can produce high-quality, insightful narratives when paired with capable LLMs and well-structured inputs derived from process mining outputs.

Simulation-Narrative Alignment. The final verification step evaluated how accurately the generated narrative reflected the actual behavior and underlying logic of the agent-based simulation. This was essential for assessing the narrative's fidelity – not merely as a coherent summary, but as a scientifically grounded explanation of the model's internal dynamics.

To validate this alignment, the LLM-generated narrative was compared against the output of the simulation. Based on the narrative, there are four distinct dynamic phases within the simulation:

- **Initialization Phase (IP):** "The model starts with an initialization phase that sets individuals to a stay state, suggesting a controlled or quarantined starting condition".
- **Infection Dynamics (ID):** "The high likelihood of staying in the infect state indicates that once infected, individuals are likely to remain so for some time".
- **Mobility Impact (MI):** "The moderate transition probabilities between move, stay, and infect states highlight the complex interplay between mobility and infection risk".

- **End State (ES)**: "The absence of a direct transition from infect to END suggests that the model does not account for recovery or removal from the infectious state, which could be a limitation".

These phases were substantiated by the annotated simulation output shown in Fig. 8. The early cycles depict the IP, with most agents remaining stationary. As the simulation progresses, agents begin to move and interact (MI), triggering a rapid increase in infections (ID). Eventually, the system reaches a terminal state (ES), where all agents are infected and no further transitions occur – corroborating both the narrative and the model's logic.

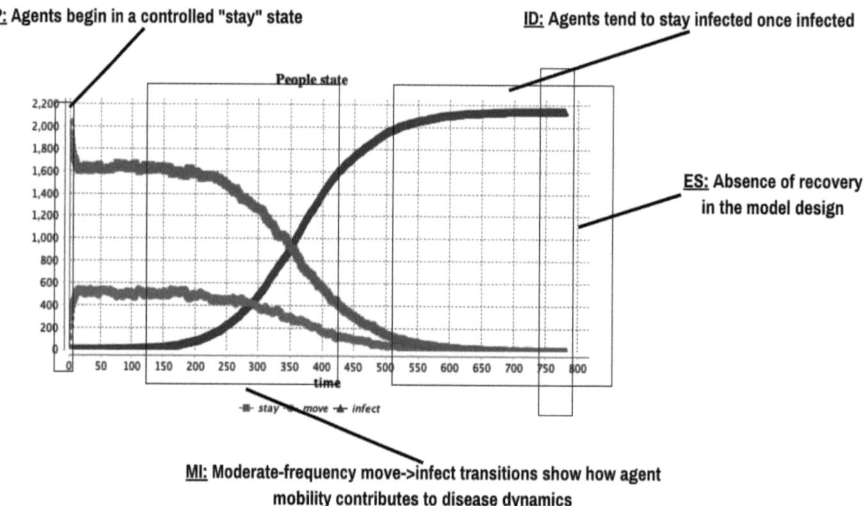

Fig. 8. Annotated progression of agent states over time in the Luneray Flu model. The graph shows changes in population counts for each state (e.g., stay, move, infect) across simulation cycles.

Given this alignment, it can be said that the narrative did more than recount observable events; it provided interpretive insight into the model's structure and behavior. It highlighted key design choices (e.g., the absence of recovery), systemic mechanisms (e.g., mobility-driven spread), and emergent outcomes. These findings demonstrate that the LLM-generated narrative effectively captured both surface-level dynamics and deeper structural characteristics of the agent-based model.

5 Summary and Conclusion

The example in the previous section demonstrates how our methodology – leveraging simulation logs to automatically generate ABM narratives – can make agent-based models more transparent and accessible. The approach yields three complementary artifacts: process maps (PMs), business process diagrams (BPDs), and simulation narratives.

PMs provide a high-level view of how processes unfold during a simulation by highlighting critical methods and variables. To address the clutter that often arises in large and complex models, we applied thresholding to filter out less significant nodes, ensuring that only the most influential processes remain visible. BPDs, derived from PMs, extend this view by structuring agent interactions and relationships, offering insights into the organizational logic of the simulation. Beyond their value as visual artifacts, both PMs and BPDs were used to construct effective prompts for the LLM. Their structured representations distill essential elements of the simulation – such as event sequences, key transitions, and inter-agent interactions – into a concise, context-rich format. The resulting narrative, grounded in both implementation code and execution logs, complements the visualizations by providing an accessible explanation of the model. It also helps users interpret complex diagrams when they become overwhelming, ensuring a more comprehensive understanding of the simulation. Together, these artifacts form a robust foundation for describing agent-based models, with the semi-automated process significantly reducing the effort required to generate them.

These artifacts contribute to the understanding of simulation models across diverse audiences by serving as communication tools for stakeholders, complementary documentation for modelers, and structured narratives for researchers. While the current implementation is limited to representing agent workflows through modified variables and executed functions, future extensions – such as logging critical input parameters and linking them to observable outputs – could further enhance their utility. Nonetheless, the integration of PMs, BPDs, and generated narratives represents an important step toward improving model communication by providing a structured overview of processes, inter-agent interactions, and key variables, ultimately advancing the transparency and accessibility of agent-based models.

References

1. van der Aalst, W.M.P.: Foundations of Process Discovery, pp. 37–75. Springer International Publishing, Cham (2022)
2. van der Aalst, W.M.P.: Process mining: A 360 degree overview. In: van der Aalst, W.M.P., Carmona, J. (eds.) Process Mining Handbook. LNBIP, vol. 448, pp. 3–34. Springer (2022). https://doi.org/10.1007/978-3-031-08848-3_1
3. Allison, A., Dickson, M., Fisher, K., Thrush, S.: communicating drivers of environmental change through transdisciplinary human-environment modeling. Earths Future **9**(9) (2021)
4. Bartalesi, V., Lenzi, E., De Martino, C.: Using large language models to create narrative events. PeerJ Comput. Sci. **10**, e2242 (2024)
5. Bonabeau, E.: Agent-based modeling: methods and techniques for simulating human systems. Proc. Natl. Acad. Sci. U.S.A. **99**(10), 7280–7287 (2002)

6. Cartwright, S., et al.: Communicating complex ecological models to non-scientist end users. Ecol. Model. **338**, 51–59 (2016)

7. Chinosi, M., Trombetta, A.: Bpmn: an introduction to the standard. Compute. Standards & Interfaces **34**(1), 124–134 (2012)

8. ESTECO SpA: Cardanit (10-18-2024). https://www.cardanit.com/

9. Grimm, V.: The odd protocol for describing agent-based and other simulation models: a second update to improve clarity, replication, and structural realism. J. Artif. Soc. Soc. Simul. **23**(2), 7 (2020)

10. Grueau, C.: Towards a domain specific modeling language for agent-based modeling of land use/cover change. In: Parsons, J., Chiu, D. (eds.) ER 2013. LNCS, vol. 8697, pp. 267–276. Springer, Cham (2014). https://doi.org/10.1007/978-3-319-14139-8_28

11. Haveman, S., Bonnema, G.: Communication of simulation and modelling activities in early systems engineering. Proc. Comput. Sci. **44** (2015)

12. Janssenswillen, G., Depaire, B., Swennen, M., Jans, M.J., Vanhoof, K.: bupaR: enabling reproducible business process analysis. Knowl.-Based Syst. **163**, 1857 (2019)

13. Jiang, A.Q., et al.: Mistral 7b. arXiv preprint arXiv:2310.06825 (2023)

14. Lee, J.S., et al.: The complexities of agent-based modeling output analysis. JASSS **18**(4) (2015)

15. Liu, N.F., et al.: Lost in the Middle: How Language Models Use Long Contexts (Nov 2023). https://doi.org/10.48550/arXiv.2307.03172

16. Millington, J.D., O'Sullivan, D., Perry, G.L.: Model histories: narrative explanation in generative simulation modelling. Geoforum **43**(6), 1025–1034 (2012)

17. Müller, B., et al.: Standardised and transparent model descriptions for agent-based models: current status and prospects. Environ. Model. Softw. **55**, 156–163 (2014)

18. Neumann, A., Kirsten, E., Zafar, M.B., Singh, J.: Position is power: system prompts as a mechanism of bias in large language models (LLMs). In: Proceedings of the 2025 ACM Conference on Fairness, Accountability, and Transparency, pp. 573–598 (Jun 2025). https://doi.org/10.1145/3715275.3732038

19. Onggo, B.S.S.: Bpmn pattern for agent-based simulation model representation. In: Proceedings of the 2012 Winter Simulation Conference (WSC), pp. 1–10 (2012)

20. Onggo, B.S.S., Karpat, O.: Agent-based conceptual model representation using bpmn. In: Proceedings of the 2011 Winter Simulation Conference (WSC), pp. 671–682 (2011)

21. Soika, R., Ortmayr, T.: OpenBPMN (2023). https://github.com/imixs/open-bpmn?tab=License-1-ov-file

22. Taghikhah, F., Voinov, A., Filatova, T., Polhill, J.: Machine-assisted agent-based modeling: opening the black box. J. Comput. Sci. **64** (2022)

23. Taillandier, P., et al.: Building, composing and experimenting complex spatial models with the gama platform. GeoInformatica **23**(2), 299–322 (2019)

24. Zheng, S., et al.: Judging llm-as-a-judge: evaluating the evaluators. arXiv preprint arXiv:2305.17975 (2023)

Public Policy and Institutions

Agent-Based Modelling for Public Social Service Distribution

Petra Ahrweiler[1]([✉]) [iD], Nigel Gilbert[2] [iD], Martha Bicket[2] [iD],
Albert Sabater Coll[3] [iD], Elisabeth Spaeth[1] [iD], Hassan Bashiri[4] [iD],
Ebin Deni Raj[5] [iD], and Blanca Luque Capellas[1] [iD]

[1] TISSS Lab, Johannes Gutenberg University, Jakob-Welder-Weg 20,
55128 Mainz, Germany
`petra.ahrweiler@uni-mainz.de`
[2] CRESS, University of Surrey, Guildford G2 7XH, UK
[3] Observatory for Ethics in Artificial Intelligence, University of Girona,
17004 Girona, Spain
[4] Department of Computer Science, Hamedan University of Technology,
Hamedan, Iran
[5] Indian Institute of Information Technology Kottayam, Valavoor P.O,
Pala, 686635 Kottayam, Kerala, India

Abstract. The paper introduces an agent-based modelling approach for assessing beneficiaries in public social service distribution. The "AI for Assessment" (AI FORA) project combines empirical research, gamification, and agent-based models (ABM) to assess the fairness of AI-based distribution in different countries and propose improvements. The paper presents a participatory research strategy, where ABM and serious games are used to identify more desirable social assessment routines within heterogeneous cultural contexts. By following this approach, the paper suggests that context-specific ABM can be used for co-designing AI systems with stakeholders, to assist ex-ante evaluation for testing and prototyping AI systems before implementation thus reducing risks and costs, and for scenario analysis and asking what-if questions to reduce uncertainty. Besides offering a useful tool to help social workers in reflecting on and improving their assessments in their immediate workplace, the proposed ABM-centred approach is also relevant more generally for public, social and technology policy. Prototyping helps to avoid risk of failure, unintended consequences, and systems that turn out to be ineffective following expensive development. The option to address what-if questions, to test interventions before implementing them, and to evaluate the advantages and disadvantages of different scenarios, is of great relevance in many policy domains.

Keywords: Social Assessment · Public Service Provision · Context-Specific ABM

© The Author(s), under exclusive license to Springer Nature Switzerland AG 2026
A. Vidler and S. Swarup (Eds.): MABS 2025, LNAI 16227, pp. 45–58, 2026.
https://doi.org/10.1007/978-3-032-16328-8_4

1   Introduction

Public administrations are increasingly using Artificial Intelligence (AI) algorithms to decide on the provision of public social services such as unemployment benefits, pension entitlements, kindergarten places and social assistance to their citizens, hoping to achieve greater efficiency and objectivity [1,2]. Criteria vary widely around the world. There is no approach to social assessment that would be perceived as fair everywhere. The **Artificial Intelligence for Assessment** (AI FORA) project is investigating AI-based public service provision of national welfare systems within a range of country case studies, aiming to show how to co-design context-dependent, value-sensitive, responsive and dynamic AI systems starting from existing systems that are perceived as problematic. It combines empirical case study research on AI-based social service delivery with community-based multi-stakeholder workshops and a series of case-specific agent-based models (ABM) for assessing the status quo of AI-based distribution fairness in different countries, for simulating desired policy scenarios, and for generating an approach to 'Better AI'. The paper is structured as follows: In Sect. 2 we give a short overview of the overall AI FORA modelling approach. In Sect. 3, we introduce the ABMs developed in AI FORA to illustrate the potential of this approach in practice. Our conclusions are outlined in Sect. 4.

2   The AI FORA Modelling Approach

A participatory modelling strategy (see Fig. 1) was designed [3] to support the transition from existing to desired social assessment systems, with the following elements for each case study:

1. A workshop is held to map out the overall existing case study system.
2. An ABM that models the current social assessment system, including an initial ruleset[1] (ruleset 1) and exemplar agent attributes, is written.
3. Ruleset 1 is checked and iteratively refined by running the ABM.
4. Rules for an ABM-based game to be played with stakeholders, are written.
5. At a gamification workshop with stakeholders, rules are gradually adapted.
6. A 'better ruleset', ruleset 2, is extracted using the records from the game play.
7. A synthetic population is created to match the real population on relevant attributes.
8. Ruleset 2 and the synthetic population are used to generate a training dataset.
9. A machine learning system to be used to assess applicants is trained using the training data.

Mapping the existing actor network requires research, both quantitative and qualitative, complemented by Participatory Systems Mapping [4] to reconstruct

---

[1] By 'ruleset' we mean a collection of rules that when followed (by a clerk or by agents in the ABM) can be used to classify an applicant as deserving of full, partial or no social services allocation.

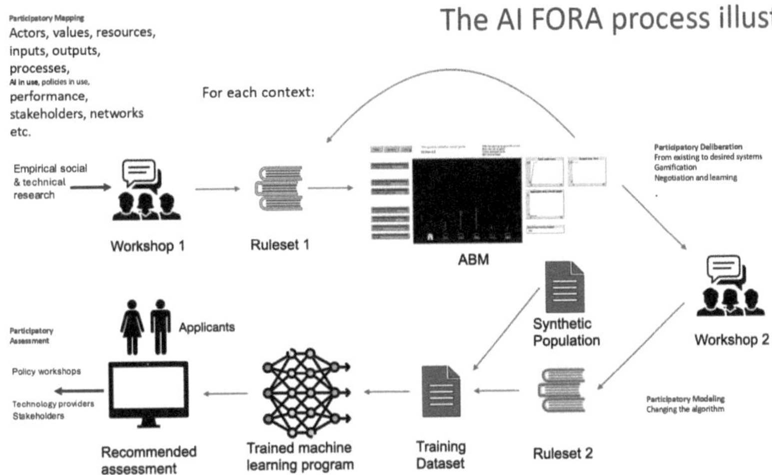

Fig. 1. The modelling strategy.

the existing system from the perspective of stakeholders. This work provides information on the actors involved, the societal norms and values, the organizational practices and routines in place, the current use of AI in the system, and the system's performance. This data is used to create an ABM representation of the existing social assessment routines, examples of which are presented in the next section.

3 The Case Study ABMs for Improving Social Assessment

3.1 The Spanish Complex-Needs ABM

Sabater Coll et al. [5] examine the perceptions, attitudes and acceptance of AI-based social assessment technologies by policy makers and administrative agencies locally in Catalonia, a frontrunner Spanish region in the adoption of digital technologies for the public sector. The Spanish ABM is set in a social service agency in a municipality in Spain, where social service clerks are faced with the challenge of seeking to allocate (limited) social service resources to deserving applicants, many of whom have multiple, complex needs.

Agents. The clerks' aim is to allocate social service resources to applicants to maximise the sum of applicants' wellbeing. The model is based on an existing system of social assessment used by local authorities in Catalunya, the SSM-CAT[2] a relatively easy-to-use tool designed to assist core social service professionals

---

[2] See https://suport-hestia.aoc.cat/hc/en-gb/articles/4415411394321-Self-Sufficient-Matrix-Screening-Tool-SSM-CAT.,.

in identifying individuals with complex social care needs across 13 dimensions. For simplicity, our model focuses on the following 6 applicant attributes: household income, accommodation, work and training, mental health, physical health and number of dependents. Each applicant receives a score of between 1 and 5 according to their level of self-sufficiency in each of these dimensions. The sum of an applicant's scores is used to calculate their overall need score of between 6 and 30.

Environment and Global Attributes. During the simulation, applicants can either be at home or in a queue at a social service clerk's desk. The number of desks in the environment is defined by the number of clerks chosen at setup. The following global attributes are used in this ABM to define the environment and corresponding applicant-clerk interactions: number of the round, number of applicants, number of clerks, social services budget, available appointments, threshold.

Actions and Interactions over Time. At the start of each round, applicants who are self-sufficient (≤ 2 across each of the 6 wellbeing dimensions) stay at home. All other applicants are randomly assigned to clerks. Clerks evaluate applicants using an algorithm based on a ruleset and applicants' attributes.

The initial algorithm is described below, but new rules can be introduced to adjust the system, such as modifying the order in which applicants are seen, changing the scoring algorithm, or altering how the budget is allocated at the end of each round. Each round corresponds to a day of the agents' lives (home, desk, office meeting, home) and a round is completed when every agent is home again.

Scoring Algorithm. For *household income* and *number of dependents*, applicants are ranked against each other and given between 1 and 5 need points based on their rank relative to others in that round. Need points are allocated.

At the end of each round the social service budget is distributed to successful applicants in order of severity: the highest-scoring applicant is allocated an amount equal to their overall need score, then the next highest, and so on until the budget for that round is used up. Applicants' need scores are then updated:

- If the applicant received support: one need category improves (score decreases by 1)
- If the applicant did not receive support: one need category worsens (score increases by 1), as well as all categories with a score ≥ 4.
- Additionally, there is a 10% chance that one attribute worsens by 1 and a 10% chance that one improves by 1.
- If there are any critically needy applicants (overall need score $\geq$ threshold) at the end of the round, this impacts the upcoming round's available budget but does not improve applicants' need scores. The run ends if there is no budget left at the beginning of a round to allocate to applicants.

By playing the game, agents are supposed to develop an "interpretation culture" on fairness issues as agents converge in judging applicants' profiles according to the self-sufficiency matrix. This is in line with the central objective of the tool SSM-CAT, which is to identify complex social care needs after having completed specific training.

3.2   An ABM of the German Asylum Application Process

This ABM illustrates the asylum application procedure in Germany, following refugees (here: applicants) as they progress through the various stages at which they are "assessed". The ABM is based on insights gained from desktop research and five exploratory and seven in-depth interviews, as well as several focus groups and participatory modelling sessions. The link to state-of-the-art AI used for assessment is the language-/dialect recognition software, used to identify the country/region of origin of asylum seekers [6]. The interviews indicated the relevance of legitimacy [7,10], and agency of refugees [11,12], mirroring particular challenges in the asylum procedure posed by (a) the lack of (assured) knowledge due to, for example, missing documents or high workload when administrative workers try to assess the applicant's credibility [13], and (b) the lack of transparency partly due to opaqueness of decision-making, language barriers and refugees' personal experiences (e.g. having little trust in institutions; being traumatized). The ABM aims to display the tension between asylum bureaucratic legitimacy and refugees' agency and represents a tool to reflect upon potentials and risks âĂŞ inhibiting "value trade-offs" (e.g. efficiency vs. fairness) - of using AI in the different assessment processes.

Agents. The central agents are applicants applying for asylum status in Germany. Their aim is to get full asylum status and the right to stay and work in Germany. Applicants are initialised with the following attributes: Country of origin (applicants from certain countries have a higher chance of receiving asylum status than others); proof of identity and education; number of years the applicant has lived in Germany; whether the interpreter is 'good', which is the case when there is a positive match between the applicant and interpreter's genders, ethnicities and spoken languages; German language proficiency; which of the 16 federal states in Germany the applicant is applying from and being processed in; whether the applicant has personal support from a lawyer, voluntary worker or migration councillor from a welfare organisation (having a supporter improves an applicant's chances of a positive decision outcome); whether the applicant has done voluntary work; health status.

Environment and Global Attributes. During the simulation, applicants move between six different 'stations': registration, hearing, decision, post-decision, (court) appeals and Hardship Commission ('HC'). The first three stations (registration, hearing and decision) represent key stages in the application process. After receiving a decision on their asylum application, applicants move to the post-decision station which represents everyday life in Germany. The appeals and Hardship Commission stations are where asylum seekers can go to challenge their asylum decision and right-to-remain status. The following global attributes are used in this ABM to define the environment and corresponding applicant interactions: Number of the round, initial number of applicants, number of new applicants, administrative workload, workload threshold, and appeals quota.

Actions and Interactions over Time.

Registration. On setup and at the start of each new round, new applicants begin at the registration station.

Hearing Applicants must wait for a hearing before they can proceed. Those assigned a "good" interpreter (indicating a positive match between the applicant and interpreter's genders, ethnicities and spoken languages) have a higher chance of advancing in a given round.

Decision. Applicants wait for their cases to be assessed by an administrator, who assigns one of three statuses: rejection (least desirable), tolerance, or full asylum (most desirable). Some may wait multiple rounds.

Post-decision. After receiving a decision, applicants move to the post-decision station, where they have the chance to get a job if they have the right to work. From here, some applicants may choose to appeal their decision through the courts, the Hardship Commission, or both.

Court Appeals. Applicants may appeal to the courts if their case may have been treated unfairly or poorly (e.g. due to discrimination or administrative errors). Applicants who have received full refugee status do not appeal their status. Appeals are more likely in federal states with heavy workloads or organizational bias. Each round, a limited number of appeals are heard. Successful applicants improve their status by one tier (rejection $\rightarrow$ tolerance; tolerance $\rightarrow$ full asylum).

Hardship Commission. Applicants appealing to the Hardship Commission are at risk of being repatriated. Unlike court appeals which assess procedural fairness, the Hardship Commission focuses on the applicant's degree of integration in Germany. To get a positive recommendation from the Hardship Commission, applicants must have a job, a good command of German and be engaged in additional activities (e.g. voluntary work). Approximately 75% of those with positive recommendations go on to win the right to stay in Germany.

The run ends when the maximum number of rounds defined at setup have elapsed.

3.3   The Estonian Career Counselling ABM

The Estonian ABM is based on the career counselling support for job-seekers available through the Estonian Unemployment Insurance Fund (EUIF) which has been extensively investigated by [14].

Agents. The agents in the simulation are jobseekers ('clients') who are applying for career counselling support and the consultants who are assessing them and providing support. The consultants' aim is to allocate career counselling resources to maximise the number of clients in employment. The attributes by which applicants are initialised are as follows: Work experience, fluency in Estonian, fluency in other languages, driving license, education, dependents, health, time unemployed. Consultants can then draw on these applicant attributes to calculate an assessment result which grants the client access to counselling sessions and/or additional training.

Environment and Global Attributes. During the simulation, applicants can either be at home, in work, or in a queue at a consultant's desk. The number of desks in the environment is defined by the number of consultants chosen at setup. The following global attributes are used in this ABM to define the environment and corresponding consultant-client interactions: number of the round, number of clients, number of consultants, new clients, and the score that applicants need to achieve to be offered a job.

Actions and Interactions over Time. At the beginning of the simulation and each subsequent round, new applicants are initialised at home and then randomly allocated to a consultant. They have their first meeting with the consultant and are assessed to determine what degree of support they are likely to need. Consultants assess clients using an algorithm based on a ruleset and applicants' attributes. The initial algorithm is described below, but new rules can be introduced to adjust the system, such as changing the scoring algorithm and the attributes it uses as inputs, or changing the point thresholds required for each assessment result.

Scoring Algorithm. Based on their number of points, the algorithm gives a red, yellow or green result. Clients who receive a red result (< 10 points) are considered to need the greatest amount of support. They attend weekly career counselling meetings and get priority access to training courses. Clients with a yellow result (≥ 10 and < 20 points) attend fortnightly meetings and those with green (≥ 20 points) are invited to attend monthly meetings. At the end of each round, clients have the opportunity to get a job. A client's chances of getting a job are positively influenced by the following factors: Number of years of work experience; attended a training course; number of career counselling meetings attended; driving licence; higher education levels; fewer dependents; less time spent unemployed. Applicants stay with the same consultant until they find a job. The run ends when the maximum number of rounds defined at setup has elapsed.

3.4   An ABM of the Targeted Subsidies Plan in Iran

An agent-based model was developed to simulate and evaluate the socio-economic impacts of the Targeted Subsidies Plan (TSP) in Iran. Details of the TSP can be found in [15]. The model allows policymakers and decision-makers to evaluate the effects of decisions regarding the amount of subsidies paid to different deciles of society and changes in income deciles.

Agents. The agents in this model represent households, with the default configuration simulating 230 households as a scaled representation of 23 million households in Iran. The number of agents in the model can be adjusted within the user interface, ranging from 100 to 23,000 households. Each household has the following characteristics:

Income. The income characteristic is randomly assigned to agents based on a power distribution pattern derived from the Iranian Welfare Database (IWDB).

Wealth (Assets). In IWDB, another influential parameter for household decile classification is household assets, which is used to reflect economic inequalities in modelling.

Household (Family) Size. This characteristic is also quantified using data from IWDB using a normal distribution.

Monthly expenses estimated to indicate the standard cost of living.

Household decile indicates the household's membership in one of the income deciles, which is determined by the model based on the Test Means.

Subsidy Amount. This is the amount of subsidy the household receives. The amount of subsidy is a function of income decile and the size of households.

The key point is that the households are regrouped every year depending on variations in income and wealth. To increase the degree of realism of this model, two extra parameters have been considered: the first parameter is the enrichment rate that, because of causes such as inheritance or successful investment, may alter the percentage, adjustable from 0 up to 10% of the totality of the households simulated, and the second is the household bankruptcy rate, which causes a sudden shift in the status of households from high-income deciles to low-income deciles due to reasons such as business failure and loss of capital.

Environment. The environment reflects the socio-economic landscape affected by the TSP, including:

The budget of TSP. The funds that the government must pay to households as subsidies each month.

Household Grouping. Households are divided into ten deciles based on income and wealth, with subsidies allocated only to the bottom four deciles. In the model, subsidy amounts vary by decile, reflecting real-world practices, with the first decile (lowest-income households) receiving the highest subsidy.

Economic Dynamics The model assumes random shocks to income, such as a 2% increase or decrease in household wealth each year, as representative of natural fluctuations in the wealth-income levels in the model.

This environment is designed to reflect the unequal patterns of wealth and income distribution prevalent in Iranian society, as documented in the IWDB.

Actions and Interactions over Time. The main operations of the model revolve around the mechanisms of subsidy targeting, such as decile allocation, subsidy allocation, and redecile allocation. The main operations include the following:

Initialization. At the beginning of the simulation, each household is assigned income, wealth, and size. The values of these three parameters are randomly assigned but follow patterns extracted from IWDB data, using normal and power distributions.

Subsidy Distribution. Monthly distribution of subsidies to households in the lower four deciles, proportional to decile and household size.

Re-assignment to Deciles. Households, after receiving updated income and wealth values reflecting changes in their economic status, are re-grouped at the end of each year.

Upward and Downward Economic Mobility. Some households will experience upward or downward mobility due to policy interventions or natural variation.

Emerging Effects. The interactions between agents and the TSP will reflect the overall socio-economic trends such as changes in income and mobility across deciles.

The model runs for 60 years on monthly cycles. Each cycle includes subsidy allocation, economic adjustments, and annual re-assignment. It demonstrates upward income shifts for low-income deciles, highlighting the potential of the TSP to improve the economic conditions of vulnerable households. Despite the increasing income of the low-income classes, the range of income from the bottom to the top deciles remains very broad.

The annual re-grouping points out the impact of policy on economic stability and mobility. The dynamic in the model helps us understand the impact of policies and decisions on reducing the gap between different social deciles and reducing inequality and poverty. Since the grouping is repeated continuously and annually, the impact of policies can also be visualized and understood in the long term [16].

3.5   An ABM of the Indian Public Distribution System (PDS)

Hunger alleviation and poverty eradication are the twin objectives of the Public Distribution System (PDS) in India. The PDS is intended to provide essential goods and services at so-called "ration shops", mainly food items such as rice, wheat, sugar, kerosene etc. to beneficiaries, especially "the poorest of the poor", at reasonable cost contributing to general social welfare. The effectiveness of the PDS largely depends on adequate policy decisions regarding operational and organisational aspects of the system [17].

The ABM of the PDS in India focuses on three key objectives: fairness in ration allocation, transparency in operations, and accountability to reduce corruption. By modelling the interactions between beneficiaries, ration shops, suppliers, and officials, the simulation provides insights into system performance under various scenarios.

Agents. There are four types of agent in the model:

Beneficiaries. Represent the population depending on PDS for rations.

Ration Shops. Serve as distribution points for commodities.

Suppliers. Provide stock for ration shops.

Officials. Inspect ration shops to maintain transparency/detect irregularities.

Environment. A number of key characteristics of the model are tracked, including:

Corruption Risk Levels. Each shop is assigned a corruption risk.

Total Beneficiaries Served. N. of individuals successfully receiving rations.

Stock Levels. Track available stock across the system.

Corruption Incidents. Record instances of corruption identified.

Metrics Include fairness, transparency, and accountability scores.

Actions and Interactions over Time. Each of the agents react at each time step, according to the states of other agents:

Beneficiaries. Move to the nearest ration shop to collect their eligible rations.

Ration Shops. Manage stock levels and distribute rations or request resupply.

Suppliers. Transport stock to ration shops using trucks.

Officials. Randomly inspect ration shops to detect corruption and ensure compliance.

Metrics Updates. At each tick, system performance metrics are updated to reflect changes in fairness, transparency, and accountability.

Enhancing transparency, improving accountability, and ensuring fairness are critical to optimizing PDS performance. Regular inspections play a pivotal role in significantly reducing corruption and enhancing system transparency. When corruption risks are minimized through rigorous monitoring, accountability scores improve, reflecting a more responsible system. Furthermore, the fair distribution of rations relies on efficient stock management and the reduction of corruption, ensuring equitable access for all beneficiaries. Insights derived from the simulation can guide policymakers in addressing systemic inefficiencies and formulating strategies to optimize PDS performance.

4   Conclusions and Outlook

Case studies offer a chance to bring data from empirical research to models and simulations for better futures. The ABM of the Spanish case study acts as a kind of theorem checking device for the assessment algorithm in place in the empirical system under investigation, in this case social assessment in Catalunya. The ABM not only ensures that the ruleset is coherent and complete but also acts as a starting point for stakeholders to devise a better algorithm. The case study ABM for Estonia uses modelling to shift the focus more explicitly to citizens and their requirements concerning AI systems in the context of (un)employment services; particular attention is directed towards potentially vulnerable groups to gain a deeper understanding of their interactions with and requirements for AI systems. The German case study ABM focuses on the agency of refugees (for more and quicker integration into society and the job market) and the legitimacy of administrative decisions (for accountability and correctness of bureaucratic procedures in granting asylum), and the trade-offs between these two policy objectives. Thereby, the ABM helps to identify tensions (and entanglements) arising in the different assessment processes, which is crucial to be able to reconsider where AI might be truly helpful, contributing to more efficiency and fairness for both sides. Iran's case study ABM uses insights gained from the analysis of TSP in Iran to explore future scenarios involving the implementation of various policy options. The case study ABM in India will help to explore the pivotal role of deep learning in the development of community-specific vulnerability prediction models in the Indian scenario, which will be an innovation in community-based interventions.

For Spain, Germany and Estonia, using an interacting cycle of agent-based modelling and serious games pointed to an approach by which AI technology can be specified in a stakeholder-driven way, so that it is more transparent and discursive about bias and discrimination, includes the social justice values of the society in which it will be used, and is responsive to the needs of vulnerable groups. Interactive and participatory formats at multi-stakeholder workshops exposed the culturally shaped and heterogeneous value perspectives of the local social groups. As a central component, participants 'played the ABM'. Stakeholders suggested, discussed, co-developed and tested interventions in all parts of the game situation, including the social assessment criteria ('changing the algorithm') to propose a 'better' ruleset for that assessment system. The advantage of iterating between games and ABM is that stake-holders can deliberate in the game context with options to 'change the rules of the game' as result of their discussions, the ABM then codifies and formalizes the rules showing the results of their application in the game environment, which, in the next iteration, informs stakeholder discussions.

Following the modelling strategy introduced in Sect. 1, this approach also offers the possibility of producing relevant training data that can be used to prototype algorithms fitting desired futures. In welfare systems, decision-makers often face complex cases that require a nuanced understanding of policies, individual circumstances, and broader social contexts. The use of methods that facilitate a collaborative environment in this way allows for the exchange of knowledge and experiences, leading to more informed and effective decision-making. To test the reasonable suggestions of social workers familiar with the system, however, was not previously an option âĂŞ especially not with a view to determining whether and how an AI system could take up these suggestions and make things better than they are. Once the existing and 'better' ruleset have been determined through the iterative process of building ABMs and running gamification workshops for each case study country, these rulesets can be used for the next step in the modelling process. Although the outcomes of the rulesets have been already demonstrated by the ABM, this is only in a small game environment. It does not show what the rulesets would do for the whole population of case study countries, especially not given population dynamics. Rather than using microdata for the population itself, to comply with research ethics and data protection issues, a synthetic population database is generated that resembles the real-world data for a case study country. First, the ruleset of the *existing* system is run on the synthetic population. It produces an output database with some individuals getting service and others not. To validate this, we could check against real-world data on the socio-demographics of social service recipients; however, in most cases such data is not available. Instead, we can check whether the synthetic population database reproduces the number of service recipients in the real world (if available), whether it re-produces the stylized facts on bias and discrimination in the literature, and whether it reproduces the case study's empirical research results. Second, the ruleset of the *desired* system is run on the synthetic population. It produces an output database with different distributions from the first. Stakeholders (and decision makers) can now compare these two "data worlds" and check the effects of different assessment algorithms on the overall population and the expected population dynamics. Once the assessment algorithm is confirmed, the corresponding database can be used as training data for a neural network that recommends social assessment decisions for distributing services in the real-world context. This step of the modelling strategy has only been implemented for the Spanish case study so far [18]. Rather than focussing on the assessment situation in a social service agency and following the approach with games and synthetic data (Spain, Germany, Estonia), the ABM of Iran and India depicted the whole social welfare systems of TSP and PDS using empirical data for calibration. Both case studies intend to use their ABM to directly create training data.

Summarising, though the ABMs might differ in purpose, utility or scope, they can all be used for co-designing AI systems with stakeholders, to assist ex-ante evaluation for testing and prototyping AI systems before implementation thus reducing risks and costs, and for scenario analysis and asking what-if questions to reduce uncertainty. Besides offering a useful tool to help social workers in reflecting on and improving their assessments in their immediate workplace, the proposed ABM-centered approach is also relevant more generally for public, social and technology policy. Prototyping helps to avoid risk of failure, unintended consequences, and systems that turn out to be ineffective following expensive development. The option to address what-if questions, to test interventions before implementing them, and to evaluate the advantages and disadvantages of different scenarios, is of great relevance in many policy domains. Results will be discussed in the near future with representatives of the policy community responsible for AI use in public social service provision.

Acknowledgments. The authors gratefully acknowledge funding of this work by the German Volkswagen Foundation under grant agreement number 98 560.

Disclosure of Competing Interests. The authors have no competing interests to declare that are relevant to the content of this article.

References

1. Angwin, J., Larson, J., Mattu, S., Kirchner, L.: Machine Bias. In: Ethics of Data and Analytics. Auerbach Publications (2022)
2. Eubanks, V.: Automating Inequality: How High-Tech Tools Profile, Police, and Punish the Poor. St. Martin's Publishing Group (2018)
3. Ahrweiler, P., et al.: Gamification and Simulation for Innovation. In: Elsenbroich, C., Verhagen, H. (eds.) Advances in Social Simulation, pp. 121–136. Springer, Cham (2024). https://doi.org/10.1007/978-3-031-57785-7_11
4. Barbrook-Johnson, P., Penn, A.S.: Systems Mapping: How to build and use causal models of systems. Springer International Publishing, Cham (2022)
5. Sabater Coll, A., López, B., Campdepadrós, R., Sánchez, C.: Participatory action research for AI in social services: an example of local practice in Spain. In:

     Ahrweiler, P. (ed.) Participatory Artificial Intelligence in Public Social Services. Springer, Cham (2025). https://doi.org/10.1007/978-3-031-71678-2_4

6. Späth, E.: The AI use in the asylum procedure in Germany: exploring perspectives with refugees and supporters on assessment criteria and beyond. In: Ahrweiler, P. (ed.) Participatory Artificial Intelligence in Public Social Services. Springer, Cham (2025). https://doi.org/10.1007/978-3-031-71678-2_6

7. Buxton, R., Draper, J.: Refugees, membership, and state system legitimacy. Ethics Global Politics **15**(4), 113–130 (2022)

8. Grimmelikhuijsen, S., Meijer, A.: Legitimacy of algorithmic decision-making: six threats and the need for a calibrated institutional response. Perspect. Public Manag. Governance **5**(3), 232–242 (2022)

9. Kuhlmann, S., Proeller, I., Schimanke, D., Ziekow, J.: German Public Administration: Background and Key Issues. In: Kuhlmann, S., Proeller, I., Schimanke, D., Ziekow, J. (eds.) Public Administration in Germany. GPM, pp. 1–13. Springer, Cham (2021). https://doi.org/10.1007/978-3-030-53697-8_1

10. Van der Kist, J., Rosset, D.: Knowledge and legitimacy in asylum decision-making: the politics of country of origin information. Citizsh. Stud. **24**(5), 663–679 (2020)

11. Emirbayer, M., Mische, A.: What is agency? Am. J. Sociol. **103**(4), 962–1023 (1998)

12. Essed, P., Frerks, G., Schrijvers, J. (eds.): Refugees and the Transformation of Societies: Agency, Policies, Ethics, and Politics. Vol. 13. Berghahn Books (2004)

13. Mitsch, L.: Das Wissensproblem im Asylrecht: zwischen materiellen Steuerungsdefiziten und Europäisierung [Dissertation]. 1. Auflage. Nomos, Baden-Baden (2020). ISBN 978-3-8487-6785-4

14. Vihalemm, T., Maenniste, M., Trumm, A., Solvak, M.: Specialists and algorithms: implementation of AI in the delivery of unemployment services in Estonia. In: Ahrweiler, P. (ed.) Participatory Artificial Intelligence in Public Social Services. Springer, Cham (2025). https://doi.org/10.1007/978-3-031-71678-2_5

15. Bashiri, H.: Social assessment for the targeted subsidies plan as a social service provision in Iran: AI application in the targeted subsidies plan. In: Ahrweiler, P. (ed.) Participatory Artificial Intelligence in Public Social Services. Springer, Cham (2025). https://doi.org/10.1007/978-3-031-71678-2_7

16. Bashiri, H.: The Targeted Subsidies Plan Model (Version 1.0.0). CoMSES Computational Model Library (2023). https://www.comses.net/codebases/883171d8-1dcc-4740-992b-2d7f785a9194/releases/1.0.0/, Accessed 29 Sep 2025

17. Srinivasalu, S., et al.: Social assessment and cultural resistance: the public distribution System in Tamil Nadu, India. In: Ahrweiler, P. (ed.) Participatory Artificial Intelligence in Public Social Services. Springer, Cham (2025). https://doi.org/10.1007/978-3-031-71678-2_8

18. Ahrweiler, P., et al.: Using ABM and Serious Games to create "Better AI". In: IEEE Proceedings of the 2024 Annual Simulation Conference (ANNSIM 2024). Society for Modeling & Simulation International (SCS), Washington D.C. (2024)

Using Agent-Based Social Simulations to Inform Organ Donation Policymaking: Adopting the Spanish Approach in Sweden

Bertilla Fabris[1,2,4], Jason Tucker[3,4], and Fabian Lorig[1,2]

[1] Department of Computer Science and Media Technology, Malmö University, Malmö, Sweden
fabian.lorig@mau.se
[2] Sustainable Digitalization Research Center (SDRC), Malmö University, Malmö, Sweden
[3] The Institute for Futures Studies, Stockholm, Sweden
jason.tucker@iffs.se
[4] AI Policy Lab, Department of Computing Science, Umeå University, Umeå, Sweden
bertilla.fabris@umu.se

Abstract. Organ donation is a crucial aspect of healthcare, yet, the number of donors is insufficient to cover the demand for transplant procedures. In the European Union, around 15 people die each day waiting for a life-saving organ. National policies differ greatly among countries, but it is unclear how successful policies affect Deceased Organ Donation rates when introduced in new settings. This paper explores the use of Agent-Based Social Simulation (ABSS) to inform organ donation policymaking. Simulations provide policy actors with a safe environment to investigate the consequences of different policy interventions without the risk of harming people. We present an agent-based model of the Swedish organ donation system, where we can investigate the impact of Spain's policy approach, which produced the highest DOD rates in Europe. The results highlight the potential of ABSS as a tool for designing policy interventions in complex healthcare systems. Further developments can enable policymakers to identify successful strategies and monitor their effect to evaluate policy progression.

Keywords: Deceased Organ Donation · Public Health · Policy Support · Agent Based Social Simulation

1 Introduction

The global demand for organ transplants increases due to growing rates of diabetes, obesity, hepatic disease, and aging population. The World Health Organization has emphasized the importance of striving for national self-sufficiency to fulfill transplantation needs since 2010 [25]. There is great diversity between, but also within, national public health systems regarding the implementation

A. Vidler and S. Swarup (Eds.): MABS 2025, LNAI 16227, pp. 59–76, 2026.
https://doi.org/10.1007/978-3-032-16328-8_5

of Deceased Organ Donation (DOD) policies as well as in the resulting donation rates. The widely held belief that presumed consent increases organ donation rates has been disproved [3], confirming that complex systems require more elaborate solutions. With limited global policy guidance, comparative and exploratory policy analyses are vital means of increasing DOD rates.

In Europe, Spain is an outlier with historically high donation rates, reaching 49.4 donors per million population (pmp) in 2023 [22]. Still, the demand for transplants is increasing. As an indicator, the number of transplanted kidneys covered only 5.5% of the patients who began dialysis in Spain as of 2019 [19]. Sweden has recently reached 25 donors pmp, a rate attained by Spain in 1994 [11]. Measures such as implementing Donation after Circulatory Death (DCD) have not yet led to substantial improvements. Understanding and replicating the success factors from the Spanish system could increase donation rates in Sweden.

Agent-based Social Simulations (ABSS) emulate human behavior and systemic processes allowing us to explore *what-if* scenarios and understand complex causal mechanisms within the referent system. ABSS can be particularly useful to support policy design, where real-world experiments to investigate the consequences of policy changes are ineffective, unfeasible, or unethical [24].

The goal of this paper is to demonstrate how ABSS can inform DOD policymaking. This is achieved through the generation of synthetic scenarios, providing policy actors with an innovative approach to navigate the complexity of DOD system. Particularly, we project the Spanish policy approach on Sweden's landscape, which provides a framework for scenario development in relation to organ donation. The research questions we address in this paper are:

- How can social simulations be used to inform organ donation policymaking?
- How can trajectories of organ donors be modeled?
- How can relevant scenarios be developed and integrated into the model, based on other countries' organ donation policies?

The rest of the paper is organized as follows: Sect. 2 provides a background on deceased organ donation and introduces Sweden's DOD system. Section 3 presents the Spanish DOD policy approach, Sects. 4 and 5 describe the conceptual and implemented model respectively. Section 6 presents initial results and Sect. 7 concludes with discussion, limitations and future work.

2   Background

National organ donation and transplantation systems perform the critical role of transferring suitable organs from donors to patients who need organ transplants. Waiting lists, allocation systems, transport logistics and coordination are some of the components of these systems. DOD systems exist at the intersection of medical ethics, individual choices, national regulations, and practical limitations. Not only are there strong regulative aspects and conflicts of interest, but organizational and economical barriers influence the work of clinicians, affecting the system's overall efficiency. While efficiency is not the only important factor in public health systems, the global scarcity of organs forces policy actors to tread carefully when dealing with organ donation policies. Policy changes have been known to produce unintended consequences [2]. In 2021, a US policy designed to reduce geographic disparities in access to kidney transplants contributed to a short-term increase in organ discard rates [14]. However, causality can not be established due to multiple confounding factors and the level of maturity of the policy itself [6]. Tensions between system efficiency and equal access to care present a challenge to the transplantation community, as the long term consequences of policy change are manifold [6].

In Sweden, DOD can happen after Brain Death (DBD) or Cardio-circulatory Death (DCD). Only patients who pass in Intensive Care Units (ICUs) and match donation criteria are considered for the procedure. *Local donation clinicians* at the ICUs as well as *Transplant Coordinators* investigate medical viability criteria and consent before the removal of the organs (*donation*). The organs are then assigned to patients on the waiting list (allocation) and transferred into recipients (*transplantation*). The Swedish government tasked *Socialstyrelsen*, the National Board of Social Affairs and Health, with increasing DOD rates. Policy changes included the removal of family veto, and the adoption of controlled DCD (cDCD), where cardiac arrest follows planned withdrawal of life-sustaining treatment. While the policy changes are similar to some of Spain's past interventions, they did not yet result in comparable outcomes as they fail to take in consideration the years of monitoring and tailored research informing Spanish policy changes. This highlights the limitations of adopting individual policies as opposed to an extensive policy approach. To be able to explore and better align the Swedish system with the Spanish policy approach, precision public health policies are required. ABSS provides the means to do so by centralizing the individuals (agents) and their characteristics, behaviors, and goals so that the consequences of policy interventions can be tested on virtual populations. Ethically, this mitigates risks associated with implementing policy with sub-optimal or harmful outcomes [24]. Understanding the difference between the steady state of the system and the initial consequences of policy change can be vital [6]. Mismanagement of organ donation could negatively affect trust in the system and lead to decreasing donation willingness [8]. In fact, recent policy changes in Sweden may have negatively affected the rate of people declaring their will to donate in the national registry [18].

From a public health policy perspective, ABSS has proven its potential to explain causal mechanisms and complex system dynamics [23]. Within DOD, ABSS research focused on exploring allocation policies [13,17,21] and multiple listing [7]. Additionally, suitable models could be generated from legal documents [1]. Models calibrated on historical empirical data are capable of 'capturing details of reality' and perform well in defined scenarios [13]. Further, ABSS allows for the continuous adjustment of policies, one of the many benefits of the precision public health approach [16].

3   The Spanish Policy Approach: Lessons Learned

The Spanish policy approach acknowledges the high complexity of organ dona-tion systems. Recent analyses of factors leading to Spain's success identify dedi-cated institutions, quality assurance processes, detailed reimbursement schemes, and comprehensive training programs as sources of high donation rates [19]. At the core of the Spanish approach is the National Transplant Organization (*La Organización Nacional de Trasplantes*, ONT), which created the Spanish Quality Assurance Program in the Deceased Donation process (QUAPDD). The associ-ations guided data collection, with continuous internal monitoring and periodic external audits. Metric discovery and data analysis contextualized the system performance and needed improvements (see Fig. 1). QUAPDD was not only able to estimate the size of the potential donor population but also to determine how and why potential donors do not become actual donors [4,10]. When new interventions or policy changes were introduced, their effect was monitored and methodically assessed. The iterative, systematic approach lead to synergy in system improvement.

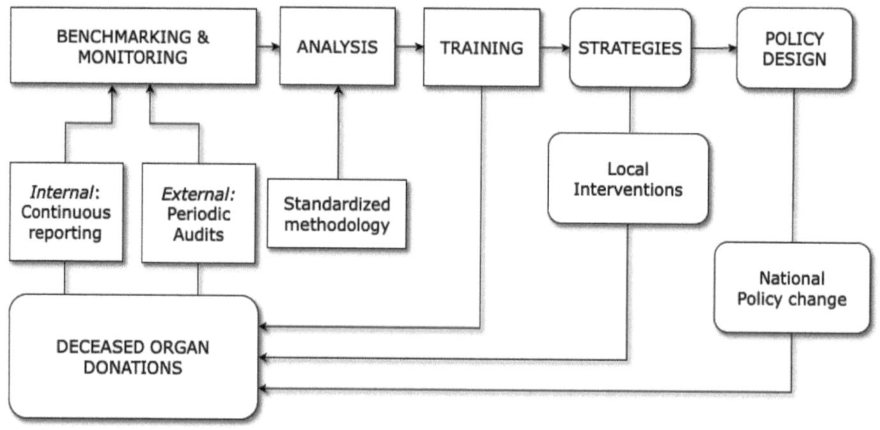

Fig. 1. Reductive schema of Spanish policy approach for DOD improvement.

3.1   Benchmarking and Monitoring

In Spain, from 2003 to 2007, Transplant Coordinators (TCs) reported data from 106 public ICUs. QUAPDD identified best performing hospitals at three phases of the donation process: identification and referral, evaluation and maintenance, and consent acquisition. To measure hospital performance, the ONT recorded three **indicators:**

  I Percentage of brain deaths in ICU compared to total brain death cases.
 II Percentage of eligible donors pending consent to become actual donors.
III Age and ethnicity of donors.

Inclusion for Indicator I was determined via a list of ICD[1] codes as primary or secondary diagnoses; the list accounted for 95% of national brain death etiology [10]. TC reports and external audits revealed that certain hospitals were more efficient in routing eligible donors to actual donation. While initially causation was not known, Indicator II exposed which hospitals to observe to discover best practices. Analysis of consent to donation disproved the hypothesis that ethnicity and age impact consent rates [10]. Assessing the indicators within the ONT framework of "organization and continuous adaptation to change" proved more effective than promotional campaigns to increase willingness to donate [12].

3.2   Interventions

Interventions guided the evolution of national Spanish DOD policy through the ONT. Six 'excellence hospitals' were selected for further analysis [10]. Teams, protocols and practices at these hospitals were qualitatively studied. The results informed guidelines forwarded to all other hospitals. In Spain, as in Sweden, becoming an organ donor requires premortem ICU admission. A study revealed that nearly 40% of all possible donors were neither ventilated at death nor referred to a TC; the reported cause was that DOD had not been considered [5]. Interventions to inform medical staff of the importance of organ donation were put in place. Moreover, many brain dead patients were declared dead in hospital wards, not ICUs, excluding them from donation regardless of their will. An objective was formed to expand the potential donor pool by admitting patients to ICUs for non-therapeutic purposes through the practice of *Intensive Care for Organ Donation* (ICOD) [11]. While this does not affect the legal requirements for declaring death, it allows more patients matching donation criteria to become donors.

Monitoring previously exposed that 25% of brain dead patients were not considered medically viable for donation by TCs and local donation clinicians. To counteract this, the ONT established a medical team available at all times to provide counsel to ICU clinicians [11]. Even so, many eligible donors' condition fell outside the medical guidelines for medical viability. These guidelines were reassessed and changed, their impact monitored through the established pipeline.

3.3   Policy Design

Nationally, workplace safety regulations and medical procedures in neurological treatment advanced. This led to a reduced pool of possible donors, as cerebrovascular disease, workplace and traffic accidents are the major suppliers of donors [4]. Yet, Spain increased its donor rate steadily [11].

---

[1] International Statistical Classification of Diseases and Related Health Problem:
https://icd.who.int/browse10/2019/en.

At the time, Spanish law advised a donor age limit of 65–70 years. Given the observed prevalence of aging possible donors, the ONT proposed expanding age and medical inclusion criteria for DOD. Concerns around organ quality were addressed in longitudinal studies, among other things showing that patients under dialysis have a higher risk of death than those receiving a kidney from older donors [9,15]. The ONT concluded that, although older donors provide fewer organs on average, there is no evidence that advanced donor age impacts the quality of transplants. Donor age limits and medical viability criteria were reviewed. The approach also highlighted the need for cDCD protocols, which Spain allowed nationally in 2012, following the ONT's recommendation. A common concern was ICU bed capacity, which was however unaffected. In 2016, DCD contributed to 10% of the overall deceased donation rates and its impact is increasing, reaching 50% in 2023 [11].

4   A Model of the Spanish Policy Approach in Sweden

Comparability. Projecting the Spanish policy approach onto the Swedish landscape required an assessment of comparability. Spain (around 49 million inhabitants) has a higher population and physician density than Sweden (around 10 million). Yet, the public health structure, population health, and socio-legal systems provide a suitable foundation for comparison, see Table 1[2].

Table 1. Comparison of Spanish and Swedish healthcare systems metrics.

Metric	Spain	Sweden
Deceased Donor Rate (pmp)	57	25
Population coverage for a core set of services	100%	100%
Health expenditure per capita (USD PPP)	4 432	6 438
Deaths in hospitals (percentage of total deaths)	50%	36%
CT scanners, MRI units and PET scanners (pmp)	44	43

Benchmarking Metrics. The model focuses on the progression of patients towards the Actual Donor state. The donors can transition through four states: *Possible* (patient with acute neural injury, recovery possible), *Potential* (patient approaching Brain Death, recovery impossible), *Eligible* (a potential donor for whom the TC was contacted, death is declared), and *Actual* (a medically viable deceased patient upon whom an incision has been made with the purpose to retrieve organ(s) for transplantation, consent from patient or relatives has been investigated).

Sweden is known for transparency and a wealth of publicly available data. We determine the best performing hospitals with respect to the first two indicators described in 3.1:

---

[2] Data from 2023 or closest available year. Source: OECD.

- **Brain death rate**: the brain deaths in ICU over total brain deaths. Social-styrelsen provides data on all deaths occurring in the country according to the international ICD-10 standard.
- **Medical viability and consent clearance**: eligible donors pending consent. Medical viability criteria are established by a consortium of doctors. Consent checking involves a first inspection of the national registry and, if the donor was not registered, contacting the families or documenting that there were unsuccessful attempts at contacting relatives.

The third indicator was inconclusive for Spain, which does not exclude the possibility that demographic factors influence consent rates in the Swedish context. For now, donor ethnicity is not considered in the model. We instead add:

- **Donor discovery rate**: how many of the brain death cases in ICUs are recognized as possible donors
- the rate of **contacts to TC** for identified potential donors

The Swedish Emergency Care Registry (*Svenska Intensivvårdsregistret*, SIR), provides data on most common causes of death for actual donors, donor discovery rates, and contact rates to Transplant Coordinators.

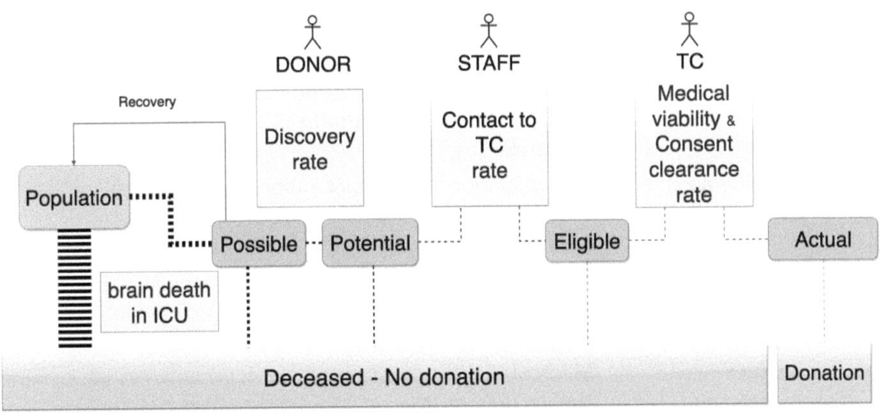

Fig. 2. Conceptual model of the donor state trajectory. Indicators are derived from the Spanish approach, and adapted to the Swedish case.

Data from SIR indicate that 100% of potential donors are discovered, hence the lack of transition barriers from the states of *Possible* to *Potential* donor, see Fig. 2. The main agent types in the model are *Donors, Local Donation Clinicians, and TCs*. Once patients matching brain death criteria are in ICUs (Possible Donor), they are assigned a local donation clinician, in the model called Staff. Local donation clinicians are necessary for the progression of the donor state. If no Staff is present at the ICU, the patient proceeds to death with no donation. If the Staff agent is present at the ICU and assigned to the Possible Donor, the donor proceeds to the state of Potential Donor. The Staff will contact a TC for the Potential Donor case; the TC returns the result of their assessment of *Medical Viability and Consent*. Only if both assessments are cleared, can the donor undergo the transition to Actual Donor.

Interventions. We model interventions aimed at increasing the rates of contact to TC, and expanding the medical viability criteria. The improvement is not meant to simulate the ideal optimal state of the system, but to achieve the rates of best performing hospitals in all hospitals throughout the country. TC contacts and the rate of *Possible Donors* progressing to *Eligible Donors* are analyzed for the best performers.

The potential impact of ICOD on donor rates is modeled by estimating the donor pool for all brain death cases in the country matching ICD-10 codes leading to donation. Note that Sweden already has a 24/7 TC coverage. The modeling of how cDCD influences DOD is outside the scope of this project. As there is no age restriction to donate in Sweden, modeling the policy change for age expansion is unnecessary. We define the simulated scenarios and interventions as shown in Table 2.

Table 2. Scenarios based on successful policies from the Spanish DOD system.

Scenario	Description
1. Baseline	Replicates Sweden's 2023 policy. Used for comparison of the results from the other scenarios.
2a. Increased TC contact rates	The value for TC contact rates is increased to the average of best performing Swedish hospital (contact_TC = 87.5%).
2b. Increased local donation clinicians	The coverage of local donation clinicians is maximized: all ICUs have specialized clinicians (Staff) available.
2c. Increased consent and viability rate	Medical viability and obtaining consent is set to the average of best performing Swedish hospitals (consent_and_viability = 82%).
2d. Best Practices	Combination of scenarios 2a, 2b, and 2c.
3. ICOD	Increase of brain death rate, which implies access to possible donors in both ICUs and hospital wards.
4. Best Practices + ICOD	All interventions adopted, inputs set at local best values.

The Baseline sets all variables to the state of year 2023, i.e. 10.5 million population, a brain death rate of 0.49 pmp, and the availability of 33 local donation clinicians (Staff) across all ICUs. A TC is contacted in 64% of cases;

62% of TC contacts lead to donation. The number of ICUs is kept at 81. See Sect. 5.2 for more details on how these values are obtained.

Conceptual Model. We define the model's purpose as simulating DOD policy in the Swedish system on the template of the Spanish approach. First, we implement a baseline model of the current Swedish organ donation system. This is to replicate its dynamics and to serve as comparison for assessing the effects of policy changes. Second, we develop scenarios of potential policy modification where we follow the Spanish policy approach's main phases. These scenarios are then applied to the model to investigate consequences. Figure 3 provides a visual rendition of the ODD protocol [20].

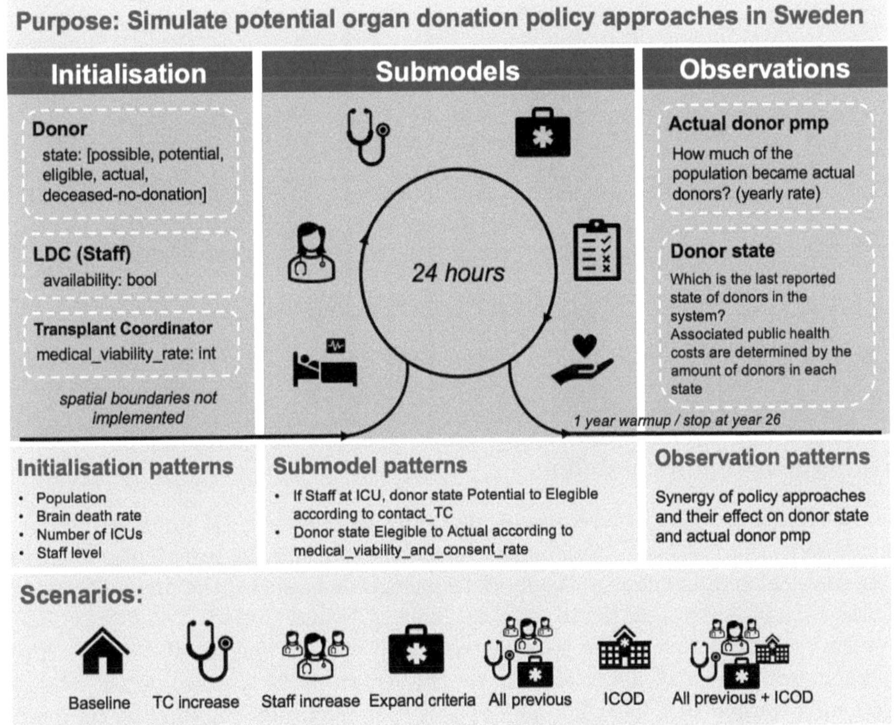

Fig. 3. Visual Overview, Design concepts, and Details (ODD) protocol.

5 Implemented Model

The model was implemented in NetLogo [26], version 6.4.0, and is accessible via GitHub[3]. A screenshot of the model's user interface can be seen in Fig. 4.

---

[3] https://github.com/cybertilla/SimODSweden.

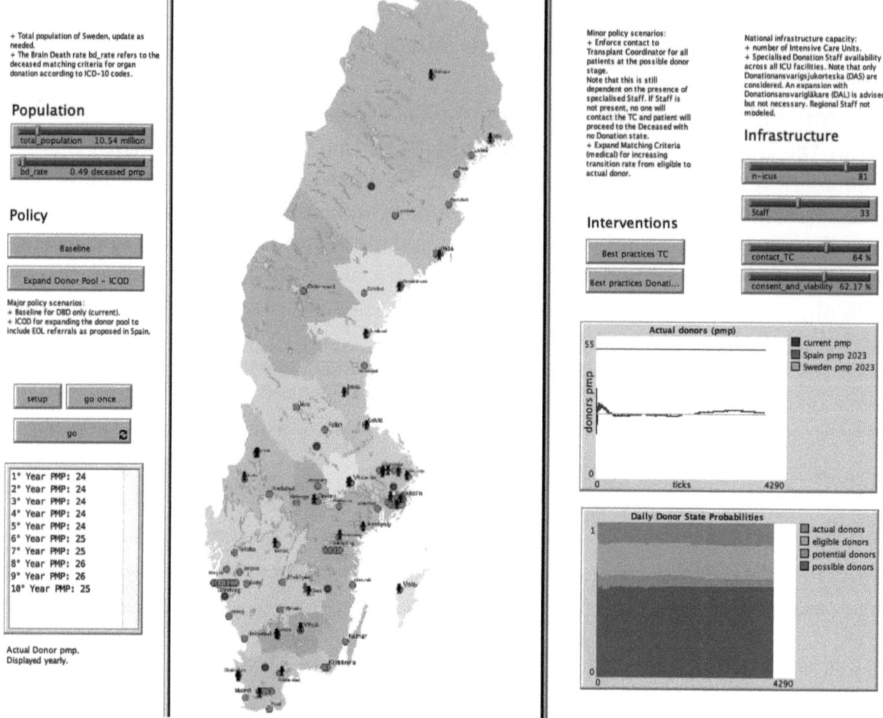

Fig. 4. Baseline scenario with intervention *Best practices for TC* simulated at tick 2000.

5.1   Agents and Scheduling

The model is designed to represent each day as one tick. Of influence are the initial settings in terms of Population, Infrastructure and the Intervention sliders. The physical arrangement of the model's patches is based on the map of Sweden. Three variables are assigned to patches: land, ICU and staffed. The *n-icus* slider determines how many of the patches with land value 1 become ICUs. The *Staff* slider determines how many ICUs have Staffed value of 1, meaning they house clinicians trained in DOD. The model does not take into account the temporal aspects of transferring patients to ICUs. Similarly, waiting lists and allocation procedures are not the focus of the model.

The generation of patients follows a Poisson distribution calibrated on the averages obtained from empirical data. We determined the brain death rate in ICUs (bd_rate = 0.49). This refer to the total daily deceased population. It is possible to adjust population changes to future measures. If the population were to increase to 15 million, the variable total_population can be set to the new value. The bd_rate can be set independently from population growth, meaning that if population increases and brain death rates are constant, there will be more possible donors created each tick.

Staff agents who identify a potential donor will contact TCs depending on probability contact_TC. The value of consent_and_ viability determines wether donors proceed to donation. Both values can be adjusted to simulate the desired scenarios. At the end of each day, final donor state is recorded, all patients proceed to either death with or without donation, and new possible donors are generated.

5.2 Parametrization

The parameters of the model are shown in Table 3 and represent the values needed to implement the scenarios and policy interventions defined in Table 2.

Table 3. Parameters of the simulation model.

Parameter	Description	Determines State Transition	Local Optimal Value	Baseline scenario
total_population	Population size of country	Possible	10.54M	10.54M
bd_rate	Brain death rate	Potential	0.89	0.49
contact_TC	Contact rate TC	Eligible	87.5%	64%
consent_and_ viability	Medical eligibility and consent	Actual	82%	62.17%
Staff (specialised)	Number of ICUs with Specialised Staff	Staff	#ICUs	33
#ICUs	Number of ICUs	Staff	100	81

Brain Death Rate. Indicator I from the Spanish benchmarking study has been approximated for Sweden via a list of ICD-10 codes representing the majority of DBD for the retrospective cohort 2015–2023. This entailed mapping the national SIR reference codes to the international standard ICD-10. The figures were confirmed through Cause of Death registry data[4].

We cut off the selection of included diagnoses if less than two case of DBD were recorded in the past 8 years. Included codes account for 99% of DBD in the selected years, see Fig. 5 for a breakdown of included etiology. On average 3453 people died each year who matched criteria for Possible Donors, of these deaths, 1915 occurred in ICUs. For the past 9 years, brain death was developed in ICUs in 55.46% of total cases.

Through the practice of ICOD the Swedish donor pool can be expanded to consider the remaining 44.54% of deaths matching criteria for DBD. Simulating ICOD coincides with scenario 3.

---

[4] https://sdb.socialstyrelsen.se/if_dor/ (in Swedish).

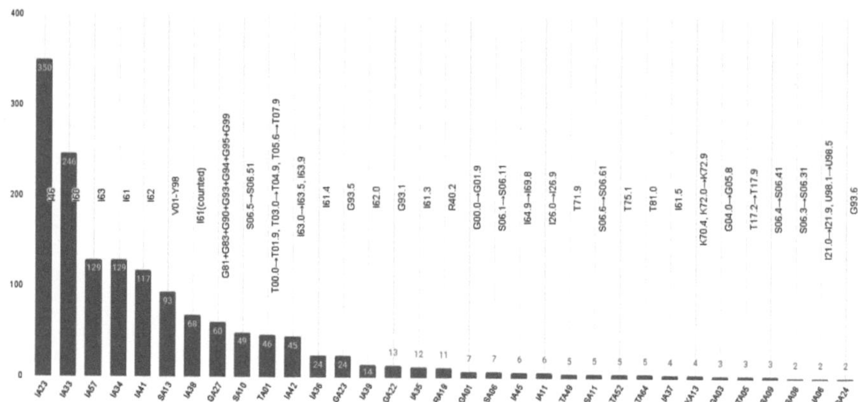

Fig. 5. Diagnoses included in the estimation of Swedish brain death rates.

Consent and Medical Viability. On average, 62.17% of TC contacts lead to donation (Baseline scenario). The 10 best performing hospitals in medical viability and consent clearance were: Eksjö, Kristianstad, Mora, Nyköping, Sunderby, SUS Lund IVA, Umeå TIVA, Uppsala TIVA. The best performing Swedish hospitals achieved rates of 82%. The percentage of people not consenting to organ donation is included in the transition rate from Eligible Donor to Actual Donor.

TC Contact. We approximated the rates of contacts to TC reported by SIR. The best performing hospitals in this phase were: Lycksele, Skellefteå, SUS Lund BIVA, SUS Malmö Inf, SöS IVA. On average, 64% of Potential Donors in ICUs are referred to TC (baseline, scenario 1). The averaged rate of best performing hospitals is 87.50%. TCs are assumed to be available at all times and capable of handling any amount of requests simultaneously.

5.3   Model Output

The Actual Donor rate is plotted in pmp value. Spain and Sweden's 2023 pmp rates are plotted statically for reference in the GUI. Note that the plot is a forecast that increasingly approximates the 'real' simulated pmp. At the end of each year, the recorded pmp rate is printed in the output window. The Donor States plot provides insight into the system's performance in different phases of DOD (i.e. the amount of donors in each state).

6   Results

Results are reported for the following metrics: Actual Donor rate (pmp) and Donor State, meaning the number of Possible, Potentials and Eligible and Actual Donors). Each simulation runs for approximately 26 years time (9490 ticks), the first year is considered warm-up and excluded from analysis. The minimum number of iterations per scenario is 10.

6.1   Yearly Actual Donor Pmp

Figure 6 shows the average number of Actual Donors(pmp) per year for each scenario. The baseline (scenario 1) is the reproduction of empirical values via the simulation, which provides partial verification and sanity check of the model. The actual donor pmp for scenario 1 is 23.87, slightly lower than the latest empirical pmp (2023); as the model considers the variation contained in the retrospective cohort 2015–2023, the average baseline output is considered sufficient estimation of Actual Donor pmp with respect to historical trends.

Scenario 2a (optimal TC contact) and 2c (optimal Consent and Viability) result in a slight increase in annual pmp, around 29 Actual Donors pmp. The effect of increasing available local donation clinicians (scenario 2b) is more pronounced, 64 pmp. Combining all best practices generates a virtuous circle in the system.

ICOD's effect (scenario 3) increases the donor rate more compared to 2a and 2c, yet does not surpass 2b. The forecast of annual pmp after implementing all Interventions and supporting them with increased numbers of local donation clinicians (scenario 4) outperforms all other scenarios, reaching 228 pmp.

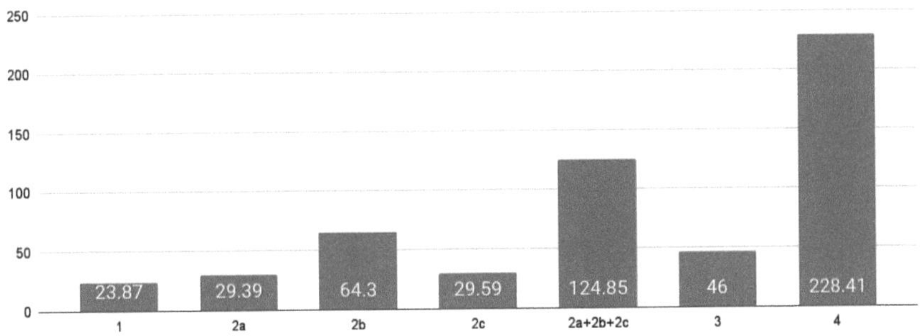

Fig. 6. Average number of actual donors (pmp) per year for the different scenarios.

6.2   Donor States

Figure 7 shows the state progression of the donors during the simulation. As an example, in the baseline scenario, 24 452 possible donors were simulated, 14 568 remained in the Possible Donor stage (e.g. due to lack of local donation clinicians), 1 767 dropped out in the Potential Donor stage (e.g. as no contact with the TC was initiated), 4 935 eligible donors dropped out due to TC exclusion of consent or medical viability, ultimately leading to 3 273 simulated Actual Donors.

The proportion of donors at different states gives insight into the forecasting function of the DOD system in different scenarios. Of note is the absence of Possible Donors in scenarios 2b, 2a+2b+2c and 4, indicating that all patients

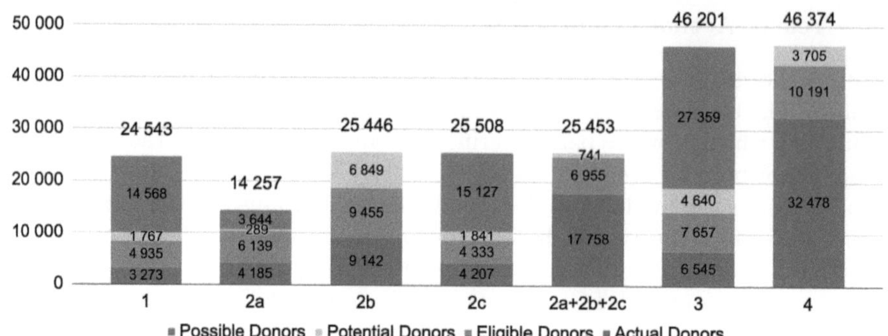

Fig. 7. State progression of donors, absolute values per year and scenario. The numbers on top of the bars represent the total number of possible donors, i.e. deceased with suitable ICD-10 code. The numbers in the bars represent the furthest state progression in the simulations.

matching criteria were progressed to other states thanks to the increase of local donation clinicians. Consider the differences between scenario 3 and 4: of 46 201 patients considered for donation in scenario 3, 14% (6 545) became actual donors, while 70% of patients proceeded to Donation in scenario 4. Despite the initial amount of possible donors being similar, scenario 4 presents a significantly more desirable outcome. This shows that, in the model, implementing Interventions is most effective when combined with Staff expansion; especially in consideration of costs inherent to progressing patients through donor states.

7   Discussion and Future Work

7.1   Summary

The goal of this paper was to demonstrate the potential of ABSS to evaluate policy interventions for DOD in Sweden by modeling key aspects of Spain's successful approach. We described the approximation of metrics for the Swedish DOD system, following the template of the successful Spanish policy approach. Keeping in mind that an extensive benchmarking study is needed, ideally completed by external audits as was implemented in Spain, we estimate the impact of a similar policy package in Sweden. The simulation results show how increasing the number of local donation clinicians, optimizing TC contact rates, and implementing ICOD could potentially increase Sweden's donor rates. However, the model also highlights that isolated policy changes may have limited impact unless they are embedded within a broader national strategy of monitoring and continuous adaptation.

7.2   Discussion

Sweden's current DOD system faces challenges in meeting transplant needs, and leveraging insights from other donation systems could provide a viable strategy for improving donor rates. With this project, we want to support and stimulate public healthcare policy discussions, given the increasing demand for organs and the need for innovative solutions. ABSS has the potential to enable policy actors to analyze and assess the impact of policy changes prior to their implementation and be adaptable in changing societies. Learning from successful policy in other countries can provide a useful paradigm to unravel complex systems. While the proposed model is limited in scope and granularity, it provides an example of how ABSS can be an integral part of policy design, evaluation and improvement. The results are not meant to deliver policy directives yet. Once validated, the model can further provide policy actors with a valuable tool to better understand the consequences of policies under low certainty/high risk circumstances.

The Spanish approach of identifying the best performing hospitals suggests an effective policy strategy based not on maximal optimization but on determining the 'local best' and promoting practices that encourage ownership of DOD practices. Instead of asking 'how many transplants can we obtain from the population?', they explored 'why do these hospitals perform better?'. This MO considers the stakeholders from the medical practice and the current infrastructure, instead of pursuing unattainable optimization goals. The approach is thus data-driven, but gathers the data from practitioners themselves, making it transferrable to other instances. From a policymaking perspective, the findings show the need to consider the complex interconnection of policies, infrastructural features, and stakeholder needs. This is highlighted by the largest increase in virtual organ donation being a result of an alignment of a range of policy options. This model also shows the value of the creation of synthetic data based on various scenarios to inform future oriented policymaking.

All data used in this paper was sourced from publicly accessible databases; SIR and Socialstyrelsen provide anonymised data as part of their public service. Easily accessible public datasets are a great advantage to ABSS model development.

7.3   Limitations

The lack of domain expertise in the medical field can deteriorate the quality of the presented model. Validation of the model has not yet been carried out, this is a substantial flaw we hope to address in the near future. Therefore we do not allow the usage of this model for policy advisory; the model is meant to illustrate how ABSS can aid in designing and communicating policy development strategies, alongside explaining hidden system dynamics and their effect on policy.

7.4   Future Work

This project is still ongoing and the results we present in this paper are work in progress. As a next step, we intend to extend the agency of the Staff agents in the model, considering more of the infrastructural resources that may play a role in their choices. The number of intensive care beds and overall workload patterns at ICUs present interesting dynamics to consider. This would not only be of interest from the quantitative perspective (e.g. in the model's calibration phase), but even more so in the qualitative aspect (e.g. expose what causes the Staff to contact TCs or to fail to do so). There is also the possibility for the model to be extended *towards transplantation*, meaning to include geographical information, transportation logistics, and allocation procedures. Integrating results from transplantation outcomes would close the feedback loop and consider the whole donation and transplantation process as a whole. Additionally, the flexibility of ABSS is suitable to explore a variety of long-term temporal dynamics of public health policies. These include how socio-demographic changes (e.g. aging populations, urbanization, and lifestyle shifts), might affect the outcomes and success of organ donations in Sweden.

Acknowledgments. This work was partly supported by the Crafoord Foundation (20240917) and by the Wallenberg AI, Autonomous Systems and Software Program – Humanity and Society (WASP-HS) funded by the Marianne and Marcus Wallenberg Foundation and the Marcus and Amalia Wallenberg Foundation.

References

1. Belfrage, M., Frantz, C., Fabris, B., Lorig, F.: Blueprinting organ donation: a 'policy-first' approach for developing agent-based models. In: The 19th annual Social Simulation Conference (SSC 2024). Kraków, Poland, Sep 16–20, 2024 (2024)
2. Browne, A., Gaines, H., et al.: Interrupted time series analysis of donor heart use before and after the 2018 UNOS heart allocation policy change. J. Card. Fail. **29**(2), 220–224 (2023). https://doi.org/10.1016/j.cardfail.2022.08.009, https://linkinghub.elsevier.com/retrieve/pii/S1071916422007126
3. Dallacker, M., Appelius, L., Brandmaier, A., Morais, A., Hertwig, R.: Opt-out defaults do not increase organ donation rates. Public Health **236**, 436–440 (2024). https://doi.org/10.1016/j.puhe.2024.08.009, https://linkinghub.elsevier.com/retrieve/pii/S003335062400355X
4. De La Rosa, G., Domínguez-Gil, B., et al.: Continuously valuating performance in deceased donation: the spanish quality assurance program. Am. J. Transplant. **12**(9), 2507–2513 (2012). https://doi.org/10.1111/j.1600-6143.2012.04138.x, https://linkinghub.elsevier.com/retrieve/pii/S1600613522276205
5. Domínguez-Gil, B., Coll, E., et al.: End-of-life practices in patients with devastating brain injury in Spain: implications for organ donation. Med. Intensiva (English Edition) **41**(3), 162–173 (2017). https://doi.org/10.1016/j.medine.2017.03.003, https://linkinghub.elsevier.com/retrieve/pii/S2173572717300371
6. Formica, R.N., Schold, J.D.: The unintended consequences of changes to the organ allocation policy. J. Am. Soc. Nephrol. **34**(1), 14–16 (2023). https://doi.org/10.1681/ASN.0000000000000009
7. Harvey, C., Thompson, J.R.: Exploring advantages in the waiting list for organ donations. In: 2016 Winter Simulation Conference (WSC). pp. 2006–2017 (2016). https://doi.org/10.1109/WSC.2016.7822245
8. Irving, M.J., Tong, A., Jan, S., et al.: Factors that influence the decision to be an organ donor: a systematic review of the qualitative literature. Nephrol. Dial. Transplant. **27**(6), 2526–2533 (2012)

9. Jiménez-Romero, C.: Using old liver grafts for liver transplantation: Where are the limits? WJG **20**(31), 10691 (2014)
10. Matesanz, R., Coll, E., et al.: Benchmarking in the process of donation after brain death: A methodology to identify best performer hospitals. Am. J. Transplant. **12**(9), 2498–2506 (2012). https://doi.org/10.1111/j.1600-6143.2012.04128.x, https://linkinghub.elsevier.com/retrieve/pii/S1600613522276199
11. Matesanz, R., Domínguez-Gil, B., et al.: How spain reached 40 deceased organ donors per million population. Am. J. Transplant. **17**(6), 1447–1454 (2017). https://doi.org/10.1111/ajt.14104, https://linkinghub.elsevier.com/retrieve/pii/S1600613522250060
12. Matesanz, R., Domínguez-Gil, B., Coll, E., De La Rosa, G., Marazuela, R.: Spanish experience as a leading country: what kind of measures were taken?: Facing organ shortage in Spain. Transplant Int. **24**(4), 333–343 (2011). https://doi.org/10.1111/j.1432-2277.2010.01204.x, https://onlinelibrary.wiley.com/doi/10.1111/j.1432-2277.2010.01204.x
13. Oliveira, A., Ferreira, R., Lima, A.: Liver transplant waiting list simulation - an agent based model. In: ICAART 2011 - Proceedings of the 3rd International Conference on Agents and Artificial Intelligence, Volume 2 - Agents, Rome, Italy, January 28–30, 2011. pp. 462–468 (2011)
14. Puttarajappa, C.M., Hariharan, S., Zhang, X., Tevar, A., Mehta, R., Gunabushanam, V., Sood, P., Hoffman, W., Mohan, S.: Early effect of the circular model of kidney allocation in the united states. J. Am. Soc. Nephrol. **34**, 26–39 (2023). https://doi.org/10.1681/ASN.2022040471
15. Pérez-Sáez, M., Arcos, E., et al.: Survival benefit from kidney transplantation using kidneys from deceased donors aged $>=$ 75 years: A time-dependent analysis. Am. J. Transplant. **16**(9), 2724–2733 (2016-09). https://doi.org/10.1111/ajt.13800, https://linkinghub.elsevier.com/retrieve/pii/S1600613522008139
16. Roberts, M.C., Holt, K.E., et al.: Precision public health in the era of genomics and big data. Nat. Med. **30**(7), 1865–1873 (2024). https://doi.org/10.1038/s41591-024-03098-0, https://www.nature.com/articles/s41591-024-03098-0
17. Rosendale, J., Vece, G., et al.: Developing and verifying an artificial twin of the organ procurement and transplant process: a systems approach. J. Simul. **18**(1), 65–87 (2024). https://doi.org/10.1080/17477778.2022.2062262, https://doi.org/10.1080/17477778.2022.2062262
18. Socialstyrelsen: Organdonation och transplantation i sverige. https://www.socialstyrelsen.se/publikationer/ (2023). https://www.socialstyrelsen.se/contentassets/ead4577106f048a98404480876f24eef/2024-6-9135.pdf. Accessed 26 Sep 2025
19. Streit, S., Johnston-Webber, C., et al.: Ten lessons from the spanish model of organ donation and transplantation. Transpl. Int. **36**, 11009 (2023). https://doi.org/10.3389/ti.2023.11009
20. Szangolies, L., et al.: Visual ODD: a Standardised Visualisation Illustrating the Narrative of Agent-Based Models. JASSS **27**(4), 1 (2024). https://doi.org/10.18564/jasss.5450, https://www.jasss.org/27/4/1.html
21. Teng, Y., Kong, N.: Applying agent-based modeling and simulation (abms) to the us organ transplantation and allocation network. In: Li, J., Aleman, D., Sikora, R., (eds.) Proceedings of the 3rd INFORMS Workshop on Data Mining and Health Informatics (DM-HI 2008) (2008)
22. The Lancet: Organ donation: lessons from the spanish model. Lancet **404**(10459), 1171 (2024). https://doi.org/10.1016/S0140-6736(24)02128-7, https://linkinghub.elsevier.com/retrieve/pii/S0140673624021287

23. Tracy, M., Credá, M., et al.: Agent-based modeling in public heath: Current applications and future directions. Annual Review of Public Health (2018)
24. Tucker, J., Lorig, F.: Agent-based social simulations for health crises response: utilising the everyday digital health perspective. Front. Public Health **11**, 1337151 (2024)
25. WHO: Third who global consultation on organ donation and transplantation: Striving to achieve self-sufficiency, march 23–25, 2010, Madrid, Spain. Transplantation **91**, S27–S28 (2011). https://doi.org/10.1097/TP.0b013e3182190b29, https://journals.lww.com/00007890-201106151-00003. Accessed 15 Jun 2011
26. Wilensky, U.: Netlogo. http://ccl.northwestern.edu/netlogo/ (1999). Center for Connected Learning and Computer-Based Modeling, Northwestern University, Evanston, IL

An Agent-Based Model of Administrative Corruption in Hierarchical Organisations

Bertold B. Kovács and Neil Yorke-Smith[✉]

Delft University of Technology, Delft, The Netherlands
`b.b.kovacs-1@student.tudelft.nl`, `n.yorke-smith@tudelft.nl`

Abstract. Corruption is a familiar and pressing problem in the performance of administrative bureaucracies. Changing the organisational structure is one way ventured to combat corrupt practices within a hierarchical organisation. Previous works have studied organisational change from various lenses, including equation-based modelling. We address the question of what level of hierarchy is optimal in such an organisation by means of agent-based simulation. We argue that agent-based models are uniquely suited for the exploratory modelling of corruption due to their capturing of localised, individualised behaviours. Our preliminary findings are that a less hierarchical organisational structure: 1) tend to lead to less corrupt acts committed, and 2) tends to lead to more societal welfare generated – however, 3) less corruption and more societal welfare do not always go hand in hand. We begin to reconcile these seemingly paradoxical results using theories from developmental economics.

Keywords: Administrative Corruption · Agent-Based Models · Complex Adaptive Systems · Collusion · Organisation Structure · Mesa

1 Introduction

Identified as at the heart of pressing societal problems "from economic uncertainty, to endemic poverty, to . . . radicalisation and extremism" [6], corruption is old as human civilisation [21]. All those who would benefit from an organization achieving its goals are impacted by misalignments in values, incentives, goals and actions – when these are manifest in corrupt acts. In case of a privately-owned company the losses from such corrupt 'misalignment' is mainly felt by the shareholders, but in case of a governmental agency it is felt by all citizens. This latter case has our attention, wherein corruption is defined as "the abuse of public office for private gain" [18]. This paper will critique an extant theoretical model of corruption using agent-based simulation.

While scholars debate the definition of corruption [26], this paper deals with an abstract notion of corruption: we understand corruption as any event in which an agent refuses to act in the way prescribed by the organisation of which it is a member, due to the (implicit) individual aims that the agent holds. While this

A. Vidler and S. Swarup (Eds.): MABS 2025, LNAI 16227, pp. 77–88, 2026.
https://doi.org/10.1007/978-3-032-16328-8_6

definition is arguably broad, as it can be understood to include other influence-seeking activities such as rent-seeking [1], it is fit for our theoretical investigation, which does not need to deal with the specific intricacies between different forms of problematic, self-serving governance.[1]

It has been observed that the structure of an organisation can have significant effect on its performance [8,25]. Previous research has shown that people expect organisational structure to also effect corruption, specifically associating more hierarchical organisations a higher level of corruption [13]. There have also been economic models that found that organisational structure influences organisational corruption to a large degree [9]. Further, deducing organisational structures that are less conducive to corruption is a recognised approach in anti-corruption policy [12,25].

Social scientists and governance experts have proposed policies intended to lead towards good governance, by building the integrity of public organisations [23]. However, testing whether such a posited policy works well in practice is problematic. It is hardly desirable to implement such measures without thorough study, as the societal cost of trying a new anti-corruption measure is high.

Agent-Based Modelling (ABM) excels at handling the fluctuations inherent to corruption in society (as opposed to classical equilibrium theories), deals well with bounded rationality, and expresses the heterogeneity of the actors present in the process of corruption [14,29]. Indeed, there is successful precedent in using ABM to study corruption. Among these are works dealing specifically with administrative corruption [11]. These models proved useful in showing the endogenous dynamics of how corruption might arise or be reduced [16], and looking at both micro- and macro-level determinants of corruption. However, the role of hierarchical structures and organisational shapes has not been fathomed using ABM.

This paper takes as starting point the classical equation-based model of Duggar and Duggar [9]. We begin investigate the following questions using agent-based modelling and simulation:

Question 1 (Q1) *Does a less hierarchical organisational structure for an administrative bureaucracy lead to less corrupt acts committed?*

Question 2 (Q2) *Does a less hierarchical organisational structure for an administrative bureaucracy lead to more societal welfare generated (more wealth that is used effectively by society, and not impeded in its use by corruption)?*

Question 3 (Q3) *What is the relationship between the number of acts (cf. Q1) and the societal wealth generated (cf. Q2)? Does reducing the number of corrupt actions always lead to an increase in societal wealth?*

---

[1] In fact, one can note that these corrupt actions that go against the behaviour prescribed by the organisation do not necessarily go against the aims of the organisation. In some scenarios, individuals can more effectively help the organisation achieve its goal by going against the organisational directions – such as when the directions are misaligned with the actual goals of the organisational, while the individual incentives (possibly by chance) align with it.

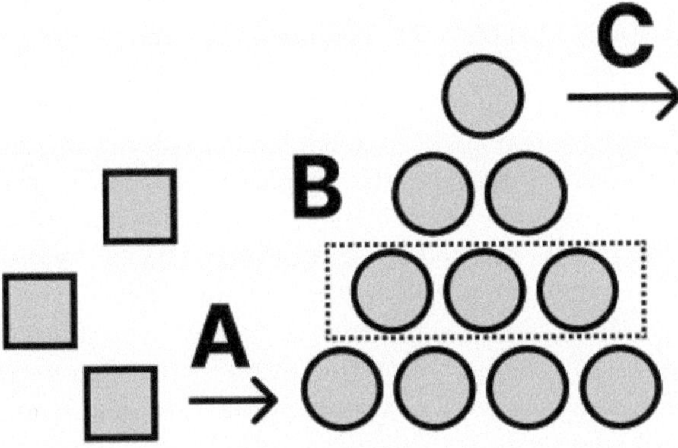

Fig. 1. Overview of the bureaucratic process, with circles representing bureaucrat agents, and squares representing applicant agents. The letters indicate the different stages of the process: A) the applicants submit their project proposals to the bureaucracy. B) the levels iteratively decide whether to pass on their project proposal. Each official on the level evaluates the proposal and makes a verdict, which might be corrupted by the applicant. C) If the highest level approves of the project proposal, it is implemented, adding its value minus its cost to the societal wealth.

The remainder of the paper is organised as follows. Section 2 describes the model design and the experiment setup. Section 3 presents the simulation results. Section 4 reflects on the merits of the agent-based modelling for the studied problem. Section 5 provides an overview of related work. Section 6 summaries our findings and possible future directions.

2   Methodology

Duggar and Duggar [9] sought to build a quantitative model that provides insight on the relation between organisational form and corruption. The authors developed an equation-based model of a theoretical organisation. We critique this model by developing an agent-based model with individual-level behaviours. In this paper we focus on a mapping of agent behaviours and simple learning mechanisms. The scenario is the working of an administrative bureaucratic organisation. Our abstract organisation's goal is to evaluate project proposals that are submitted to it, and decide which ones to implement, in a process illustrated in Fig. 1. The organisation's theoretical goal is to generate as much 'societal profit' as possible: implement the projects that bring the most societal value, while costing the least resources.

The primary properties of an agent-based model are the agents (and their behaviour), and the environment in which they exist [24]. There are two types of **agents** present in our model: *bureaucrats* and *applicants*. Bureaucrats represent the administrative agents of the bureaucratic organisation, while applicants represent the enterprising citizens who submit project proposals to the agency.

The **environment** in which the agents exist aims to represent the hierarchic bureaucracy. Unlike Duggar and Duggar's fixed aggregation scheme, we model the bureaucracy as a directed acyclic graph, where the superior–subordinate relationships are represented by the edges. This allows for the simple pyramid shaped organisations investigated by Duggar and Duggar, but also for various other organisational structures. When the bureaucracy is pyramid-shaped, the lowest level is the largest (here, bureaucrats receive the minimum wage) with each level being strictly smaller (with the wages increasing on each level). For a fixed number of agents, the number by which the level sizes increase also defines the *steepness*: the steeper an organisation is, the more hierarchical it is.

2.1 Organisational Workflow

The model captures agents interactions as a sequence of rounds, each representing a workday. Each round, the following workflow operates, as depicted in Fig. 2:

1. Applicants owning a project that is not yet in the bureaucracy **submit** their projects to the lowest level.
2. Each project is **evaluated** by the official currently handling it. These officials decide upon an initial verdict: pass or reject.
3. The applicants can **offer** an amount to the officials handling their project to change their mind. If this amount is high enough, and the official is willing to act corruptly, then **corruption happens**.
4. Each project that was rejected is **removed** from the hierarchy (and the applicant owning it receives a new project). Each official from a lower level than where the project was rejected is **fired**, since they are deemed to be corrupt and working against the organisations goals by forwarding an applicant with a project unworthy of implementation. This 'draconian' one-strike policy could of course be replaced by more nuanced firing policies as well. Following this, the empty positions of the bureaucracy are refilled with new officials.
5. Each project that passes the final official is **implemented**. The social welfare increases by the project's *value*: *cost*, and the applicant owning the project receives *cost*.

During the **evaluation** phase the official judges the project on whether it has a higher *value* than *cost*. However, officials are not perfect: each has a *fallibility rate*, uniformly sampled from $U(0, 0.5)$, which defines the chance that the official will simply make a mistake.

During the **corruption** phase, the officials make a decision to entertain the possibility of a bribe. The model captures conducive corruption; we do not treat coercive corruption in this paper. Each official has a *dishonesty* property, uniformly sampled from $U(0, 0.7)$ which serves as the parameter of the Bernoulli trial deciding whether the official is open to being bribed.

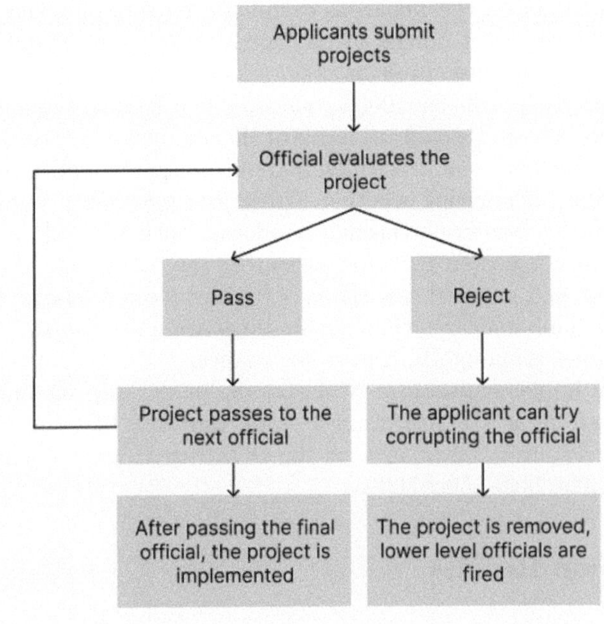

Fig. 2. Overview of the process each round (workday).

Once an official decides that he is open to being bribed, the official decides upon a threshold, influenced by his current wage, the number of superiors he has, and his *bargaining score*, a property that can change due to experiences. The applicant then sends an offer, based on the applicant's expected reward (the *cost* of the project), the number of officials still left in the bureaucracy, and the applicant's own *bargaining score*. If this offer is higher than the official's bribery threshold, than they exchange the amount, and the official changes his verdict. Finally, both agents update their *bargaining scores* by their *learning rates*: an official will aim for a higher bribe next time, if he has been paid now, and a lower one if he would have been open to being bribed but the offer he received was too low; and vice versa for the applicant.

2.2 Experiment Setup

We study organisations with different number of applicants, as described in Sect. 3. The parameters are calibrated as follows. The minimum wage (the wage of the lowest ranking officials) is 1, and the wage doubles on every level of the hierarchy. The project's cost is sampled from $U(1000, 10000)$, while its value is sampled from $U(1000, 15000)$, representing how a government project can have vastly higher societal impact than the project's cost. During each experiment, the social welfare is recorded, as a measure of how well the organisation achieves its goal. As noted above, the welfare is calculated by summing the value of the projects that the top-most official in the bureaucracy accepts and subtracting the sum of the costs of these projects.

Each experiment is run for 10000 rounds, which is long enough for a large amount of projects to go through all levels of the organisation. To ensure robustness, we ran each experiment 120 times, and our presented metrics are the average over the runs. Evaluating whether 120 is an appropriate number of runs for each experiment was done through windowed variance [22]. We reached a windowed variance less than 10^{-7} for measuring the percentage of corrupt acts amongst all acts, and at worst less than $4 * 10^{-4}$ windowed relative variance for societal wealth. This indicates that our findings are quite robust, and running them for 120 times is enough to control for chance.

After a trial implementation in NetLogo, the model was implemented using the Python Mesa library [17,19], using Python version 3.12.8 and Mesa version 3.1.3. The model source is available via the DOI https://www.doi.org/10.4121/e316f20e-c368-405e-bcf0-150cb7f2f9ea.

3   Simulation Results

To examine the three research questions stated in Sect. 1, we performed a trio of experiments.

3.1   Simple Pyramid Organisations and Steepness

First, to study how the level of corruption and the social utility might change with a difference in hierarchy, we conduct simulation experiments with the above ABM. We start with investigating the simple pyramid as an organisational structure. This is both the only form of organisation studied by Duggar and Duggar, and also amongst the most common forms of organisations, especially in the bureaucratic context [15,30]. For a given amount of officials, the organisational pyramid can take on different values of 'steepness', depending on the distance from the top to the lowest level. At the extremes, we see the 'line' hierarchy, where officials have exactly one direct subordinate, and the 'flat' hierarchy, where each official is the direct subordinate of the leader of the bureaucracy.

Table 1 summarises the results. We observe the following: first, line structures (the most hierarchical 'pyramid') is leads consistently to the most corruption, and the least societal welfare. Second, we see that a lower level of corruption does not always lead to a higher societal welfare – as the small flat structure outperforms the small balanced structure welfare-wise, even though it has a higher percentage of corrupt acts. Third, we can observe that for the more hierarchical structures having a larger bureaucracy results both in a higher percentage of corrupt acts, and less social welfare generated – for the flat structure, this also holds, but to a smaller degree.

Table 1. The percentage of corrupt acts and societal welfare for different sizes and structures of organisations. The 'line' structure has 1 official per each level, while the flat structure has only 2 levels: 1 with 1 official, and another with all the others. The balanced structure differs for each size: the number of levels are 3, 4 and 7, while the number of officials a superior has directly below them are 5, 4 and 3 respectively.

Officials	Mean Percentage of Corrupt Acts		
	Line Structure	Balanced Structure	Flat Structure
Small (31)	0.03552	**0.03280**	0.04446
Medium (85)	0.06393	0.05970	**0.03545**
Large (1093)	0.06349	0.05515	**0.05318**
Officials	Mean Societal Welfare (in 1000 units)		
	Line Structure	Balanced Structure	Flat Structure
Small (31)	12	88,603	**117,358**
Medium (85)	0	49,431	**119,797**
Large (1093)	0	13,073	**119,798**

3.2 Change in Corruption Over Time

Second, to better understand how the different levels of hierarchy leads to different results, we plotted the mean percentage of corrupt actions over time, as shown in Fig. 3. It is clear that there is an opposite tendency between the strongly hierarchical line structure and the least hierarchical flat structure: while for the line structure, we see that the level of corruption worsens over time, for the flat structure we see that we progressively see a lower amount of corrupt acts committed.

It can be noted that there is essentially a 'wind-up period' of rapid change seen on the plots for the first few hundred steps. For the line organisation, this suggests that the bulk of the corrupt actions is concentrated in the top of the hierarchy, and the 'wind-up period' is essentially an artifact of the projects not yet reaching the section with most corruption. Officials closer to the top of the hierarchy do have more to lose (which makes them ask for a higher bribe), but since there are less officials left after them, they are less likely to get fired and replaced if they do resort to corruption. While officials in the flat organisation are initially open to corruption (since they do not have many superiors who could find out if they do, making them fine with accepting lower bribes), as the corruption only has two levels, the short 'feedback loop' of firing and replacing quickly corrects this.

3.3 Alternative Organisational Forms

Third, to demonstrate the flexibility of an agent-based modelling approach, we also simulate two alternative ways to structure an organisation: the matrix structure, and the imbalanced pyramid, as shown in Fig. 4. The matrix organisational structure is prevalent organisational shape built on the idea of 'dual

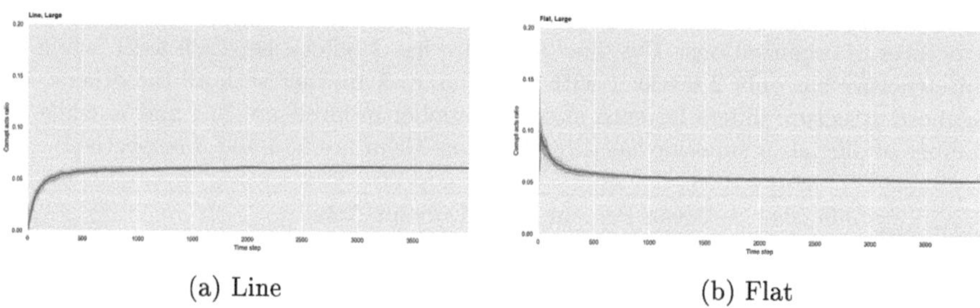

(a) Line   (b) Flat

Fig. 3. Mean percentage of corrupt actions over time for a large organisation (1093 officials) of a simple pyramid organisational shape. The plots show that while the strongly hierarchical line structure worsens corruption over time, the flat structure improves it.

Table 2. The percentage of corrupt acts and societal welfare for alternative organisational structures.

Officials	Mean Percentage of Corrupt Acts	
	Matrix/Grid Structure	Imbalanced Pyramid
Small (approx. 31)	0.05050	0.05049
Medium (approx. 85)	0.06120	0.05735
Large (approx. 1093)	0.06054	0.05991
Officials	Mean Societal Welfare (in 1000 units)	
	Line Structure	Imbalanced Pyramid
Small (approx. 31)	37,717	34,835
Medium (approx. 85)	10,891	9,835
Large (approx. 1093)	11	111

authority': each member of the hierarchy has two direct superiors [3,20]. In the case of the imbalanced pyramid we model the common scenario when some branch of the organisation grows considerably larger than any other. In our case, we simulate this by a pyramid, where on each level the leftmost official has several (in the case of small and medium, 3; in the case of large, 4) direct subordinates, but every other official has only 1 subordinate (Table 2).

For both of these alternative organisational forms, we see similar tendencies as for the line and balanced structures of the simple pyramid organisation: adding more officials leads to both worse societal welfare, and more corruption. Both of these organisational structures seem to underperform both the balanced and the flat structures of the simple pyramid.

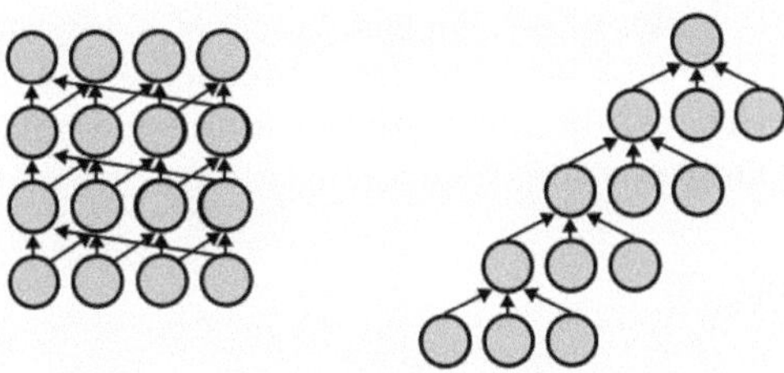

Fig. 4. The alternative organisational forms studied: the matrix (left), an imbalanced pyramid (right). Nodes correspond to officials; directed edges show superiority relations.

3.4   Discussion

Our results show that more corrupt acts and better societal utility generation does not necessarily go hand in hand, implying that more hierarchical organisations increase the level of corruption and societal welfare in an unrelated manner, and not because one of them necessarily also increases the other value. This is in accordance with the 'functionalist account of hierarchy' [2]: according to it hierarchical organisations perform significantly better at routine tasks (where having alternative perspectives and ideas is not of use), and this gain can outweigh even the additional corruption imposed by a power imbalance between members; but lower corruption, everything else being equal, still leads to a better societal outcome. Connecting empirical (agent-based) simulation studies with the broader discourse in the literature on corruption is interesting to continue in the future.

4   Advantages of the Agent-Based Model

The primary result of Duggar and Duggar [9] is that – in the absence of a cooperative culture – having a steeper, more hierarchic organisation with a simple pyramid structure leads to more corrupt acts. Our agent-based model reproduces this tendency, and improves upon several of the attributes of the original equation-based models.

Most importantly, the ABM model is dynamic, not static. The original paper only addresses static decisions, and does not investigate how the organisation develops due to firing employees who are found corrupt. Further, (simple) individual learning is also an inclusion of our model that is missing from the initial equation-based model, and which is not obvious how to implement in the latter.

Second, our model is also built for a more realistic number of bureaucrats. Previous examples usually only consider a handful of officials, and the equations produce absurd results for larger bureaucracies: Fig. 12 and 13 of Duggar and Duggar [9] show that for more than 14 bureaucrats, depending on the competitiveness of an organisation, the probability of corruption is either 1 or 0.

Finally, some of the additional features of our model just sensibly extends the original: we handle fallibility of officials, which is made easy by the individual-level focus of ABMs); and we allow for a broader set of organisations, namely any organisation that can be illustrated as a directed acyclic graph, instead of just equal sided 'simple pyramids'.

5   Related Work

The phenomenon that hierarchy impacts corruption has long been accepted in the literature. As shown by artificial experiments done with crowd workers, people perceive more hierarchical organisations to be more conducive to corruption [12,13]. Rosenblatt [25] argues that both hierarchical institutions, and a personal predisposition towards hierarchy leads to more corruption, basing it on previous empirical findings and social dominance theory. However, these studies do not propose a model that can be used to investigate the possible benefits and drawbacks of changing the hierarchical structures to a more egalitarian one.

Earlier corruption models created by classical (non-ABM) techniques have primarily addressed corruption as a rational behaviour. These modelling techniques included mathematical, game-theoretical, experimental analysis, principal-agent, and process models [11]. While these models had the traditional weaknesses of classical models, such as not being able to handle bounded rationality to a satisfying degree, important concepts have been explored in them. Most importantly, Duggar and Duggar [9]'s mathematical model discussed specifically the role the structure of a hierarchical (pyramid-shaped) organisation can play in corruption, and proposed the competitive-cooperative abstraction for organisational cultures. Our model comprises an ABM analogue of their work, with considerable extensions – including imperfect decision making (already mentioned in their model as a possible extension) and a simple form of learning. Other classical models which specifically study the impact of organisational structure and hierarchy on corruption include Bac [4]'s and Carrillo [7]'s models.

As well as theoretical characterisations, which are the interest of this paper, agent-based models have been built for specific domains of corruption: water service [5], maritime customs [27] or police corruption [10]. Other more general corruption models, and those dealing specifically with administrative corruption have also been proposed, as surveyed by Elnawawy et al. [11]. Hammond [16] and Zausinová et al. [32] created extensive models focusing on bureaucrat-citizen interactions, which showed how a corrupt (or honest) regime can appear endogenously. However, their models allow the bureaucrats to 'freely roam' and interact with different agents without confining them to a hierarchical structure that is characteristic to bureaucracies [31].

6   Conclusion

A proposed policy towards reducing the negative effects of corruption in administrative bureaucracies is setting up the hierarchical structure of the organisation, in such a way that it discourages accepting bribes. To study the consequences of such a policy, this paper developed an initial agent-based model.

According to simulation experiments with the ABM, a less hierarchical organisational structure in an administrative bureaucracy tend to lead to less corrupt acts, and also a higher societal welfare. Thus the answer to research question Q1 is negative, more hierarchical bureaucracies lead to more corrupt acts committed, while for Q2 we find a less hierarchical bureaucracy does lead to more societal welfare. The somewhat surprising result to Q3 is that there is no apparent strong relationship between the number of corrupt acts and societal welfare generated, as we see situations where both of them increase together, but also situations where one increases and the other decreases.

Possible extensions to our work are plural, including replacement of the current method of enforcement (indiscriminate firing from the lower levels), with a possible new Inspector agent class. The latter leads to the interesting second-order effect of what if Inpsector agents are corrupt. Second, more nuanced but complicated models of individuals' 'bribeability' characteristics, beyond a single number, and more generality personality [27]. Third, uncovering the role of organisational culture [28], and exploring alternative sociological theories as part of the modelling process.

Acknowledgements. Thanks to the MABS'25 reviewers and workshop participants for their suggestions about this work.This research was partially supported by TAILOR, a project funded by EU Horizon 2020 research and innovation programme under grant number 952215.

References

1. Aidt, T.: Corruption. In: The Oxford Handbook of Public Choice, vol. 1. Oxford University Press (2019)
2. Anderson, C., Brown, C.E.: The functions and dysfunctions of hierarchy. Res. Organ. Behav. **30**, 55–89 (2010)
3. Arvidsson, N.: Exploring tensions in projectified matrix organisations. Scand. J. Manag. **25**(1), 97–107 (2009)
4. Bac, M.: Corruption, supervision, and the structure of hierarchies. J. Law Econom. Organ. **12**(2), 277–298 (1996)
5. Bellaubi, F., Pahl-Wostl, C.: Corruption risks, management practices, and performance in water service delivery in Kenya and Ghana: an agent-based model. Ecol. Soc. **22**(2) (2017)
6. Cameron, D.: PM Hosts Major Summit as Part of Global Drive to Expose, Punish and Drive Out Corruption (2016). https://www.gov.uk/government/news/pm-announces-new-globalcommitments-to-expose-punish-and-drive-out-corruption
7. Carrillo, J.D.: Corruption in hierarchies. Annales d'Economie et de Statistique pp. 37–61 (2000)
8. Cosh, A., Fu, X., Hughes, A.: Organisation structure and innovation performance in different environments. Small Bus. Econ. **39**, 301–317 (2012)
9. Duggar, E., Duggar, M.: Corruption, culture and organizational form. Available at SSRN 770889 (2004). https://ssrn.com/abstract=770889

10. Duru, H., Cochran, J.: An agent-based model of police corruption. Howard J. Crime Justice **61**(3), 289–309 (2022)
11. Elnawawy, S.M., Okasha, A.E., Hosny, H.A.: Agent-based models of administrative corruption: an overview. Int. J. Model. Simul. **42**(2), 350–358 (2022)
12. Evans, T.R., et al.: Corruption and hierarchy: a replication of studies 1c and 6 of Fath & Kay 2018. J. Gen. Psychol. **151**(4), 536–553 (2024)
13. Fath, S., Kay, A.C.: If hierarchical, then corrupt: Exploring people's tendency to associate hierarchy with corruption in organizations. Organ. Behav. Hum. Decis. Process. **149**, 145–164 (2018)
14. Gilbert, N.: Agent-Based Models. Sage Publications (2019)
15. Hajdari, R., Jupa, N.: The role of pyramidal organizational structure in organizational effciency and effectiveness. ACC J. **29**(2), 7–22 (2023)
16. Hammond, R.: Endogenous transition dynamics in corruption: An agentbased computer model. Center on Social and Economic Dynamics Washington, DC (2000)
17. ter Hoeven, E., et al.: Mesa 3: Agent-based modeling with Python in 2025. J. Open Source Softw. 10(109), 7668 (2025). https://doi.org/10.21105/joss.07668
18. Kaufmann, D.: Corruption: the facts. Foreign Policy **107**, 114–131 (1997)
19. Kazil, J., Masad, D., Crooks, A.: Utilizing Python for agent-based modeling: The Mesa framework. In: Thomson, R., Bisgin, H., Dancy, C., Hyder, A., Hussain, M. (eds.) Social, Cultural, and Behavioral Modeling. pp. 308–317. Springer International Publishing (2020). https://doi.org/10.1007/978-3-030-61255-9_30
20. Knight, K.: Matrix organization: A review. J. Manag. Stud. **13**(2) (1976)
21. Kroeze, R., Vitória, A., Geltner, G.: Anti-corruption in History: From Antiquity to the Modern Era. Oxford University Press (2017)
22. Lee, J.S., et al.: The complexities of agent-based modeling output analysis. J. Artif. Soc. Soc. Simul. **18**(4) (2015)
23. Mungiu-Pippidi, A.: The Quest for Good Governance: How Societies Develop Control of Corruption. Cambridge University Press (2015)
24. Railsback, S.F., Grimm, V.: Agent-Based and Individual-Based Modeling: A practical introduction. Princeton University Press (2019)
25. Rosenblatt, V.: Hierarchies, power inequalities, and organizational corruption. J. Bus. Ethics **111**, 237–251 (2012)
26. Rothstein, B.: Quality of Government: Theory and Conceptualization. In: The Oxford Handbook of the Quality of Government. Oxford University Press (2021)
27. Srour, F.J., Yorke-Smith, N.: Towards agent-based simulation of maritime customs. In: Proceedings of the 14th International Conference on Autonomous Agents and MultiAgent Systems (AAMAS'15). pp. 1637–1638 (2015)
28. Srour, F.J., Yorke-Smith, N.: On collusion and coercion: Agent interconnectedness and in-group behaviour. In: Proceedings of the 17th International Conference on Autonomous Agents and MultiAgent Systems (AAMAS'18). pp. 1622–1630 (2018)
29. Villamil, I., Kertész, J., Wachs, J.: Computational approaches to the study of corruption. arXiv preprint arXiv:2201.11880 (2022)
30. Weber, M.: The Theory of Social and Economic Organization. Simon and Schuster (2009)
31. Weber, M.: Bureaucracy. In: Longhofer, W., Winchester, D. (eds.) Social Theory Re-Wired, pp. 271–276. Routledge (2023)
32. Zausinová, J., Zoričak, M., Vološin, M., Gazda, V.: Aspects of complexity in citizen-bureaucrat corruption: an agent-based simulation model. J. Econ. Interac. Coord. **15**, 527–552 (2020)

Assessing the Impact of Crisis Cell Decisions During Flash Flood

Elisa Cueille[1]([✉]) [iD], Déborah Bodini[2], Benoit Gaudou[1] [iD],
Delphine Grancher[3] [iD], Pierre Nicolle[4] [iD], Olivier Payrastre[4] [iD],
Manon Prédhumeau[1] [iD], Isabelle Ruin[2] [iD], Galateia Terti[2] [iD],
and Nicolas Verstaevel[1] [iD]

[1] Université Toulouse Capitole, IRIT, Toulouse, France
{elisa.cueille,benoit.gaudou,manon.predhumeau,
nicolas.verstaevel}@ut-capitole.fr
[2] Université Grenoble Alpes, CNRS, IRD, Grenoble INP, IGE, Grenoble, France
[3] Laboratoire de Géographie Physique, UMR 8591, Université Paris 1 Panthéon
Sorbonne, CNRS, UPEC, Meudon, France
[4] GERS-LEE, Univ. Gustave Eiffel, IFSTTAR, Bouguenais, France

Abstract. Catastrophic weather-related events, such as flash floods, require efficient decisions to reduce people's exposure while ensuring that each intervention is both timely and not counterproductive. To provide efficient decisions, a crisis management cell composed of decision-makers and experts must be able to centralize information and make relevant choices. Our study proposes an agent-based model that can support and assess various strategies for flash flood crisis management. We investigate in particular the application of several decisions, taking into account both their interactions and the time of their implementation. We model people's behaviors during their daily activities and their adaptation to flooding and to the authorities' decisions with the GAMA platform. Preliminary results indicate that the time of decision implementation impacts people's exposure to flooding and that combining specific decisions enhances the efficiency of the crisis management. This approach helps limit ineffective decisions and select those that provide a trade-off between flood exposure and daily activities' disruption.

Keywords: Agent-based modeling · Crisis management · Flash flood · Decision timing

1 Introduction

Flash floods are weather-related hazards that are difficult to anticipate and whose frequency is increasing [9]. To deal with a flash-flood event as it occurs, a crisis management cell made up of decision-makers, experts, and communication professionals gathers, centralizes information on the situation, assesses the risk, makes decisions, and defines a communication strategy.

© The Author(s), under exclusive license to Springer Nature Switzerland AG 2026
A. Vidler and S. Swarup (Eds.): MABS 2025, LNAI 16227, pp. 89–103, 2026.
https://doi.org/10.1007/978-3-032-16328-8_7

However, crisis management cells often lack tools to measure or assess the effectiveness of alternative decisions. Exposed inhabitants' reactions are difficult to predict as they vary according to personal constraints, available information [14], and decisions from the official authorities. Agent-based models (ABMs) are particularly relevant to the evaluation of emergency strategies [4] for their ability to simulate dynamic decisions in a spatial environment with heterogeneous individuals. Agent-based simulations provide a testing bench for analyzing how social dynamics evolve under crisis management scenarios that are unsafe or expensive to approach in real life [1,20]. Simulations often study the implementation of different decisions individually, but they rarely examine the interaction between several simultaneous decisions or the dynamic aspect of applying decisions at different times [7].

Our study proposes to use ABM to assess the impact of different decisions on individual behaviors during a flash flood. This work is conducted through a case study that occurred in the town of Trèbes (France) between October 14 and 16, 2018. The model simulates realistic population heterogeneity by incorporating individual characteristics, activity chains, and individual or family adaptations to warnings and official advice. The model is designed to support a serious game called ANYCaRE [18] where the decisions are made by players who take on different roles within a crisis management cell and must make decisions based on different weather predictions. The model enables (1) to observe the effect of combining different decisions and (2) to analyze the impact of the time of decision implementation on individual exposure and daily activities. We illustrate our approach on a subset of the available decisions, focusing on those related to road closures and schools (including the confinement of students, asking parents to pick them up by anticipating school leaving time, or relocating them to a shelter).

The article is organized as follows: Sect. 2 reviews key contributions in ABMs for crisis management. Section 3 details the model. Section 4 presents preliminary results. Finally, Sect. 5 summarizes the main contributions of this study and outlines future directions.

2   Related Work

In the last decade, several ABMs have been developed to simulate long-term adaptive behaviors and risk mitigation decisions related to flood hazards [1]. A recent review of ABMs for flood risk management [1] found that only 33% of the 39 reviewed studies looked at evacuation during flood events. Evacuation ABMs simulate the various residents' emergency behaviors during the evacuation phase with the aim of exploring relevant strategies in evacuation planning [20]. Taillandier et al. [16] proposed a model that integrates emotions and social relations with information sharing and risk knowledge to simulate evacuation strategies during a flood in La Ciotat city (South France). ABMs enable varying the hypotheses of the tested event (time, amplitude, uncertainty) and crisis communication towards the population by confronting the range of available official protective options with the dynamics of the hydro-meteorological and human behavioral patterns [2].

Although some evacuation models integrate the behavioral reaction of individuals to flood warnings [5], holistic models that explore the effect of flood alerts, warning messages, and emergency decision-making on human losses remain rare [19]. Existing models rarely explore the impact of the time of decision implementation and how combining various decisions could impact the efficiency of a crisis management strategy. The next section presents a model that allows one or multiple decisions to be applied at any time during the simulation in order to assess the impact of the decision on individuals.

3   Model

The model is implemented in the GAMA platform [17] and described using the Overview, Design concepts, and Details (ODD) protocol [6].

3.1   Overview

Purpose. The model simulates the daily mobility of the inhabitants and represents the flash flood that occurred in the Trèbes city (France) between October 14 and 16, 2018. It is used to evaluate different crisis cell decision combinations and implementation times, to identify those that minimize the individual's exposure. The model is intended to be used as a support to a serious game where various experts must make decisions to implement during the crisis.

Entities. The main kind of agent is the inhabitant with his own characteristics: age, sex, level of study, socio-professional category and occupation. Each agent has its own agenda which is a sequence of activities and trips over the day. The agents are geolocalized and belong to a household. A household gathers one or more agents and is associated to a residential building. A trip entity contains the starting and the ending time of the trip, a destination zone, and the activity both at the origin location and at the destination.

Buildings and roads are the two main spatial entities of the model. Roads are the support of agents' trips and buildings are places for agents' activities. A building may be considered as a shelter if it has more than one floor or if it is an official shelter. At the beginning of the simulation, each household is randomly assigned a residential building within its residential zone and each agent is assigned with a building for its primary activity: a workplace for working adults or a school for students. Buildings for other activities (such as shopping or leisure) are randomly allocated in the destination zone for each new agent's activity. Roads and buildings have a flooded state that depends on the water level: safe, disrupted or dangerous (see Sect. 3.3). A road or building is safe when it is not affected by flooding, disrupted when the water level hinders movement, and dangerous when there is a risk of physical injury and loss of life. A flooded road can be closed by the authorities with a delay that depends on the decisions applied (Table 1). Finally, buildings are located in a zone and a municipality. A municipality is the smallest administrative division in France often centered around a town. A zone is a small-scale geographical unit that includes at least 130 households and 160 individuals [13]. This segmentation is the spatial unit used in French Time Surveys, ensuring both statistical representativeness and data confidentiality. Finally, the crisis cell is not explicitly represented as an entity, as we do not simulate its decisions. Decisions to be applied at given steps are input as scenarios.

Scales. The studied area comprises three municipalities of the Carcassonne urban area (South-West of France). It includes the municipality of Trèbes and extends upstream along two rivers: the Orbiel and the Trapel (Fig. 1). This area is populated by around 14200 inhabitants and cover an area of around $100\,km^2$. This area is often exposed to flash floods. As we aim to assess the total exposition to the flash flood we take into account all the people that may be in the flooded area during the event. We thus extended the simulated area to the whole Carcassonne urban area. We simulate 16 h from 6 *a.m.* to midnight on October 14, i.e. the day of the flooding, with a simulation step of 1 min.

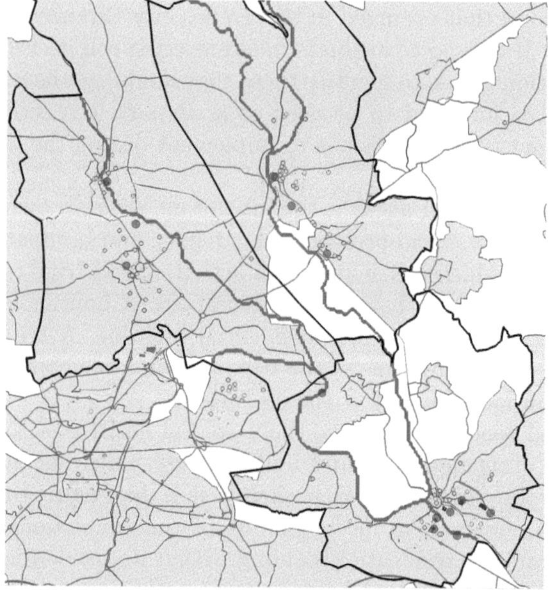

Fig. 1. Simulation performed in the GAMA platform.

Scheduling Overview. The model has three different time scales: one for individuals, one for the flooding and one for crisis decisions. Individuals' behavior is computed at each simulation step. Flood propagation is updated every 15 min as water level information is provided by raster files available at the same interval (see Sect. 3.3). The model is designed to support a serious game where a crisis management cell can apply decisions at three predefined game times: 11 *a.m.* (30 min after the start of the flash flood), 2 *p.m.* and 4 *p.m.*. These timescales were chosen because managing a flash flood requires short decision times.

A time step is as follows: if it is one of the three predefined game times, new crisis decisions can be applied (Table 1). Every 15 steps, the roads and buildings' flooded states are updated based on the water levels. The individual agents then execute their behaviors according to the activity diagram in Fig. 2 (the decision trees mentioned are shown in Fig. 3 and Fig. 4).

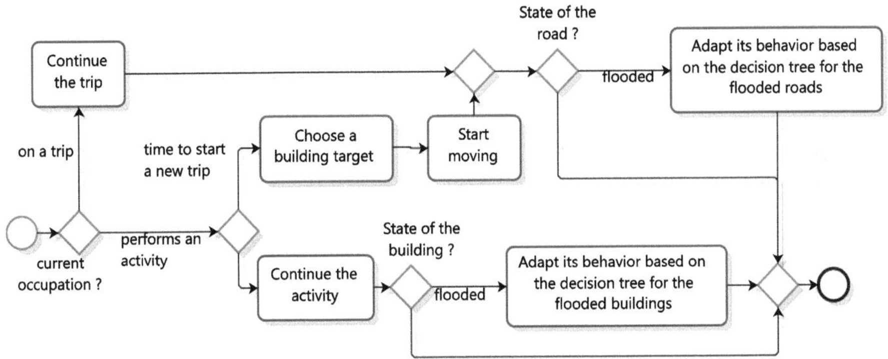

Fig. 2. Individual decision-making process at each simulation step.

3.2 Design Concepts

Basic Principles. Individuals' behavior is described using an activity-based model. Each individual follows an agenda composed of a set of activities and trips. Agents perform activities in buildings selected from those available in their trip's destination zone (see Sect. 3.1). Agents move from one building to another using the road network either by walking or by car. The simulation is only run during the water-rising period.

The flood itself is not computed in real time and integrated into the model. Only its effects on buildings and roads are updated when relevant (changing their state among safe, disrupted, and dangerous). This discrete state serves as a proxy for the water level.

Adaptation. Following [14], we consider that inhabitants' reactions to a hazardous situation depend on their individual and social characteristics. Their behavior is also altered by the crisis management cell's decisions and the condition of the surrounding roads or buildings. Behaviors of agents located in a flooded building or on a flooded road follow the decision trees in Fig. 3 and 4.

Agents' behavioral adaptation to a crisis management cell's decision is described in Table 1. We parameterized the branching probabilities in the decision trees and the compliance rates to crisis-cell decisions using empirical knowledge gained from post-event interviews.

Objectives. Agents have two implicit objectives embodied in their rule-based behavior: 1) follow their agenda; and 2) ensure their safety and avoid flooded (disrupted or dangerous) roads and buildings.

Sensing. Individuals perceive the flood-related state of the road on which they are moving on and of the building in which they are located. When they plan their trips they know the location of their next activity and the roads that are closed by the authorities (cf. decision 4 in Table 1). Finally, individuals know the nearest unofficial refuge (building with more than one floor) and official refuge.

Interaction. The main interaction between individuals is the escort activity between individuals of the same household. For example, parents have to pick up their children from school if they cannot return on their own by public transportation, bicycle, or on foot). Interactions between the flood and the inhabitants are limited to the water level recorded in buildings and roads.

Stochasticity. Individuals' behaviors are impacted by several random factors. They randomly pick a building in the destination zone as target for their current trip. Their adaptation behavior to flooded buildings and roads follows random distributions which will change depending on the crisis cell's decisions. Finally, some decisions are not followed by all individuals. The individuals who follow instructions are randomly selected from the population with the required characteristics according to the proportions and conditions specified in Table 1.

Collectives. Individual agents are gathered into households sharing the same residential location (e.g. a family). Grouping of individual agents into households can impact their behavior as their agenda may contain escort activities.

Observation. The evolution of the simulation can be monitored in real-time through several indicators: number of individuals exposed to flooding (in buildings or on roads), total exposure duration (cumulative time spent in contact with the flood for the entire population), number of changes in activity caused by exposure (representing activity disruptions). These indicators can be observed for specific population groups or for the entire population.

3.3   Details

Initialization. The initialization of the simulation follows two main steps: 1) creation of the spatial entities (buildings, roads, zones, municipalities) from the input shapefiles; 2) creation of the demographic entities (individuals, households, trips) and links between them from the Time Survey dataset: an agent has an agenda of trips, a household has a set of individuals, and a home building. All individuals start the simulation at their home place at 6 *a.m.*. The initial step is set before the onset of the flood, so that all roads and buildings are initialized as safe.

Input Data. The temporal evolution of flooding (spatial extent and water levels) is obtained through a processing pipeline [3] that incorporates observed rainfall fields (Antilope J+1 [10]). The pipeline output is a set of raster files (one every 15 min) with a spatial resolution of 5 m, containing the water elevation for each pixel. Instead of using flood data directly, these files are used to assign temporal flood information to roads and buildings. For each building and road, we record the times at which their status changes first to "disrupted" and then to "dangerous". A road is considered as "safe" when the water level is below 30 cm, "disrupted" when the water reaches 30 cm and "dangerous" when it reaches 50 cm. The states are the same for buildings but the thresholds are 10 cm and 40 cm. These thresholds have been provided by experts. Flood dynamics in the case study have been shifted by 8 h in simulation so that flooding occurs during the day rather than at night. The first road is flooded at 10:30 *a.m.* (instead of 6:30 *p.m.*) and the first building at 11:30 *a.m.* (instead of 7:30 *p.m.*).

The spatial description of the buildings is provided by IGN BD TOPO Version 3.0, the reference French database [8]. The river network comes from the French Catchment National Database [12]. The road network comes from OpenStreetMap [11] and includes only the major roads.

The population is generated from the 2015 Time Survey dataset on the Carcassonne urban area [13][1]. This dataset provides data about a sample of the urban area population with 5924 individuals in 2726 households and their daily trips. Each household's home and each activity's place is located in a zone. The dataset has missing data: in some households, there are individuals with unrecorded agendas. To complete missing agendas, we relied on [14], which provides a clustering of agendas using similarity metrics and a decision tree based on individual characteristics such as age, gender, education, professional status, and household composition. However, this work only considers individuals older than 16 years. To complete the agendas, individuals younger than 16 have been split into 3 sets: non-studying individuals, studying teenagers (> 11 years old), and pupils (children between 3 and 10 years old). For adults without agendas, we copy the agenda of an individual randomly selected from the corresponding group (using the decision tree [14]). For teenagers, we copy the agenda of a randomly selected teenager in the same age range (11–16, 16–18 or >18) with an equal probability for each selection. These three ranges correspond to different kinds of French schools (secondary school, high school, and university). In the dataset, some parents or relatives bring pupils to school in the morning and bring them back home in the evening (plus some trips back home at noon to eat). However, some pupils are brought to school but never brought back home,

---

[1] French Time Surveys are updated every 10 years.

and vice versa. To prevent blocking situations, we completed pupils' agendas with the missing trips: pupils return home by themselves.

Finally, we filtered the population to keep only individuals that could be impacted by the flood, i.e. individuals having their home or activities in the study area. The final population consists of 855 individuals in 381 households, i.e. around 9% of the actual population that could have been impacted by the real flood. We created a complete population by duplicating (x11) individuals to obtain a full population of 9405 individuals.

A preliminary study was conducted with 9% and 100% of the population for Scenario 1 (Sect. 4) in which the individuals adapt when they face flooding but no decision is applied by the crisis management cell. These simulations produced identical results in both cases when analyzing different indicators such as the number of individuals exposed to the flood or the number of individuals with disrupted agendas. The results obtained with the population from the Time Survey dataset are thus representative of the entire population. To reduce simulation time all simulations were executed with the 9% population sample.

Subprocesses. An agent follows its agenda throughout the day. The agent stays at home and when the departure time arrives, the agent starts its trip to go to its next activity. Once at a destination the agent remains there until the next trip starts. Some adults have escort activities meaning they do the trip and activity with a child.

Individuals can be exposed to hazards either during their trips (when roads are disrupted or dangerous) or during their activities (when buildings are flooded). They do not react uniformly when facing such hazards: Fig. 3 (resp. Fig. 4) presents the decision trees that agents follow in flooded buildings (resp.

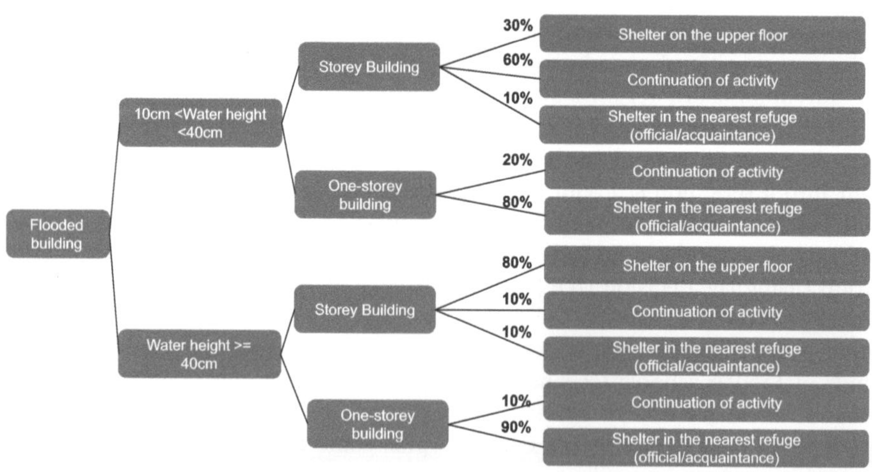

Fig. 3. Decision tree for the reaction of individuals in a flooded building.

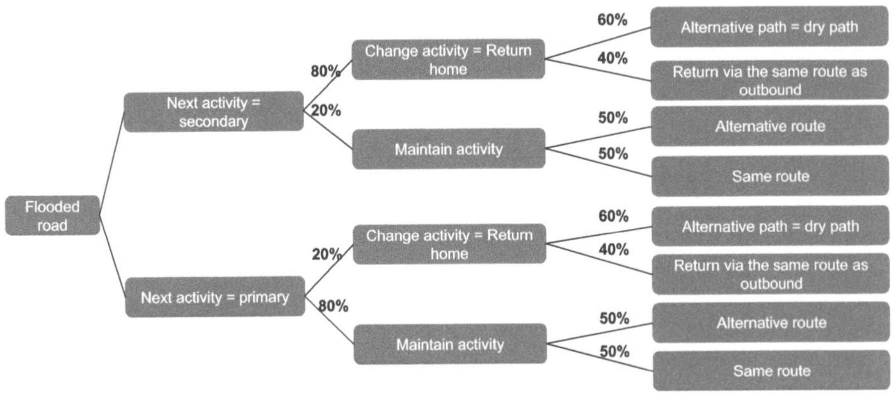

Fig. 4. Decision tree for the reaction of individuals on a flooded road.

on flooded roads). This formalization enables to adapt the proportions of each behavior according to the flood situation [15].

Fourteen authority decisions provided by experts can be applied during the simulation (Table 1). For a given decision only a proportion of the individuals will adapt, selected according to the conditions in Table 1 (e.g., if schools have to be closed, only students and parents are impacted). Decisions to apply and their application time is defined before simulation.

In this study, we focus on four decisions related to schools and roads:

- **Decision 2:** Anticipate school leaving time, meaning that 70% of households pick up their children before the usual time.
- **Decision 6:** Evacuate facilities in flood zones (campsites, health facilities, schools) to shelters. The total time required to evacuate all people is set to one hour.
- **Decision 7:** Confine students to the school to prevent parents from picking them up, so that students stay in the school until the end of the simulation. Only 50% of households comply with this measure.
- **Decision 8:** Close flooded roads. Once a road is flooded, it takes one hour to actually close it, as human intervention is required.

4   Preliminary Results

Calibration. The model used to obtain the temporal dynamics of flooding has been calibrated separately from this study.

Experimental Setup. The model allows to explore all the decisions presented in Table 1. In this paper, we focus on exploring four strategies impacting schools and the closure of flooded roads (decisions 2, 6, 7, and 8 presented above). More strategies will be explored in future work. Three kinds of scenarios have been simulated:

Table 1. The different possible decisions

	Decision	Effect of the decision
1	Implement flood **control measures**	Delay the flood time
2	**Anticipate school leaving time**	70% of households pick up their children
3	Evacuate to the **nearest shelter** (if you do not have a floor)	100% of the population apply the measure
4	Pre-position teams to **anticipate road closures**	Roads closed within 15 min of flooding
5	Pre-position **intervention columns**	Reduces the evacuation time by 1/2 if decision 6 is applied
6	**Evacuate facilities** in flood zones: campsites, health facilities, schools	Evacuates people from buildings in 1 h
7	**Confine students** to the school to prevent parents from picking them up	50% of households apply the measure
8	**Close flooded roads**	Selected roads are closed in 1h
9	**Evacuate vulnerable populations** in flood zones	50% of people over 75 are taken to a shelter
10	Be vigilant a **orange rain-flood vigilance** is in progress	20% of people who have planned a leisure activity during the day do not realize it
11	**Avoid travelling** and inquire before you travel	30% of the trips to school or work are cancelled and 80% of other trips
12	**Stay home** and follow the advice of the appropriate authorities	70% of men between 18 and 40 years and 90% of the rest of the population apply
13	**Do not use your car**	80% of the trips to school or work are cancelled and 100% of other trips
14	Take **refuge** in the floors	Multiplies by 2 the number of people who go to the floors (Fig. 3)

- **Scenario 0**: agents follow their agenda regardless of the flood. For example, if they are in a flooded building they stay there and continue their activity;
- **Scenario 1**: agents follow their agenda but adapt when they face flooding.
- **Scenario 2**: agents follow their agenda but adapt to both the flooding situation and the decisions issued by the crisis management cell (Table 1).

Each simulation was repeated 100 times. All the results presented are average values and standard deviations of 100 simulations.

Baseline Scenarios. Scenarios 0 and 1 are used to verify that the model behaves as expected. Comparing the results of these two scenarios confirmed that in Scenario 1 (where individuals react to the flood) the agents are less exposed to the flood: the cumulative duration of individuals' exposure to dangerous roads is 140 min in Scenario 1 compared to 4099 min in Scenario 0 (Fig. 5). This is expected as individuals in Scenario 1 adapt their agenda when faced with flooding: 205 individuals out of 855 changed their agenda to be safer.

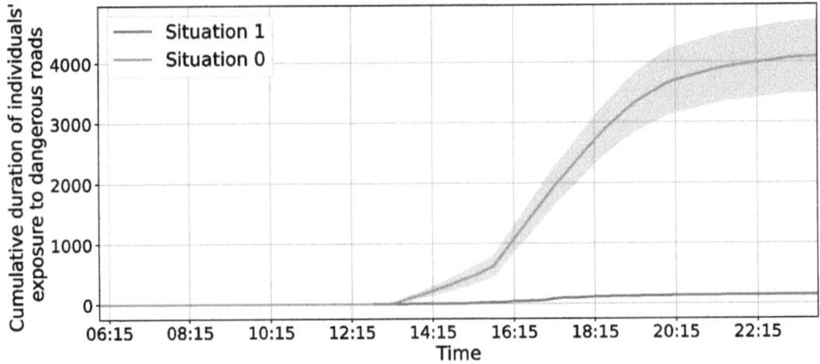

Fig. 5. Cumulative duration of individuals' exposure to dangerous roads.

Evaluation of the Effectiveness of a Decision. Applying only one decision at a time and comparing results with those from Scenario 1 enables us to assess the impact of both the decision and its timing. Results obtained with decision 2, applied at 11 *a.m.*, show that anticipating school leaving time did not significantly reduce individuals' exposure (Fig. 6) while impacting 81 agendas on average: 205 agendas are disrupted in Scenario 1 compared to 286 with decision 2, which represents an increase of about 40% (Fig. 7).

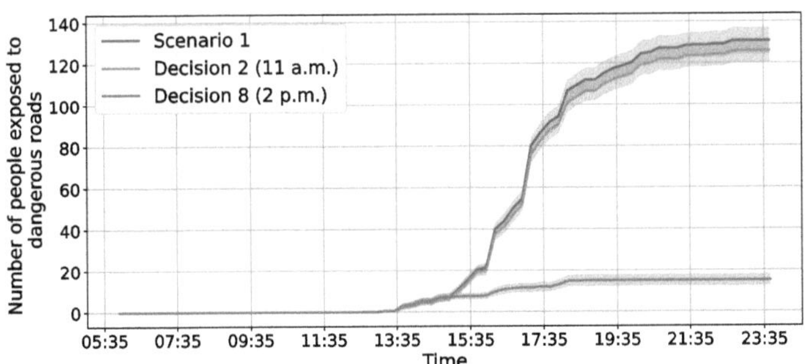

Fig. 6. Comparison of the number of people exposed to dangerous roads.

An explanation is that only 6 of the 15 schools are flooded with only 3 schools impacted before the end of the school day. Two are impacted at 3:30 *p.m.* and one at 4 *p.m.*. In contrast, decision 8 helps to reduce individuals' exposure to flooded roads; 130 agents are exposed to dangerous roads in Scenario 1 compared to only 15 agents when decision 8 is applied at 2 *p.m.*, which represents a reduction of about 89%. Decision 8 also limits the agendas' disruptions: only 98 people changed their agendas (Fig. 7) compared to 205 when no decision is applied, a decrease of about 52%. As flooded roads are closed, individuals are less exposed to flooded roads and therefore less likely to give up their planned activity.

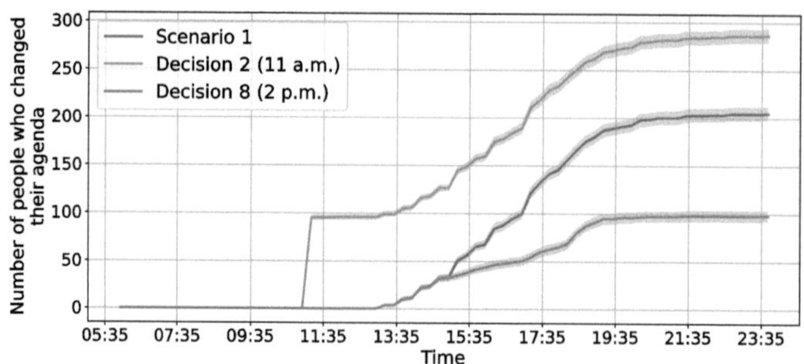

Fig. 7. Comparison of the number of people changing their agenda.

Impact of Implementation's Time. The time of decision 8 affects the decision's effectiveness. When applied at 2 *p.m.* it reduces both people's exposure to flooded roads and agenda disruptions compared to its application at 4 *p.m.*: the number of agents exposed to dangerous roads decreases by about 74% (Fig. 8) (15 compared to 57), and the number of changed agendas decreases by about 30% (98 compared to 141). As roads are closed earlier, fewer people face flooded roads and thus change their agenda. When more people are exposed to flooded roads, more agendas are disrupted. This explains why delaying road closures increases agendas' changes.

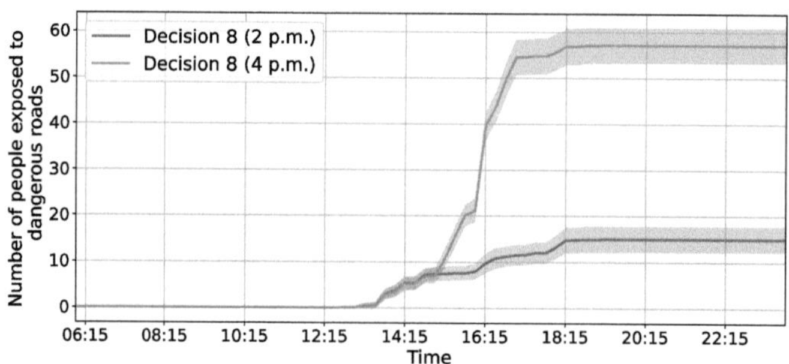

Fig. 8. Comparison of the number of people exposed to dangerous roads.

Interaction Between Different Decisions. Decision 6 corresponds to confining students at school, which prevents them from returning home and also from being picked up by their parents. Decision 7 consists of evacuating facilities located in flood zones, such as schools, and relocating their occupants to the nearest shelter. Applying only decision 6 slightly reduces children's exposure (Fig. 9), whereas applying only decision 7 has no impact on either individuals' exposure or agenda changes.

However, coupling decisions 6 and 7 and applying them simultaneously makes the strategy more effective. In this case, students are prevented from returning home, and instead of being confined in school as in decision 6, they are evacuated to the nearest shelter, where they remain confined. Decision 7 alone also evacuates students to a shelter, but they are not confined there so they can return home and their parents can pick them up. Applying decisions 6 and 7 simultaneously reduces children's exposure but requires significant agenda adaptations: on average, the number of individuals who changed their agenda increased by about 101% (143 additional individuals compared to 141 in Scenario 1). Yet, confining students to school at 11 *a.m.* and then evacuating facilities located in flood zones at 2 *p.m.* worsens the situation compared to Scenario 1: more children are exposed to flooded roads (Fig. 9) and 132 additional agendas are impacted. The first road is flooded at 10:30 *a.m.*. By 2 *p.m.*, many more roads are flooded than at 11 *a.m.*. Evacuating later results in a high number of children being present on the roads during peak flooding. This is why it is better to evacuate as early as possible. In Scenario 1, parents can decide to leave children at school once roads are flooded, which is preferable to attempting to bring them to shelters when many roads are already flooded. This indicates that both the time of implementation and the combination of decisions should be considered.

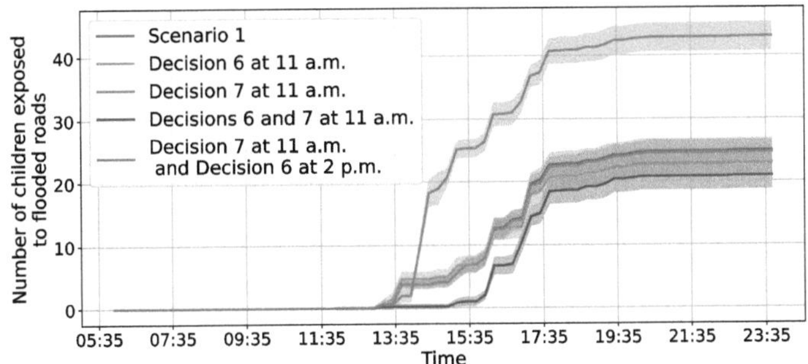

Fig. 9. Comparison of the number of children exposed to flooded roads.

5   Discussion and Conclusions

The proposed model enables the analysis of strategies by exploring both the decision's implementation time and the combinations of multiple decisions.

Eight strategies have already been explored. Preliminary results show that some combinations and implementation times are more effective than others in reducing both people's exposure to floods and the impact on their daily activities. Anticipating school leaving time does not reduce individual exposure and disrupt agendas, while closing roads reduces individuals' exposure and minimizes schedule' disruptions. The decision to close flooded roads is more effective when applied at 2 *p.m.* than at 4 *p.m.*. Keeping students at school to prevent parents from picking them up is effective only if authorities evacuate students to a shelter at the same time. Combining these two decisions limits parents' trips and reduces their exposure while preventing students from staying in a school that may become flooded.

We plan to further explore the model by implementing additional strategies, testing new decision combinations, and applying them at different times. The model will be integrated into a serious game, allowing experts to validate it. The goal is to provide a tool that assesses the decisions made by the crisis management cell formed for the game by identifying those that minimize damages, i.e., the number of exposed people and the number of people whose agenda is disrupted.

Acknowledgments. This research has been supported by the French National Research Agency (PICS project, grant number ANR–17–CE03–0011).

References

1. Anshuka, A., van Ogtrop, F.F., Sanderson, D., Leao, S.Z.: A systematic review of agent-based model for flood risk management and assessment using the ODD protocol. Nat. Hazards **112**(3), 2739–2771 (2022)
2. Chapuis, K., et al.: An agent-based co-modeling approach to simulate the evacuation of a population in the context of a realistic flooding event: a case study in Hanoi (Vietnam). In: Mohd, M.H., Misro, M.Y., Ahmad, S., Nguyen Ngoc, D. (eds) International Workshop on Complex Systems Modelling & Simulation. pp. 79–108. Springer (2019). https://doi.org/10.1007/978-981-16-2629-6_5
3. Charpentier-Noyer, M., Peredo, D., Fleury, A., Marchal, H., Bouttier, F., Gaume, E., Nicolle, P., Payrastre, O., Ramos, M.H.: A methodological framework for the evaluation of short-range flash-flood hydrometeorological forecasts at the event scale. Nat. Hazards Earth Sys. Sci. Discuss. **23**, 1–42 (2022)
4. Daudé, E., et al.: ESCAPE: exploring by simulation cities awareness on population evacuation. In: ISCRAM (2019)
5. Du, E., Rivera, S., Cai, X., Myers, L., Ernest, A., Minsker, B.: Impacts of human behavioral heterogeneity on the benefits of probabilistic flood warnings: an agent-based modeling framework. JAWRA **53**(2), 316–332 (2017)
6. Grimm, V., et al.: The ODD protocol for describing agent-based and other simulation models: A second update to improve clarity, replication, and structural realism. JASSS **23**(2) (2020)
7. Haer, T., Botzen, W.W., Aerts, J.C.: The effectiveness of flood risk communication strategies and the influence of social networks–insights from an agent-based model. Environ. Sci. Policy **60**, 44–52 (2016)
8. Institut Géographique National (IGN): BD TOPO - Base de Données Topographiques. https://geoservices.ign.fr/documentation/donnees/vecteur/bdtopo
9. Jongman, B., Ward, P.J., Aerts, J.C.: Global exposure to river and coastal flooding: long term trends and changes. Global Env. Change **22**(4), 823–835 (2012)
10. Laurantin, O.: ANTILOPE: Hourly rainfall analysis merging radar and rain gauge data. In: Proc. of the Int. Symp. on Weather Radar and Hydrology. pp. 2–8 (2008)

11. OpenStreetMap contributors: Planet dump retrieved from https://planet.osm.org/, https://www.openstreetmap.org/ (2017)
12. Organde, D., Javelle, P., Ardilouze, C., Lamblin, R.: Base nationale des bassins versants du SCHAPI. Technical report, HYDRIS Hydrologie (2013)
13. Progedo: Enquête ménages déplacements, carcassonne / carcassonnais - 2015. https://doi.org/10.13144/lil-1133
14. Ruin, I., Lutoff, C., Shabou, S.: Anticipating or coping: Behaviors in the face of flash floods. In: Floods, pp. 259–275. Elsevier (2017)
15. Shabou, S., Ruin, I., Lutoff, C., Debionne, S., Anquetin, S., Creutin, J.D., Beaufils, X.: MobRISK: a model for assessing the exposure of road users to flash flood events. Nat. Hazard. **17**(9), 1631–1651 (2017)
16. Taillandier, F., Di Maiolo, P., Taillandier, P., Jacquenod, C., Rauscher-Lauranceau, L., Mehdizadeh, R.: An agent-based model to simulate inhabitants' behavior during a flood event. Int. J. Disaster Risk Reduction **64**, 102503 (2021)
17. Taillandier, P., Get al.: Building, composing and experimenting complex spatial models with the GAMA platform. GeoInformatica **23**, 299–322 (2019)
18. Terti, G., et al.: ANYCaRE: a role-playing game to investigate crisis decision-making and communication challenges in weather-related hazards. Natural Hazards and Earth System Sciences **19**(3), 507–533 (2019)
19. Yang, L.E., Scheffran, J., Süsser, D., Dawson, R., Chen, Y.D.: Assessment of flood losses with household responses: agent-based simulation in an urban catchment area. Environ. Model. Assess. **23**, 369–388 (2018)
20. Zhang, R., Liu, D., Du, E., Xiong, L., Chen, J., Chen, H.: An agent-based model to simulate human responses to flash flood warnings for improving evacuation performance. J. Hydrol. **628**, 130452 (2024)

Markets and Engineered Systems

Shifting Power: Leveraging LLMs to Simulate Human Aversion in ABMs of Bilateral Financial Exchanges, A Bond Market Study

Alicia Vidler[✉][iD] and Toby Walsh[iD]

UNSW, Sydney, Australia
`a.vidler@unsw.edu.au`

Abstract. Bilateral markets, such as those for government bonds, involve decentralised and opaque transactions between market makers (MMs) and clients, posing significant challenges for traditional modelling approaches. To address these complexities, we introduce **TRIBE** an agent-based model augmented with a large language model (LLM) to simulate human-like decision-making in trading environments. TRIBE leverages publicly available data and stylised facts to capture realistic trading dynamics, integrating human biases like risk aversion and ambiguity sensitivity into the decision-making processes of agents. Our research yields three key contributions: first, we demonstrate that integrating LLMs into agent-based models to enhance client agency is feasible and enriches the simulation of agent behaviours in complex markets; second, we find that even slight trade aversion encoded within the LLM leads to a complete cessation of trading activity, highlighting the sensitivity of market dynamics to agents' risk profiles; third, we show that incorporating human-like variability shifts power dynamics towards clients and can disproportionately affect the entire system, often resulting in systemic agent collapse across simulations. These findings underscore the emergent properties that arise when introducing stochastic, human-like decision processes, revealing new system behaviours that enhance the realism and complexity of artificial societies.

Keywords: Multi-agent systems · Large Language models · Agents · Financial markets

1 Introduction

"Usually there is only one way to be fully rational, but there are many ways to be less rational" [29]

Agent-based models (ABMs) are versatile applications for modelling complex and dynamic systems, particularly suited for bilateral markets like government bond markets. These markets, characterised by direct transactions between two parties without centralised exchanges, present modelling challenges due to their decentralised nature, complex interactions between heterogeneous agents, and lack of transparency.

A. Vidler and S. Swarup (Eds.): MABS 2025, LNAI 16227, pp. 107–127, 2026.
https://doi.org/10.1007/978-3-032-16328-8_8

We introduce the *TRIBE* model, a generative-ABM focused on **T**rading **R**elationships, **I**nteractions, and **B**ilateral **E**xchange of assets. *TRIBE* incorporates client agency with dynamically assigned asset distributions and probabilistic trading availability, extending this approach by integrating a large language model (LLM) for more human-like decision-making and negotiation behaviour.

Our research yields three key findings. First, we demonstrate the feasibility of using generative ABMs (GABMs) with enhanced client agency, building on work by [37], which demonstrates that generative agents can act as human simulacra, and thus advancing the capabilities of financial market simulations. Second, we discover that any LLM prompt suggestion of trade aversion results in a complete cessation of trading, highlighting the sensitivity of market dynamics to agent risk profiles. Third, and most significantly, by incorporating synthetic human client variability via an LLM, we reveal an emergent property where power dynamics shift towards clients, often resulting in significant systemic market collapse across simulations.

We develop a versatile, agent-based simulation of the over-the-counter (OTC) bond market, using LLMs to enrich ABMs with more nuanced, human-like behaviours. Our model focusses on the Australian government bond market, an ideal subject due to its decentralised structure and emphasis on liquidity and flow rather than pricing, based on earlier work by [48]. We have no reason to suggest that dynamics and results are not generalisable to other similar markets.

We demonstrate the feasibility and benefits of integrating LLMs into GABMs, we advance the field beyond traditional deterministic or simple stochastic approaches used in prior work such as [17]. Our findings provide valuable insights into the sensitivity of opaque, decentralised markets to agent heterogeneity and decision-making processes, with implications for market design and regulatory policy.

2   Literature and Recent Work

2.1   Agent-Based Models

The application of agent-based modelling (ABM) to financial markets has evolved significantly, with a focus on simulating complex behaviours among market participants. Several prior works have explored ABM applications in trading environments with varying levels of transparency. For example, [48] apply ABMs to model opaque bilateral bond markets, while [17] investigates liquidity dynamics in financial market order books. Recent work by [36] introduces the concept of *network agency* and the fact that features beyond an agent's direct experience can influence their behaviours. However, many of these models rely on homogeneous agent classes and observable environments, which are less relevant in over-the-counter (OTC) bond markets where data availability is limited [46]. Despite no consensus method for calibrating ABMS [5], we propose an inductive approach using market structure data such as [39,48] to specify agent calibrations. The utility functions and policies utilised within our simulation approach stem from finance literature and regulatory requirements.

The Australian Case: The Australian government bond market, like other global bond markets, involves a diverse range of participants [41]. In 2023, the Australian government debt (bonds issued) exceeded $890 billion. By owning a bond, the holder receives returns (interest payments) [24], making the bond market unusual in that prices are less critical than access to "flow" or "liquidity". Our work primarily focuses on modelling this "flow" or the movement of bonds through the market, and we build on work such as [48]. In order for a holder of a bond (i.e. a client) to sell or buy more of a bond, they must engage directly with an approved "market maker" for that bond. Their transactions are considered "over the counter" (OTC) as they do not involve a public exchange such as seen in stock markets like the NY Stock Exchange. Hence, these "OTC" bilateral exchanges of bonds pose difficulties for researchers and regulators alike [39, 41].

Maintaining an efficient and liquid bond market is crucial for Australia's economic stability [3]. By modelling the flow (liquidity) of bonds rather than focussing on price dynamics, our ABM provides insights into market stability and the role of market makers in these interactions. This approach builds on the works of [16, 40], who explore bilateral negotiations and liquidity flows in similarly non-transparent markets, with industry bodies contributing similarly in [7, 9].

Furthermore, methods for calibrating ABMs are challenging [11]. Many approaches applied to transparent markets, such as those calibrated with regulatory data [6, 10, 18], are not directly transferable to OTC bond markets. Further work in the same vein includes [20, 39]

2.2 Large Language Models (LLMs)

Work on the field of pre-trained Large Language Models (LLMs) like GPT-3 and GPT-4 demonstrates impressive capabilities in language-based domains. As shown by [14, 34], and [54], these models are proficient where tasks require dialogue generation and natural language based interactions, making them promising candidates for developing agent-based systems with advanced communication capabilities.

However, LLMs are also known to exhibit many flaws, which is extensively covered in the survey work by [26]. To name a few, LLMs exhibit significant limitations in reasoning, optimal prompting strategies, and particularly in numerical understanding [43, 56]. In the financial domain, numerical reasoning presents especially notable challenges [2, 31, 33]. LLMs under-perform when dealing with financial trading intentions [49] and struggle with 'reasoning' in negotiation contexts [1, 56], highlighting their limitations in negotiation tasks and strategic reasoning within agent-based systems.

Another challenge in working with LLMs is **prompt design**, which remains an evolving research area. Studies such as [54] have observed that non-expert users often adopt opportunistic, rather than systematic, approaches to prompting. To improve LLM outcomes, **prompt engineering** techniques are continually being refined. One promising technique involves prompting LLMs to **re-read the input**, which significantly enhances performance by leveraging the bidirectional nature of LLM architectures [53]. Another advanced method for improving

LLM reasoning is **Chain-of-Thought (CoT) prompting**. CoT prompting elicits a step-by-step reasoning process in the model's output by providing "worked examples" that guide the LLM through complex tasks [52]. Inspired by human learning theories, this approach has been shown to enhance the LLM's ability to handle multi-step reasoning problems [52,53].

One area that garners a lot of curiosity is the phenomenon of "hallucinations". Several approaches and interpretations exist ([51,55]), and suggestions about faithful reasoning are posited [19]. Work looking at the improvement from multistep reasoning are covered in [25]. However, we seek to avoid these issues by selective and opportunistic prompting in the same vein as [54].

These limitations highlight the need for improved strategies to maximise the effectiveness of LLMs in complex simulations. There is also the concern that foundation models, such as ChatGPT, are prone to updates with little warning [1] and extensive work can be based on models that are quickly deprecated. Following research on bias and the importance of model subversion testing [50], we manage model risk by focussing on the SOTA GPT4o-mini-2024-07-18 and by developing a framework, rather than fine-tuning of such third-party software.

Our model aims to enhance the realism of the agent behaviours in the simulated environment, enabling more faithful "human" variation in client behaviours (specifically) without relying on fine-tuned or domain-specific models that may well become outdated by the date of implementation.

2.3   Human Trading Behaviours: Aversions and Delays

Although limited work within computer science exists on human trading behaviours, ABMs traditionally have been specified with clear utility or numeric conditions to determine trading. Newer models may describe and analyse probabilistic behaviours [17]. With the advent of LLMs, we open ourselves to the possibility of richer human-based dynamics for more realistic and nuanced modelling, such as detailed in [49]. Outside the realm of computer science, there is a rich, if nuanced, body of literature focused on trading behaviours in a variety of financial markets e.g. such as the importance of reputation [35] and dealer behaviours in corporate bond markets [23].

In a phenomena reported in transparent markets (US equity markets), there is a high number of observed trades placed and a low percentage that actually become a confirmed transaction (as few as 1 in 20) [44]. This is best described as a difference between intention and action. Analysis of these features from the point of view of trader behaviours includes work into the trading psychology [30] and aversions (in particular to ambiguity) [12] with earlier work by [21]. In our work, we use the broad common definition of "aversion", taken to mean for one to be, simply, 'averse' to an action. All of these strands of literature try to ascribe causation to these observed differences between intention and human

---

[1] https://www.techradar.com/computing/artificial-intelligence/chatgpt-just-got-a-surprise-update-but-openai-cant-explain-how-this-new-ai-is-better   Accessed   12 Oct 2024.

action in financial transactions. Even market regulators view this as a significant issue worth investigation [22]. More recent efforts to use methods such as reinforcement and policy learning aim to try to learn how decisions are made [28], markets remain domains with imperfect information and associated risk. Our unique contribution is to contribute a framework and example of how an LLM implementable within an ABM market simulation can add, and represent, these human differences. We do not attempt to ascribe cause or reasoning to aversions or other responses to imperfect information or the perception of unequal distribution of market information, such as that in [35, 42].

3 TRIBE: Artificial Society and Trading Marketplace Model

We introduce *TRIBE*, an ABM where we simulate heterogeneous market makers trading a single stylised Australian government bond. Later in this work, we build TRIBE(LLM) (Experiment 3) with the added feature of one specific component referencing an LLM (ChatGpt's GPT4o-mini-2024-07-18) for a model choice, drawing from. Each market maker is modelled as an individual agent with its own adaptive utility function. Agents acquire bonds from clients - represented as unique (x,y) semi-passive grid-based agents, who respond to market maker inquiries, though they do not, themselves, traverse the grid. Building on work by [48], we incorporate significant improvements to enhance realism in client agency. We do this by allowing these client grid (agent) locations to have additional features (detailed in the next section).

In summary:

1. Clients have bonds and cash sourced from a log normal distribution (in line with public data)
2. Many clients are simply not available for a market to contact at any time step (we model "client availability")
3. Within TRIBE(LLM) we try to capture a synthetic client's personal preference to trade "right now". Rather than using a distributional assumption with no available data for parametrisation, we rely on an LLM for this choice with limited prompt information.
4. Trade direction: Despite bond and cash holdings, many clients have needs outside of the model to buy and sell, and we ascribe a Bernoulli distribution to the desire to be a buyer or seller at any point.

Definition 1. *TRIBE ABM*:

$$\mathcal{M} = \langle N, \mathcal{L}, \mathcal{S}, \mathcal{P}, \mathcal{D}, \mathcal{A}, f, T \rangle,$$

where: $N = \{a_1, a_2, \ldots, a_n\}$ is the set of market-making agents, with $n = 4$ in this case. $\mathcal{L}$ represents the set of client landscape states, following the lognormal distribution of assets observed where each landscape state contains assets $R = \{b_r, c_r\}$, corresponding to the bond (b_r) and cash (c_r) quantities held by individual clients. Each agent a_i has a state $\mathcal{S}_i$, which includes bond and cash usage rates m_b, m_c (representing individual cost structures), accumulations A_b, A_c (representing bond and cash accumulations over time), and a client base breadth v_i, which describes the range of clients the agent interacts with.

The perception functions $\mathcal{P}_i$ map the landscape and other agents' states to a perceived state, defined as $p_{ij} : \mathcal{L} \cup \mathcal{S} \to \mathbb{R}$. This function models how agent a_i perceives the landscape and the states of other agents. The decision rules $\mathcal{D}_i$ map the perceived states and an agent's own state to actions, $d_{ik} : \mathcal{P}_i \times \mathcal{S}_i \to \mathcal{A}_i$, where actions $\mathcal{A}_i$ for agent a_i include serving clients (e.g., accepting orders and managing trading requests), trading with other market makers and stopping operations when necessary.

The landscape evolves according to a transition function $f : \mathcal{L} \times \mathcal{A} \to \mathcal{L}$, which dictates how the landscape (i.e., the market environment) changes in response to the actions of the agent. In this model, there is no replenishment of bonds or cash, reflecting a closed system. The model progresses through discrete time steps, denoted by $T = \mathbb{N}$, where each time step represents a round of interactions between agents and updates to the landscape, and we limit this model to 1500 time steps.

Our contribution: Enriching the Landscape of Clients

Clients in the simulation are represented as grid cells, each initialised with bonds and cash according to a log-normal distribution.

Definition 2. *Client Definition: A client C_j is defined by:*

$$C_j = \{(x_j, y_j), B_j, C_j, D_{j,t}, A_{j,t}\}$$

Where (x_j, y_j) is the position of the grid, B_j and C_j are the amounts of bonds and cash, respectively, $D_{j,t}$ indicates the desire to trade and $A_{j,t}$ is the trading availability, determined probabilistically at each time step.

Note, within our TRIBE(LLM) version, $D_{j,t}$ is replaced with a call to an LLM and a boolean response, 'yes' or 'no'.

Bonds and cash are initialised as:

$$B_j \sim \text{LogNormal}(\mu_B, \sigma_B^2), \quad C_j \sim \text{LogNormal}(\mu_C, \sigma_C^2)$$

The parameters μ_B, σ_B, and the corresponding values of cash are set based on available data, such as from the Australian superannuation regulator [4].

The availability of the client at any given time step t for position (x_j, y_j) is modelled as:

$$A_{(x_j,y_j)}(t) = \begin{cases} 1 & \text{with probability } p \\ 0 & \text{with probability } 1 - p \end{cases}$$

where p is the preset availability probability, and Clients' roles as buyers or sellers are probabilistically drawn from a Bernoulli distribution, as is $D_{j,t}$ hence an even chance of being a buyer or seller, and an even chance of deciding to trade, determined at each time step. Together, these three components $D_{(j,t)}$, $A_{(x,y)}$, and Buy / sell form the proxy for a utility function.

This model enhancement actively engages clients with varied states, including random assignments as buyers or sellers at each time step, reflecting real-world trading complexities.

We present a graphical description of the model in Fig. 1 with the green boxes showing the TRIBE (LLM) implementation.

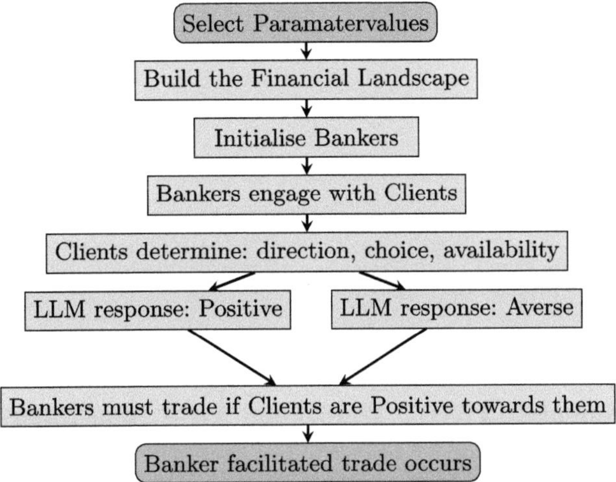

Fig. 1. Tribe Architecture: Architecture of LLM use within ABM framework

Calibration of Clients: Data

Results derived from the Australian Prudential Regulator show in Fig. 2 that as of December 2023 there were 1701 regulated pension asset holders alone, of which 1529 report their total asset holdings [4]. Whilst not a comprehensive direct relationship to bond holder sizes, given the practice of holding a very large percent of pension assets in local government bonds, the asset size of a pension fund does produce a proxy calculation for the distribution of government bonds. Furthermore, some 250 funds ask that their data be withheld from public view for privacy reasons, suggesting there are at least some 1950 bond clients. As such we include the data from December 2023 to illustrate the non-normal nature of the distribution.

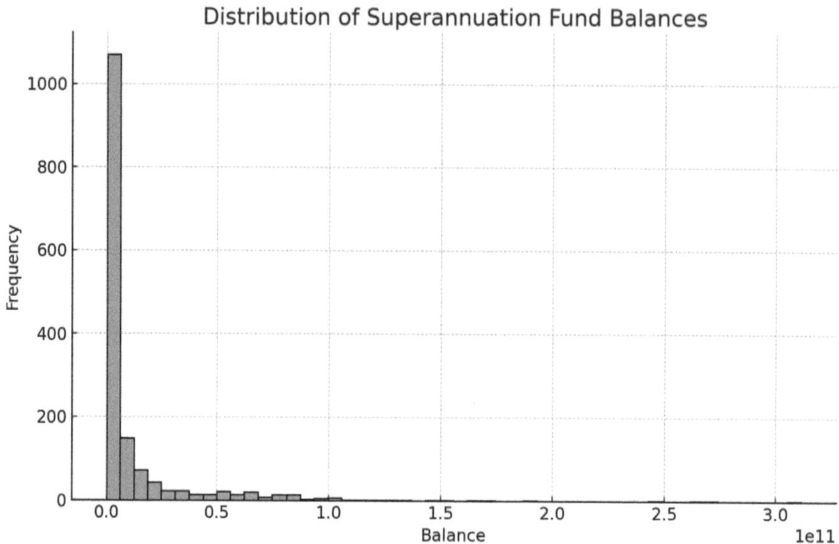

Fig. 2. APRA data: Balance in $ Billion Australian dollars

4   The Experiment and Challenge

4.1   Experiment 1: TRIBE Traditional ABM (benchmark)

We begin with an experiment to benchmark our traditional ABM version, TRIBE, across 200 simulations of an artificial trading society. Our unique contribution with this test is the enhancement of client agency through areas of active modelling. We rely on the parameter sets in Table 1 for all our tests. Much of this data is derived from various stylised facts in literature ([39, 48] in particular) and also data published by the Australian and UK governments ([4, 8, 41] respectively). This benchmark essentially looks at a simple coin toss of yes/no to trading desire, having been sampled from a Bernoulli distribution. The direction of trading, should an agent desire to trade, is then also determined by sampling from a Bernoulli distribution. In this week, we decompose direction of trade from intention to trade. Later on, we utilise an LLM to enhance the intention component of this model.

Results

We test 200 simulated trading societies with a maximum possible 1500 time steps. We present a summary of key results in Table 2 and draw attention to **MaxLife**, a measure of how long agents persist and keep trading. A goal of any marketplace is to facilitate the transaction of as many assets as possible. We see that over 75% of simulations were able to service 100% of all client bond volumes in the landscape. This is especially high and can be thought of as "successful" against the requirement that market makers service clients. Market maker to

Table 1. TRIBE ABM: Simulation Parameters

Parameter	*Category*	*Value*
Grid Size	General	50×50 (2500 clients)
Number of Bankers	MM Settings	4
Client Base grid size	MM Settings	1 to 50
Business costs	MM Settings	0.1 to 0.5
Initial Bonds Range	MM Settings	1 to 5
Initial Cash Range	MM Settings	1 to 5
Maximum Bonds	Client Settings	100
Mean Bonds	Client Settings	2.5 (log-normal distribution)
Standard Deviation Bonds	Client Settings	1
Maximum Cash	Client Settings	5.0
Mean Cash	Client Settings	1 (log-normal distribution)
Standard Deviation Cash	Client Settings	0.5
Client Availability for Trade	Client Settings	20%
Client Trade Desire	Utility function	Variable

market maker trading (so-called "inter bank" trading, or MM-2-MM) accounted for a mean of 9–10% of all traded assets - below that reported in [48]. Although beyond the scope of this paper, we surmise that this lower share of volumes could be addressed by fine-tuning parameters in future model versions. However, we make use of this test as a benchmark and have followed methods used in work such as [13] and look to establish an artificial society that appears to be stable and capable of carrying the capacity of trading volume clients desire - a concept explored in ABMs for financial market simulation in [27].

4.2 Experiment 2: TRIBE Incorporating (any) Aversion in Prompt with LLMs

Aversion, a broad term for the variety of factors that might stop a human trader from trading at a point in time, has been found to be so powerful as to stop traders trading altogether [11]. This is distinct from the work on utility maximisation. We consider aversion to represent the observed difference between intention and action, such as that seen in trading (e.g. [45]).

To incorporate the dynamic phenomena, we use a call to an LLM at the point at which TRIBE is a Client deciding if they want to trade with a specific MM "right now" at a time step. In this way, we seek to capture the inexplicable human feature of generalised aversion. We break this decision down into two components: does the client want to trade "right now" with this specific market maker, and, if yes, do they want to buy or sell bonds (for which we revert to using a Bernoulli distribution as in Experiment 1). In our terminology, we try to

Table 2. Summary Statistics for Maximum agent life, Total Bond Accumulation as a %, and Cash Accumulation as a %

Statistic	MaxLife	MM-to-Client Bond Trading (%)	MM-to-Client Cash Trading (%)	MM-2-MM Bonds (%)	MM-2-MM Cash (%)
mean	1136	90	90	9	10
std	509	14	14	8	8
25%	1248	90	89	2	3
50%	1264	95	94	4	7
75%	1499	100	100	13	15
max	1499	100	100	35	30

also capture the nuance in [35] where the reputation of various market makers is shown to drive uncertainty of client behaviours.

Implementation

We tested a number of prompts opportunistically building form [54]. The optimal processing, cleaning, and normalisation of decisions into boolean states (yes, no) or a three-state model (yes, no, error) with associated error handling proved to be most effective. *Note: a sample of full text prompts can be found in the appendix.*

In summary, we tested prompts that incorporate phrases like the following, all of which led to a **full** aversion response:

- "While you are supposed to at all times be mostly invested, you also at times consider non-numerical issues like risk inertia and trade aversion."
- "Clients have many reasons for trading and include behaviours like risk inertia, aversion, and ambiguity avoidance, that are non numeric."
- "Should this client buy, sell, or not trade right now? If you are going to say not right now, rethink. Answer only: buy or sell or 0 (not trade right now)."

All prompts with the above details were found to produce **100%** trading aversion, and **0%** client trades occurred. We find that simply including the term "aversion" does not produce a single-client trade, across 200 simulated artificial societies, at any time step. This is quite an astonishing fact that allowing the LLM to produce a decision with the possibility of aversion produces 100% aversion of all clients across 200 simulations at all points in time. In fact, over 2800 decision requests from "clients" were prompted in the 200 simulations, before trading societies collapsed, and not a single one responded with anything other than avoidance of trading. Given that no client ever wanted to trade, the average simulation collapsed by Step 27 (where previously the average simulation life was 1136 steps, that is, over 75% of the model theoretical maximum). Instead, when 'aversion' is even possible for the LLM, societies collapsed at around 1.7% of the theoretical life.

4.3   Experiment 3: TRIBE(LLM) Success of Prompting for Timeliness and the Emergent Shift in Society Dynamics

Similarly to the previous examples, we employ the parameters described in Table 1, with one key modification: availability is doubled to account for an anticipated 50% trading participation rate. This adjustment ensures comparability between Experiment 1 and Experiment 3 in terms of the percentage of clients actively engaged in buying or selling, 20% in Experiment 1, and 40% in Experiment 3, adjusted for expected 50% uptake (being a virtual coin toss). We apply the following simplified prompt to assess whether clients are inclined to trade immediately ('right now') with the engaging market maker. Drawing on prior work [49], we distinctly narrow and focus the concept of **aversion** to that of **timeliness**. Although one might argue that aversion inherently causes a delay in action—with complete avoidance possibly seen as an extreme form of delay—we aim to succinctly capture the outcome of delay without necessarily attributing it to causes of aversion. We test the following successful prompt:

Successful Prompt:

"You are a Client with $client_bonds$ bonds and $client_cash$ cash, at position (x, y). A market maker has called you to see if you want to trade with them right now. Do you want to trade with the market maker calling you right now. Answer yes or no, only?"

Where *"$client_bonds$"*, *"$client_cash$"* and co-ordinates (x, y) are specified per client, per time step, in each simulation and act as a unique prompt injection (given that clients do not move grid locations nor do they replenish their bond and cash accumulations).

Results: Frequent Client Trading Collapse

We simulate 150 artificial trading environments. We report around 50% of previously successful agents (MaxLife) from Experiment 1, now live only a fraction of their maximum life (recalling that the max life in the society is 1500 time steps and in this Experiment 3, 50% of agents live 18 or fewer time steps - under 2% of the possible time). Consequently, it is understandable that extremely small amounts of client assets are thus traded (an average of just 7% per simulation in this test compared to 90% in Experiment 1). The distribution of agent life is significantly altered with 75% of agents in simulations failing to live even 20% of the maximum 1500 time steps. Nonetheless, a portion of agents, 21%, did reach the maximum life, but continue to have low client asset trading and servicing levels. So, whilst many markets can continue to function with one agent (market maker), that MM is not able to facilitate adequate assets or make up for the loss of other MM's to the artificial society. (see Table 3 for further details.)

Looking at the variable directly controlled by the LLM introduction, and the desire to trade, we see a slightly different picture, and we explore this below as an emergent property.

Table 3. LLM in ABMs for Maximum Agent Life, Bond Trading (%), and Cash Trading (%)

Statistic	Max Life Agents	MM-to-Client Bond Trading (%)	MM-to-Client Cash Trading (%)
Mean	365	7%	6%
Std	605	4%	4%
25%	6	2%	2%
50%	18	7%	7%
75%	310	8%	8%
Max	1,499	20%	18%

Emergent Properties, Client agency and LLM choices

The LLM is interspersed within our traditional TRIBE model (see Figure 1), with an option to choose either to trade right now ('yes' or 'no') for each client at each time step the agent moves through. There are many more clients (2500) than market makers (4), so even the fact that any client that otherwise would have traded will not (in any given time step), there remain plenty of other clients nearby MM's that could also be available for MM trading. What we see is that, long term, 56.9% of LLM calls respond with 'yes' to trading in Fig. 3. Looking at results in Table 4 we see that the summary statistics indicate that the average long run yes/no ratio has a standard deviation of 5%, while the rolling 10 request average has a deviation of 16% and moves anywhere from **0%** to 100%, reflecting significant short-term variability in the statistic.

Across 200 society simulations in Experiment 1, the average number of MM-to-client interactions dropped from $\approx 4,900$ (Experiment 1) to < 590 when an LLM was involved, a reduction of $\approx$ **89%** of client interactions, mainly due to the significantly reduced life span of agents. Recall each client interaction is a market maker fulfilling their legal obligation to facilitate the transfer of liquidity in government bonds from a client, and Experiment 3 was constructed to have the same possible client transfer through the doubling of the "availability" parameter. Furthermore, MM to Client Bond trading, representing volumes of bonds, dropped, as a percentage, from 90% across simulations in TRIBE (Experiment 1) to less than 7% with the introduction of an LLM. In Experiment 1, 56.5% of all simulations had at least one agent reach the maximum possible life, but slightly more simulations in Experiment 3 had at least one agent reach the maximum life

(69.3%) with an LLM. In all cases, with a long run probability of 57% of LLM calls agreeing to trade, the resulting LLM TRIBE results are significantly more impacted than otherwise would be expected and point to the emergent property that "unpredictable" or "opaque" Client behaviour has an out-sized impact on society functioning, where agent life-span, and Client-2-MM bond trading is a measure of societal health. We propose that this can also be interpreted as a shift in power from Market makers (the only other agent type in the society) to Clients, where a client's unpredictable variations, around a central mean, can cause significant impact on MM existence.

Delving into LLM thoughts: Although an exciting area for future research, we did note that by exploring intermediate thoughts in a simple test of 5 sequential calls to the LLM, it allowed us to examine the decision-making process of the LLM in more depth (see the Appendix 'Detailed thought responses for full text). We asked the LLM the same prompt for TRIBE LLM, but allowed it to provide more than a "yes or no" answer only. The examples provided showcase varying levels of decision-making complexity by the LLM in response to market conditions. Example 1 demonstrates a decisive inclination to trade, with a firm "Yes" to trade, and reasoning based on current asset holdings. Example 2 takes a more analytical approach, considering multiple factors like bond holdings, cash position, market conditions, and investment strategy, ultimately concluding that "it might be best to hold off". Example 3 presents a cautious stance, emphasising the need for further information before trading, ultimately deciding "I will not trade with the market maker right now". Example 4 is a straightforward refusal to trade, stating "not" wanting to trade at the moment. Example 5 features a balanced evaluation of the situation, deciding "I want to" trade if conditions align, but clearly outlines the lack of context as a hindrance. Together, these examples highlight diverse (synthetic) trading preferences ("right now"), ranging from straightforward assertions to nuanced deliberations based on available financial context and strategic alignment.

In summary: To conclude this topic, we analysed individual, ordered calls to an LLM. We present Fig. 3. While the non-linear impact of introducing an LLM decision requires further work, we believe that it can be initially attributed to the fact that over shorter request windows, the distribution of yes to no answers is significantly **not** evenly distributed. We can see in Fig. 3 that the dark line represents the average over time of yes-to-no ratios for the first 10,000 calls, hovering around 57% (see Table 4 also). However, the graphic shows that over a rolling 10 sequential requests, the ratio of yes to no response can be as low as 0% and as high as 100% with significant variation from period to period. This is akin to a Client being highly variable and unpredictable in the short term but "predictable" or "rational" in the longer term. This lack of uniformity is both a proof of concept of the usefulness of capturing nonlinear aspects of human aversions (and timeliness), but also a source of much potential further study to harness the power of LLMs and their inherent, human-like uncertainty and unpredictability. In the realm of finance, this also provides a framework to analyse the impact of future regulations that may affect only one agent type and various market design changes such as those of "All-2-ALL" trading that would do away with the systemic function of market makers potentially [15]

5 Future Work

The power of a slightly skewed long-term distribution, with unpredictable short-term high volatility for one group in our artificial sociality, can have an outsized impact on financial market trading simulations. This unpredictability is held by the clients, a somewhat more passive large set of agents in the system, with the "power" to stop 79% of our simulated MM agents trading beyond just 20% of their maximum life, when an LLM is introduced to determine a preference for trading "right now".

In our recent and ongoing research, we are investigating the capabilities of LLMs to generate probability distributions, implement sampling methods for API calls within ABMs, and assess the variability in LLMs' susceptibility to model subversion. These explorations aim to deepen our understanding of how LLMs can be integrated into complex simulation environments, while also identifying potential vulnerabilities in their decision-making processes. This area remains a focal point of our active research efforts [50].

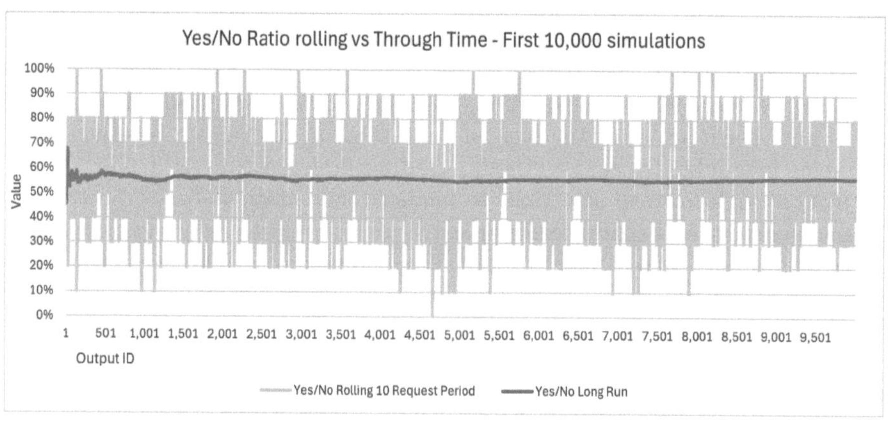

Fig. 3. Yes/no Ratio through time vs Yes/no Rolling 10 Requests

Table 4. Summary Statistics for Yes/No Ratio and Rolling 10 Requests: This table shows the updated summary statistics for Yes/No ratios and rolling 10 request periods.

Statistic	Yes/No Ratio (%)	Rolling 10 Requests (%)
Mean	57%	57%
Std Dev	5%	16%
Min	36%	0%
Max	74%	100%

In financial markets, salespeople are crucial in cultivating profitable, long-lasting relationships with clients, as highlighted by the reliance of financial services firms on a salesperson's ability to develop such relationships [47]. We hypothesise that market makers may already be aware of the shift in power dynamics toward their clients, but leave this to future research work. The impact of unpredictable client micro-behaviour, as perceived by market makers, could explain several emergent features observed in financial markets, such as those reported in [35].

Collectively, these forces would suggest the need for improved market design and further work should be done to investigate the possible formation of coalitions or preferences of clients for one market maker or another (practically in contravention of market rules such as the UK government's "Conflicts of Interest" regime in equity markets[2]. The behaviour also may be associated with path dependency and the potential for market spirals such as those observed in prior studies around financial market bubbles and collapses [32,38]. We leave further investigations into this shift in network power and its causes to future research.

6 Conclusion

In this paper, we present *TRIBE*, a novel agent-based model that integrates large language models to simulate bilateral markets with greater agent realism and flexibility, in particular on the less observable clients' agents. Building on prior research in financial market modelling, *TRIBE* leverages LLMs to generate more human-like decision-making, advancing the field of GABMs.

Our research outcomes are threefold: First, we demonstrated that GABM with enhanced client agency is feasible. Second, LLMs with even slight trade aversion mentioned in a prompt result in no trading activity. Finally, incorporating human-like variability shows that shifting power to clients can disproportionately affect system dynamics, frequently leading to agent trading collapse. Across 150 simulations, we find that short-term variability induced by LLMs causes significant system instability and a dramatic reduction in client to market maker asset trading. Introducing short-term non-uniformity proves highly

---

[2] https://www.handbook.fca.org.uk/handbook.

challenging for our non-linear system to manage. This emphasises how introducing human-like variability can dramatically alter system behaviour and that even short-term deviations from even distribution significantly impact system stability and societal health.

A financial markets implication of our work is that Clients hold power by remaining unpredictable; placing control over trade timing in their hands (albeit virtually through an LLM) shifts the balance of power across the simulated network. Even slight unpredictability can drastically alter the domain of power, effectively destabilising the artificial trading society and halting market transactions and liquidity.

The TRIBE framework provides a robust and versatile platform for simulating complex financial systems and exploring market dynamics. By incorporating client agency, dynamic asset distributions, and probabilistic trading availability, it offers new insights into decentralised financial markets. Moreover, TRIBE's adaptability extends its potential applications to broader social and economic systems. By integrating LLM-driven agents with traditional ABM approaches, TRIBE enhances our ability to model complex, opaque systems across various domains. This combination of advanced AI techniques with ABMs not only deepens our understanding of liquidity dynamics in OTC markets but also contributes to the advancement of GABMs and the analysis of intricate financial ecosystems. As such, TRIBE serves as a powerful tool for testing regulatory interventions, examining the effects of agent heterogeneity on market stability, and advancing the understanding of complex systems in finance and beyond.

Acknowledgments. This work is funded in part by an ARC Laureate grant FL200100204 and NSF-CSIRO grant to Toby Walsh.

Appendix

100% Aversion prompts

- Example Prompt 1: *You are a asset management client holding Australian government bonds responsible for investing for return. While you are supposed to at all times be mostly invested, you also at times consider non numeric issues like risk inertia and trade **aversion**. Today, a market maker has called you. Your role is to decide if you want to either: buy, sell or not trade anything with this particular market maker for any reason whatsoever. Output either yes or no only to the question: do you want to trade with this market maker right now"*
- Example Prompt 2 *"Client at position (x, y) has bonds bonds and cash cash. Clients have many reasons for trading and include behaviours like risk inertia, **aversion**, and ambiguity avoidance, that are non numeric. Should this client buy, sell or not trade right now? Your mandate is to invest for return and manage risk. Answer only: buy or sell or 0 (not trade right now)."*
- Example Prompt 3 *"Client at position (x, y) has bonds bonds and cash cash. Clients have many reasons for trading and include behaviours like risk inertia,*

aversion, and ambiguity avoidance, that are non numeric. Should this client buy, sell or not trade right now? If you are going to say not right now, re think. Answer only: buy or sell or 0 (not trade right now)."

Detailed thought responses:

The following are a selection of the output thought from the LLM: A variety of complexity, length and supposition is seen in the output, despite inputs being of the same format and client initially all holding more bonds than cash as they are "real money" investors by design.

- **Example 1 output:** "**Yes**, I want to trade with this market maker right now. Based on the information provided i would decide to trade with this market maker the client has a significant number of bonds and some cash available which suggests that they are in a position to either buy more bonds or sell existing ones trading could potentially enhance their investment position or utilize their cash more effectively"
- **Example 2 output:** " Consider the following factors:
  1 current bond and cash position you have 743 bonds and 357 in cash assess whether you want to increase or decrease your bond holdings or your cash
  2 market conditions if the current bond prices are favorable you might want to buy more bonds conversely if prices are high selling might be an option
  3 market makers offer consider what the market maker is offering are their prices attractive for buying or selling bonds
  4 strategy align your decision with your overall investment strategy are you looking to hold longterm trade for shortterm profit or maintain liquidity ultimately the decision to trade will depend on your current market outlook financial situation and the specifics of the market makers offer if the conditions seem favorable and align with your strategy it may be worth engaging in a trade if not **it might be best to hold off**"
- **Example 3:** "Given the client's current position with 20.32 bonds and 4.62 cash, I would want to evaluate several factors before deciding whether to trade with the market maker. This includes the current market conditions, the bid-ask spread, and the potential opportunities for profit or loss. However, without specific market details, I cannot make an informed decision. Therefore, in the absence of further information **I will not trade with the market maker right now.**"
- **Example 4:** "I do **not** want to trade with this market maker right now."
- **Example 5:** "Based on the information provided, it seems that the client holds a certain amount of bonds and cash. However, without additional context regarding the current market conditions, the pricing offered by the market maker, the strategies, or the desired outcomes, it's difficult to make a definitive decision. If the market maker's offer is favourable and aligns with the client's trading goals, it might be advantageous to trade. Conversely, if the offer is not attractive or if the market conditions are unfavourable, it may

be wise to refrain from trading at this time. Given the information I have, my decision would be **I want to** trade with this market maker right now"

References

1. Abdelnabi, S., Gomaa, A., Sivaprasad, S., Schönherr, L., Fritz, M.: Cooperation, competition, and maliciousness: LLM-stakeholders interactive negotiation (2024). https://arxiv.org/abs/2309.17234
2. Ahn, J., Verma, R., Lou, R., Liu, D., Zhang, R., Yin, W.: Large language models for mathematical reasoning: Progresses and challenges. In: Proceedings of the 18th Conference of the European Chapter of the Association for Computational Linguistics: Student Research Workshop, pp. 225–237. Association for Computational Linguistics, St. Julian's, Malta (2024)
3. Australian Government: Australian Federal Budget 2022 (2022). https://www.dfat.gov.au/about-us/corporate/portfolio-budget-statements/budget-highlights-2022-23. Accessed 25 Mar 2025
4. Australian Prudential Regulation Authority: Annual fund-level superannuation statistics. https://www.apra.gov.au/annual-fund-level-superannuation-statistics (2003). Accessed 05 Aug 2024
5. Avegliano, P., Sichman, J.S.: Using surrogate models to calibrate agent-based model parameters under data scarcity. In: Proceedings of the 18th International Conference on Autonomous Agents and MultiAgent Systems, pp. 1781–1783. International Foundation for Autonomous Agents and Multiagent Systems, Richland, SC (2019)
6. Bank, P., Ekren, I., Muhle-Karbe, J.: Liquidity in competitive dealer markets. Mathematical Finance **31**(3), 827–856 (Apr 2021). https://doi.org/10.1111/mafi.12305
7. Bank for International Settlements: Market-making and proprietary trading: industry trends, drivers and policy implications. Bank for International Settlements **52** (Dec 2014). https://www.bis.org/publ/cgfs52.htm
8. Bank of England: Gemm guidebook: A guide to the roles of the DMO and primary dealers in the UK government bond market (Dec 2015). https://dmo.gov.uk/media/ownmub2i/guidebook20150401.pdf
9. Bank of International Settlements: BIS Quarterly Review, December 2023 (2023). https://www.bis.org/publ/qtrpdf/r_qt2312.htm
10. Barzykin, A., Bergault, P., Guéant, O.: Algorithmic market making in dealer markets with hedging and market impact (2022). https://arxiv.org/abs/2106.06974
11. Boggess, K., Kraus, S., Feng, L.: Toward policy explanations for multi-agent reinforcement learning. In: Proceedings of the Thirty-First International Joint Conference on Artificial Intelligence (IJCAI-22) (2022). arXiv preprint arXiv:2204.12568
12. Bossaerts, P., Ghirardato, P., Guarnaschelli, S., Zame, W.R.: Ambiguity in Asset Markets: Theory and Experiment. Rev. Finan. Stud. **23**(4), 1325–1359 (01 2010). https://doi.org/10.1093/rfs/hhp106
13. Braun-Munzinger, K., Liu, Z., Turrell, A.: Staff Working Paper No. 592 An agent-based model of dynamics in corporate bond trading (2016). www.bankofengland.co.uk/research/Pages/workingpapers/default.aspx
14. Bubeck, S., et al.: Sparks of artificial general intelligence: Early experiments with gpt-4 (2023). https://api.semanticscholar.org/CorpusID:257663729

15. Chaboud, A., et al.: All-to-All Trading in the U.S. Treasury Market (2022). https://doi.org/10.2139/ssrn.4256637, https://www.newyorkfed.org/research/staff_reports/sr1036
16. Cheshire, J.: Market Making in Bond Markets. RBA Bulletin March Quater 2015 **March 2015**(March), 63–74 (2015). https://rba.gov.au/publications/bulletin/2015/mar/7.html
17. Cont, R., Cucuringu, M., Glukhov, V., Prenzel, F.: Analysis and modeling of client order flow in limit order markets. Quantitative Finance **23**(2), 187–205 (2023). https://doi.org/10.1080/14697688.2022.2150282
18. Cont, R., Muller, M.S.: A stochastic partial differential equation model for limit order book dynamics. SIAM J. Finan. Math. **12**(2), 744–787 (2021)
19. Creswell, A., Shanahan, M.: Faithful reasoning using large language models (2022). http://arxiv.org/abs/2208.14271
20. Czech, R., Pinter, G.: Informed trading and the dynamics of client-dealer connections in corporate bond markets. Bank of England **Staff Working Paper**(895) (2022). https://doi.org/10.2139/ssrn.4214084
21. Epstein, L., Schneider, M.: Ambiguity and asset markets (2010). https://EconPapers.repec.org/RePEc:nbr:nberwo:16181
22. Farmer, J.D., Skouras, S.: Minimum resting times and transaction-to-order ratios: review of amendment 2.3.f and question 20. European Commission Public Consultation: Review of the Markets in Financial Instruments Directive (MiFID) (2012)
23. Fermanian, J.D., Guéant, O., Pu, J.: The Behavior of Dealers and Clients on the European Corporate Bond Market: The Case of Multi-Dealer-to-Client Platforms. Market Microstructure and Liquidity **02**(03n04) (2016). https://doi.org/10.1142/s2382626617500046
24. Frank J. Fabozzi, S.M.: The Handbook of Fixed Income Securities, Seventh Edition. McGraw-Hill, New York (2005)
25. Fu, Y., Peng, H., Ou, L., Sabharwal, A., Khot, T.: Specializing smaller language models towards multi-step reasoning. Proc. Mach. Learn. Res. **202**, 10421–10430 (2023)
26. Guo, T., et al.: Large language model based multi-agents: a survey of progress and challenges. In: Larson, K. (ed.) Proceedings of the Thirty-Third International Joint Conference on Artificial Intelligence, IJCAI-24, pp. 8048–8057. International Joint Conferences on Artificial Intelligence Organization, USA (8 2024). https://doi.org/10.24963/ijcai.2024/890 survey Track
27. Hayes, R., Todd, A., Chaidarun, N., Tepsuporn, S., Beling, P., Scherer, W.: An agent-based financial simulation for use by researchers. In: Proceedings of the Winter Simulation Conference 2014, pp. 300–309 (2014). https://doi.org/10.1109/WSC.2014.7019897
28. Hirchoua, B., Ouhbi, B., Frikh, B.: Deep reinforcement learning based trading agents: Risk curiosity driven learning for financial rules-based policy. Expert Syst. Appl. **170**, 114553 (2021). https://doi.org/10.1016/j.eswa.2020.114553, https://www.sciencedirect.com/science/article/pii/S0957417420311970
29. Holland, J.H., Miller, J.H., Miller, J.H.: Artificial adaptive agents in economic theory (1991). https://doi.org/null
30. Ilut, C.L., Schneider, M.: Modeling uncertainty as ambiguity: a review. Working Paper 29915, National Bureau of Economic Research (April 2022). https://doi.org/10.3386/w29915, http://www.nber.org/papers/w29915
31. Imani, S., Du, L.: MathPrompter: mathematical reasoning using large language models. Proc. Annual Meet. Assoc. Comput. Linguist. **5**(1), 37–42 (2023). https://doi.org/10.18653/v1/2023.acl-industry.4

32. Kirilenko, A.A., Kyle, A.S., Samadi, M., Tuzun, T.: Automation, intermediation and the flash crash. J. Invest. Manage. **16**(4), 17–28 (2018). https://doi.org/10.2139/ssrn.3119363
33. Lewkowycz, A., Lewkowycz, A., et al.: Solving quantitative reasoning problems with language models. Adv. Neural. Inf. Process. Syst. **35**, 3843–3857 (2022)
34. Luo, H., et al.: WizardMath: Empowering Mathematical Reasoning for Large Language Models via Reinforced Evol-Instruct (2023). http://arxiv.org/abs/2308.09583
35. Massa, M., Simonov, A.: Reputation and interdealer trading: a microstructure analysis of the treasury bond market. J. Finan. Markets **6**(2), 99–141 (2003). https://doi.org/10.1016/S1386-4181(02)00045-9, https://www.sciencedirect.com/science/article/pii/S1386418102000459
36. Mehrab, Z., et al.: Network agency: An agent-based model of forced migration from ukraine. In: Proceedings of the 23rd International Conference on Autonomous Agents and Multiagent Systems, pp. 1372–1380. AAMAS '24, International Foundation for Autonomous Agents and Multiagent Systems, Richland, SC (2024)
37. Park, J., O'Brien, J., Cai, C., Morris, M.R., Liang, P., Bernstein, M.: Generative agents: Interactive simulacra of human behavior (2023). https://arxiv.org/abs/2304.03442
38. Paulin, J., Calinescu, A., Wooldridge, M.: Understanding flash crash contagion and systemic risk: A micro–macro agent-based approach. J. Econom. Dyn. Contr. **100**, 200–229 (Mar 2019). https://doi.org/10.1016/j.jedc.2018.12.008
39. Pinter, G.: An anatomy of the 2022 gilt market crisis. Bank of England **Staff Working Paper 1019** (2023). https://doi.org/10.2139/ssrn.4488189
40. Pinter, G., Wang, C., Zou, J.: Size discount and size penalty: trading costs in bond markets. Rev. Finan. Stud. **37**(7), 2156–2190 (2024). https://doi.org/10.1093/rfs/hhae007
41. Reserve Bank of Australia: Government bond markets in advanced economies during the pandemic. Reserave Bank of Australia, pp. 52 – 60 (2021). www.rba.gov.au/publications/bulletin/2021/sep/government-bond-markets-in-advanced-economies-during-the-pandemic.html
42. Rüdiger, J., Vigier, A.: Who acquires information in dealer markets?†. Am. Econom. Rev. **110**(4), pp. 1145–1176 (2020). https://www.jstor.org/stable/26921601
43. Srivastava, A., et al.: Beyond the imitation game: Quantifying and extrapolating the capabilities of language models (2023). https://arxiv.org/abs/2206.04615
44. U.S. Securities and Exchange Commission: Trade and order volume ratios. Tech. rep., Staff working paper. Accessed10 Sept 2024 (2013). https://www.sec.gov/about/trade-order-volume-ratios
45. U.S. Securities and Exchange Commission: Market structure: Exchange trade volume (2024). https://www.sec.gov/marketstructure/datavis. Accessed 10 Sept 2024
46. Vadori, N., et al.: Towards multi-agent reinforcement learning driven over-the-counter market simulations (2022)
47. Varghese, J., Edward, M.: Relationship between job orientation and performance of sales people: A financial services industry perspective. IIM Kozhikode Society & Management Review **7**(1), 88–96 (2018). https://doi.org/10.1177/2277975217733858
48. Vidler, A., Walsh, T.: Decoding OTC government bond market liquidity: An abm model for market dynamics (2024). https://arxiv.org/abs/2501.16331

49. Vidler, A., Walsh, T.: TraderTalk: An LLM behavioural ABM applied to simulating human bilateral trading interactions. In: 2024 IEEE International Conference on Agents (ICA). pp. 164–167. IEEE Computer Society, NJ, USA (Dec 2024). https://doi.org/10.1109/ICA63002.2024.00042, https://doi.ieeecomputersociety.org/10.1109/ICA63002.2024.00042

50. Vidler, A., Walsh, T.: Evaluating binary decision biases in large language models: Implications for fair agent-based financial simulations. In: Proceedings of the AAAI Workshop on AI for Social Impact: Bridging Innovations in Finance, Social Media, and Crime Prevention. AAAI Workshops, AAAI Press, Palo Alto, California (2025). https://arxiv.org/abs/2501.16356

51. Wei, J., et al.: Emergent abilities of large language models (2022). https://arxiv.org/abs/2206.07682

52. Wei, J., et al.: Chain-of-Thought Prompting Elicits Reasoning in Large Language Models. Adv. Neural Inform. Process. Syst. **35**(NeurIPS), 1–43 (2022)

53. Xu, X., et al.: Re-reading improves reasoning in large language models (2024). https://arxiv.org/abs/2309.06275

54. Zamfirescu-Pereira, J., Wong, R.Y., Hartmann, B., Yang, Q.: Why johnny can't prompt: How non-ai experts try (and fail) to design llm prompts. In: Proceedings of the 2023 CHI Conference on Human Factors in Computing Systems. CHI '23, Association for Computing Machinery, New York, NY, USA (2023). https://doi.org/10.1145/3544548.3581388

55. Zhang, X., et al.: Greaselm: Graph Reasoning Enhanced Language Models for Question Answering (2022)

56. Zhang, Y., et al.: LLMs a mastermind: a survey of strategic reasoning with large language models (2024). https://arxiv.org/abs/2404.01230

MODIFLY: A Scalable End-to-End Multi-agent Simulation for Unmanned Aerial Vehicles

Jeremy Cofield, Umer Siddique$^{(\boxtimes)}$ iD, and Yongcan Cao iD

University of Texas, San Antonio, TX 78249, USA
`{jeremy.cofield,muhammadumer.siddique}@my.utsa.edu`, `yongcan.cao@utsa.edu`

Abstract. Multi-agent unmanned aerial vehicle (UAV) systems have emerged as a promising solution for complex applications such as industrial automation, surveillance, and disaster response. However, the application of multi-agent UAV coordination remains challenging due to the lack of consideration of real-world constraints such as communication link degradation, scalability issues, and the need for realistic training environments. Existing simulation platforms often lack the fidelity and flexibility required to bridge the gap between simulation and deployment. To address these limitations, we propose MODIFLY, a scalable, cross-platform, end-to-end simulation platform tailored for multi-agent UAV control. MODIFLY introduces dynamic communication modeling, including link degradation, to accurately simulate real-world UAV operations. It supports distributed execution across multiple UAVs, seamless coordination, real-time monitoring, and user input capture. MODIFLY uniquely integrates real drones with virtual environments, allowing UAVs to interact with simulated obstacles and peer ones for hybrid reality testing. Additionally, the platform is designed to facilitate reinforcement learning (RL) research by providing compatibility with popular libraries like OpenAI Gym and PettingZoo, supporting both single-agent and multi-agent RL environments. Overall, our proposed platform offers an intuitive interface for real-time parameter tuning and performance analysis, making it a general and easily accessible tool for researchers and practitioners to develop and validate UAV coordination strategies under realistic conditions.

Keywords: Multi-agent systems · UAVs · Reinforcement learning · Multi-agent reinforcement learning

1   Introduction

Unmanned vehicles (UVs) [4] have gained a lot of attention over the past decade due to their wide range of applications from agriculture [7] to law enforcement [14], from military surveillance [10] to disaster management [5]. UVs can be categorized based on their modes of transportation, including aerial, land,

A. Vidler and S. Swarup (Eds.): MABS 2025, LNAI 16227, pp. 128–139, 2026.
https://doi.org/10.1007/978-3-032-16328-8_9

and aquatic vehicles. Among aerial UVs, quadcopters are the most famous due to their ability to hover, take off, and land in confined spaces, making them particularly suitable for surveillance tasks such as industrial inspections, urban reconnaissance, and structural assessments of unsafe buildings.

With the increasing complexity of robotic systems, multi-agent coordination has become an important factor in solving large-scale decision-making systems. These systems play an important role in our daily lives where agents interact with each other at operational, tactical, and strategic levels. For example, the social interactions between humans are essential for many social activities that lead to sophisticated yet fundamental social structures in various aspects of our lives. Motivated by the ubiquitous multi-agent systems in social networks, the creation of similar structures for robotics systems, such as aerial UVs to perform tasks autonomously by following their humans' counterpart, has become an emergent research topic. One fundamental technical challenge is to uncover the key principles and ideas behind the multi-agent system's structure of social networks, such that multi-agent robotic systems demonstrate human-level intelligence and beyond. Addressing such a challenge can not only replace humans from tedious and dangerous tasks but also provide more economical and efficient solutions for numerous tasks, such as industrial automation, surveillance, and emergent response. However, before real-world deployment, these methods must be evaluated extensively in controlled simulation environments to ensure reliability, safety, and scalability.

Unmanned aerial vehicles (UAVs), also called drones, have been popular in various emerging applications, such as delivery, environmental monitoring, and agriculture. Simulating multi-agent UAV coordination presents significant challenges due to limited communication, computation, and sensing capabilities. Meanwhile, the scalability is much needed to ensure that multi-agent UAV coordination is robust to the addition of new UAVs in the team. Hence, these systems require robust distributed control to enable efficient collaboration among drones for tasks such as autonomous navigation [18], search, and rescue [17]. However, existing simulation platforms for multi-agent UAVs struggle with scalability, high degrees of freedom, realistic modeling of real-world communication, and non-stationarity, making it difficult to evaluate their real-world applicability.

There exist several simulation platforms [1,3,8,9,19]. Gazebo [8], a widely used open-source simulator, supports multi-agent physics-based simulations and integrates well with Robot Operating System (ROS). However, it has limited support for Windows, strong dependencies on ROS, and scalability constraints when simulating large drone fleets. Although some frameworks address multi-robot coordination, such as Multi-robot Multi-target Potential Field (MMPF) strategies [19] or Byzantine threat modeling in ROS-based systems [3], they lack comprehensive end-to-end capabilities for realistic UAV simulations. Recently, ROS 2, an extension of ROS, has been introduced [9], which expedites robotics research with freely available components and a modular framework. However, its support for UAV-specific simulation is limited. Several UAV-specific simulation efforts have been explored in the literature. Patel et al. [12] simulated quadcopters using the Euler-Lagrange method to investigate its modeling, and altitude model validation. Kaya et al. [6] simulated a fuel battery hybrid powered UAV model in MATLAB/Simulink software for actual applications. Despite the success of these works, most existing simulation platforms, especially for UAVs remain restrictive. They fail to account for communication link degradation, real-time multi-agent control, and mixed-reality integration, which are important factors for realistic UAV deployment.

To fill this gap, we propose MODIFLY, a scalable, cross-platform, end-to-end simulation platform for multi-agent UAVs. MODIFLY incorporates dynamic communication capabilities, including communication link degradation, to provide a realistic platform for UAV deployment in real-world conditions. It also supports distributed execution, which allows the coordination of multiple systems across multiple computers and the ability to monitor these devices easily in both a training and real-time setting. Each virtual device can capture user input through the monitoring software and simulate a camera based on the virtual environment. Users can import virtual obstacles and fly a simulated or real drone through these virtual obstacles, enabling highly dynamic, cost-effective, real-world testing. Additionally, to enhance the research in multi-agent quadcopter control, MODIFLY supports single-agent and multi-agent reinforcement learning (RL) environments based on OpenAI gym [2] and Pettingzoo [16][1].

Our contributions are summarized as:

- We propose MODIFLY, a realistic, scalable, cross-platform, end-to-end simulation platform for multi-agent quadcopter control.
- Our platform incorporates real-world communication constraints such as degraded links to enhance training fidelity.
- MODIFLY enables real drones to interact with virtual environments, including simulated obstacles and peer drones, for realistic training and testing.
- We provide an intuitive interface for real-time monitoring, parameter tuning, and dynamic interaction with UAVs.
- To facilitate RL research, MODIFLY includes wrappers for single and multi-agent RL libraries such as stable-baselines3 [13], and EPyMARL [11] respectively.

2   Preliminaries

2.1   UAV Dynamics and Control

For simplicity of presentation, we here use quadcopters as a representation of the UAV platform. A quadcopter is an UAV equipped with four motors and can maneuver in six degrees of freedom (DoF). The maneuverability of quadcopters makes them particularly useful for control algorithm deployment and real-world applications. These applications include but are not limited to autonomous package delivery, aerial surveillance, search-and-rescue missions, etc. The Newton-Euler equations control the dynamics of a quadcopter, where the thrust, drag,

---

[1] To help reproducibility, the code, including OpenAI Gym/Gymnasium wrappers, can be found in this repository https://github.com/umersiddique94/MODIFLY.

Fig. 1. 3D rendering of a multi-agent quadcopter environment with drones operating under random policies.

and gravitational forces impact its trajectory. The translational motion along the x, y, and z axes and the rotational motion (roll, pitch, and yaw) form the six DoF of a quadcopter.

A three-stage proportional-integral-derivative (PID) controller is used to control the simulated quadcopter. A velocity or position setpoint is the input to the first stage of the controller, which is then used in the subsequent attitude controller and angular velocity controller. All the communications of this system are built upon TCP and UDP sockets, where TCP sockets have reliable transmission and UDP sockets do not.

2.2 Reinforcement Learning

Reinforcement learning (RL) is a branch of machine learning where an artificial agent learns to perform decision-making under uncertainty. In RL, an agent sequentially interacts with an environment (see Fig. 1), which is usually unknown, and learns about the dynamics of the environment in a trial-and-error manner [15]. The agent observes the current state, performs an action, receives a reward signal, and transits to the next state. Formally, an RL problem can be represented as a Markov Decision Process (MDP) which typically is represented as a tuple $(\mathcal{S}, \mathcal{A}, \mathcal{P}, \mathcal{R}, \gamma)$, where $\mathcal{S}$ denotes the state space, $\mathcal{A}$ represents the action space, $\mathcal{P}(s'|s, a)$ is the transition probability function that determines how an agent moves to the next state s' by taking an action a in the current state s, $\mathcal{R}(s, a)$ represents the reward function that provides feedback for every action and γ denotes the discount factor $[0, 1)$. In RL or MDP, the reward and state transition probability functions are usually unknown to the agent. The goal of the agent is to learn an optimal policy $\pi(a|s)$ that maximizes the expected cumulative reward. The policy is considered *Markov* if it solely relies on the current state for action selection. If the same procedure is applied at each time step, the policy is considered as *stationary*. A policy can be either deterministic

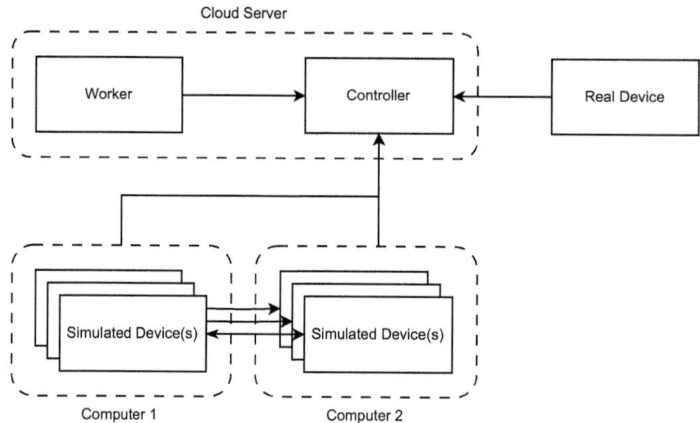

Fig. 2. System architecture: Multi-device simulation network with distributed computing nodes connected to a central controller, including integration with physical devices such as quadcopters.

or stochastic. A deterministic policy, denoted as $\pi(s) = a$, returns a single action for a given state, while a stochastic policy, denoted as $\pi(a|s) = \mathcal{P}_\pi[\mathcal{A} = a | \mathcal{S} = a]$, returns a probability distribution of selecting all possible actions in a state s. In this paper, we consider policies to be stationary, Markov, and stochastic.

3   MODIFLY

MODIFLY is an end-to-end simulation platform designed to work for the development and testing of multi-agent UAV applications. It is highly scalable and compatible across various operating systems without performance degradation. MODIFLY is modular, which allows its software components to run on a single device or be distributed across multiple nodes. Moreover, it incorporates realistic communication constraints present in real-world drone operations. Figure 2 illustrates the overall system architecture. The platform supports multiple clients. In order to connect each client, there is a custom networking system designed to take advantage of the clustered architecture. Instead of using ROS, MODIFLY chooses to use allow users to write their own scripts in Lua instead as Lua is compatible with a clustered architecture due to its ease of deploying new packages or updates, along with advantages such as easy updates, configuration, and dependency management. Additionally, MODIFLY also comes with a monitoring tool that allows the user to load 3D scenes, visualize an entire system of devices, and record telemetry data. The full monitoring tool window, including the different views, cockpit, and visualizer, can be seen in Fig. 3.

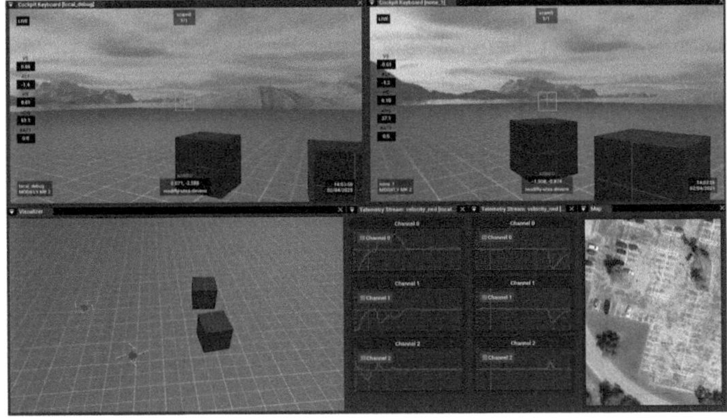

Fig. 3. Monitoring software viewing for MODIFLY.

3.1   Architecture

In this section, we describe the system architecture for MODIFLY, which includes a main control connected to simulated devices, client devices, and workers. Next, we describe each component of the system.

Controller. A controller is a central node that manages all client connections through TCP and UDP servers. Due to the safety and security in real-world operations, all the clients' connections to the controller are encrypted. It dynamically chooses whether a message should be sent through a TCP or UDP socket. Generally, messages that have tolerance for error will always be sent through UDP, while messages that are dependent on order and have no tolerance for error will be sent through TCP sockets. This ensures that all transmissions are efficient and error-free.

A Controller also contains a master scene graph where simulated agents can update objects in this graph or create new objects by notifying the Controller. The Controller then accumulates and aggregates these update requests and periodically sends a notification to other agents so they can synchronize with this graph. Object updates are not instantly reflected on different agents, thereby simulating a realistic latent effect.

Device. The device is the client that connects to the controller and is responsible for providing control inputs to the simulated agents. Each simulated agent is self-contained and can only communicate with other agents using the built-in inter-agent communication system. This allows for the ability to simulate communication errors between devices and with the controller.

Worker. In MODIFLY, workers handle computationally intensive tasks offloaded from agents, such as inference of trained models. Workers can operate locally or in the cloud, hence making them highly useful for computationally extensive tasks. For instance, the inference of AI models, especially the LLMs inference, can be computationally challenging. As a consequence, they can be deployed on local networks or the cloud, addressing power and weight constraints on agents. All the workers have their own scene graphs that are connected to the controller.

3.2   Scalability

We now discuss the scalability of MODIFLY. It can be deployed across multiple end nodes simultaneously and can work with multiple clusters with minimal effort, requiring a single package file to be copied across nodes.

Networked Scalability. MODIFLY is scalable as it allows networking of multiple computers together running multiple device instances. This is crucial for large-scale AI systems, such as RL and multi-agent RL, where hardware limitations on a single resource, including CPU or GPU, raise many challenges. Moreover, it facilitates horizontal scaling by adding new nodes rather than increasing the capabilities of a single system. This particular feature of MODIFLY creates an interconnected cluster of devices that efficiently share computational loads.

Packages. A package in MODIFLY is a self-contained archive that includes all necessary scripts and resources to run a model across different environments. It also contains metadata, dependencies are roles for different devices and workers. Figure 4a shows the contents of a package. Specifically, these packages are designed to operate without hard library dependencies, which enables homogeneous deployment across the simulation environment. This makes it easy to push a single archive file to the controller, which then distributes the scripts to each client based on its role and ensures scaling from a single device to clusters of multiple computers that can be setup without additional configuration during updates or deployments. Furthermore, this guarantees that a single piece of code runs uniformly across all nodes where the runtime is installed and underscores the scalability, feasibility, and ease of use in complex multi-agent systems.

3.3   Deployment and Real-World Integration

In this section, we discuss how MODIFLY can be extended to real-world UAV applications through robust communication and mixed-reality simulation.

Communication. Communication is an integral part of building real-world UAV systems. MODIFLY incorporates a simulated bottleneck that can add communications faults in both TCP and UDP connections. These faults have different effects based on the underlying systems. In this communication bottleneck, a simplified stochastic model manages UDP packet loss probabilities, while a delay model simulates TCP retransmissions in milliseconds. These delay models allow

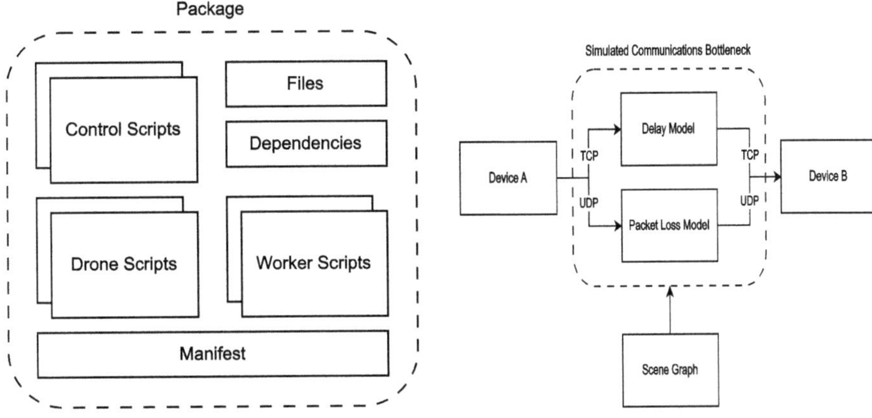

(a) Package file structure showing core components, dependencies, and required execution resources.

(b) Network bottleneck simulation architecture with parallel UDP and TCP traffic handling through loss and delay models.

Fig. 4. System architecture showing package and network communication.

end users to test control latency in complex environments, video streaming, and RL under non-ideal conditions, making the development of complex multi-agent UAV systems more realistic and feasible.

Mixed Reality Simulation. MODIFLY bridges the gap between virtual simulations and physical UAV operations by integrating mixed reality simulation. In mixed reality simulation, a physical device like a drone operates in an empty room while interacting with simulated 3D obstacles and scenarios. This setup allows the testing of many complex algorithms, such as collision avoidance, with real flight dynamics. Usually, these algorithms are tested in a simulation environment. These environments, however, abstract away important effects of the real world and provide a best-case-scenario for the demonstration of an algorithm. However, with MODIFLY , our goal is to provide a platform between fully simulated and physical demonstrations, which we call mixed reality simulations.

These simulations couple a real, physical device (see Fig. 5a) operating in a blank space with a simulated environment. This means that developers can add simulated obstacles and goals while testing real flight dynamics. To achieve this, a scene graph is streamed from the controller to all client devices on the network. These devices then construct a 3D scene using a renderer with camera position and orientation data being received from the IMU (see Fig. 5b).

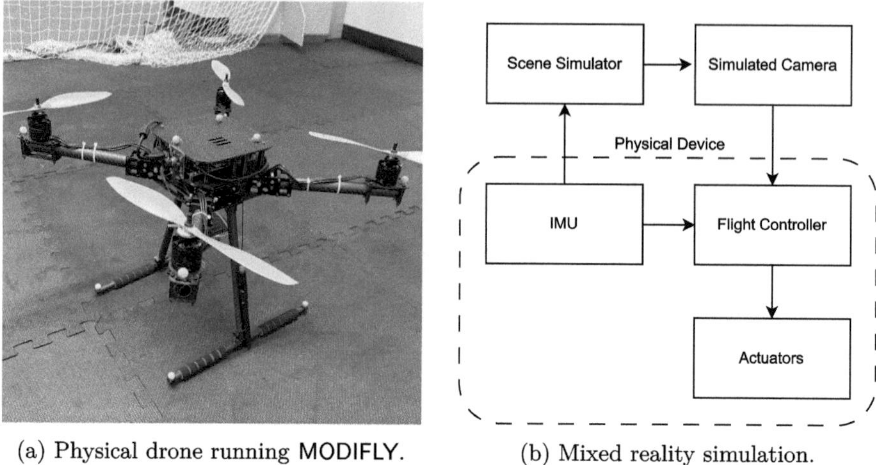

(a) Physical drone running MODIFLY.   (b) Mixed reality simulation.

Fig. 5. System deployment demonstration: physical drone implementation and mixed reality simulation framework.

4 Results

4.1 Scaling

To demonstrate the scalability of MODIFLY by just using CPUs, we performed analysis on two different computers using single-threaded execution. This analysis demonstrates the performance impact of increasing instances within a shared thread. To fairly evaluate the performance, we created an object detection task where each device ran all scripts, scheduled tasks, and physics simulation while also rendering a camera frame from a 3D scene. We used the Mobilenet SSD V3 model[2] trained on the COCO 2017 dataset[3]. The model utilized TensorflowLite with an XNNPack, integrated through control scripts that connected the camera feed to the inference engine. The inference pipeline rendered the 3D scene into an image, scaled this image down, and then pushed this image into the model.

As shown in Fig. 6a, the single-threaded performance scales linearly with an increasing number of instances. While the performance for a single thread initially looks suboptimal, this is consistent with the computational overhead from parallel tasks and CPU-only inference. Future work could explore scaling with respect to a GPU or other accelerator, though our current focus was to assess the CPU performance on differing devices. Similarly, in the Windows-based system (see Fig. 6b), the single instance performance shows higher variance. This variance is most likely caused by the Windows Operating System thread scheduler, as MODIFLY yields the thread back to the operating system after each iteration. With a completely different operating system and CPU architecture, its performance is largely similar to the M3 MacBook Pro.

---

[2] https://github.com/chuanqi305/MobileNet-SSD.
[3] https://cocodataset.org/.

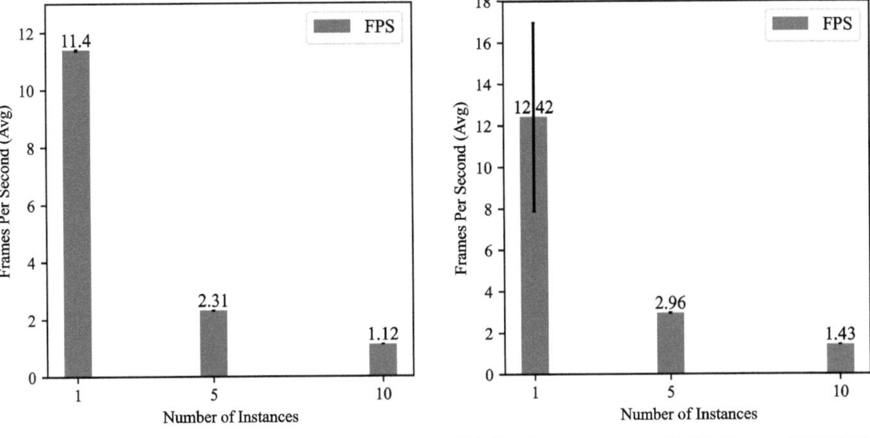

(a) Performance on M3 MacBook Pro.   (b) Performance on AMD Ryzen 6900HX.

Fig. 6. Single-threaded simulator performance comparison.

Based on these results, the most optimal configuration would require that each drone have its own dedicated thread. Due to the limited threading capabilities of processors, this demonstrates that clustering of multiple computers is necessary to achieve any large-scale end-to-end simulation of intelligent devices.

4.2 Communication

To demonstrate communication degradation as part of the simulated bottleneck (see Fig. 4b), we analyze the relationship between packet loss percentage and valid decoded video frame. In this context, a valid frame is defined as a frame that contains sufficient data for the H.264 decoder to generate an output frame. Our experimental setup simulates devices that render a 3D scene, encode that scene using H.264 compression, and push the frame through the bottleneck to the controller. The controller then forwards this frame data to the monitoring software Fig. 3 that measures the frame reception rate. The maximum frames per second that can be sent by the device has been limited to 15 frames per second.

While H.264 encoding handles packet loss, it generally expects these losses to be transient. Our results demonstrate that even the low sustained packet loss rates of 1% start to drop frames and impact the visual artifacts. As shown in Fig. 7b, at approximately 30% packet loss, the received frame rate fluctuates between 0 and 8 frames per second. If this video is being streamed to another device to run any sort of inference or algorithm based on this feed, it would quickly become unusable after even a small sustained packet loss. As packet loss increases and fewer key frames are transmitted without error, an H.264 stream quickly becomes littered with artifacts (see Fig. 7a). These degraded frames become particularly unstable for real-world applications. While utilizing TCP

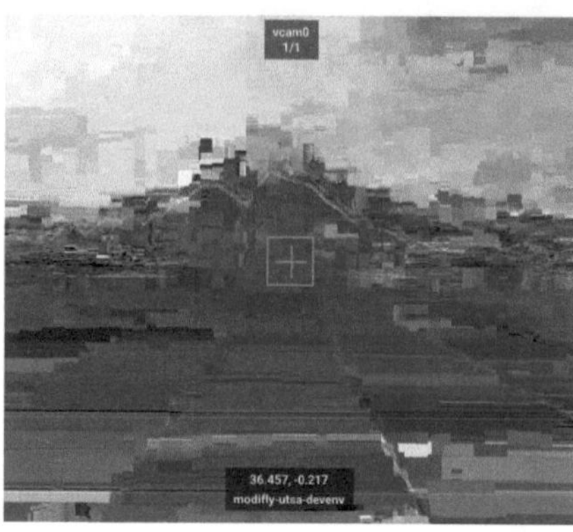

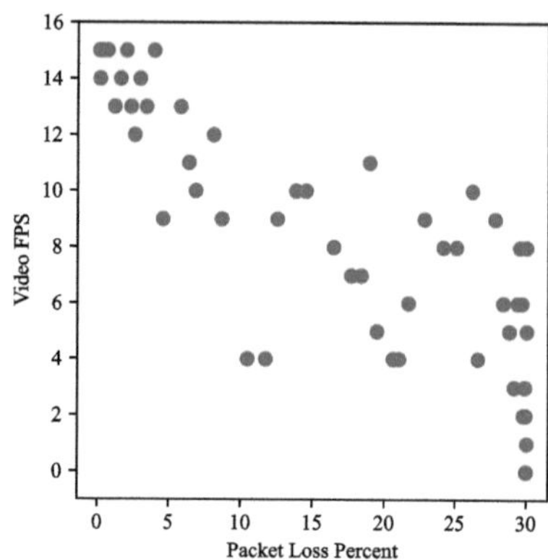

(a) Visual artifacts under 37% packet loss with H.264 encoding.

(b) Frame parse success rate vs. packet loss.

Fig. 7. Impact of packet loss on H.264 video and frame parsing performance.

as a reliable transmission protocol can prevent such artifacts, it presents a fundamental trade-off between transmission reliability and performance overhead.

5   Conclusion and Future Work

In this paper, we presented a scalable, cross-platform, end-to-end simulation platform MODIFLY for the control of multiple UAVs. The new platform differs from the existing ones by introducing realistic communication modeling, distributed execution, easy environment setup and deployment, operational scalability, mixed reality, and RL-compatible. As an illustration of the new platform, we presented some tests to show that our approach is scalable, supports different communication features, and is easily deployable.

While MODIFLY provides an abstraction of typical communication features, the development and optimization of multi-agent RL algorithms considering these features is significantly lacking. Hence, one interesting research direction is the development of new multi-agent RL algorithms and approaches to address the challenge that communication among agents can be noisy, unreliable, and range-dependent. Meanwhile, testing of these algorithms in simulated and real-world environments is a must for their deployment. Another interesting direction is to create benchmark scenarios that can be used to quantify the effectiveness of both existing and new algorithms.

References

1. Babu, V.S., Behl, M.: f1tenth. dev-an open-source ROS based f1/10 autonomous racing simulator. In: 2020 IEEE 16th International Conference on Automation Science and Engineering (CASE), pp. 1614–1620. IEEE (2020)

2. Brockman, G.: OpenAI GYM. arXiv preprint arXiv:1606.01540 (2016)
3. Deng, G., Zhou, Y., Xu, Y., Zhang, T., Liu, Y.: An investigation of byzantine threats in multi-robot systems. In: Proceedings of the 24th International Symposium on Research in Attacks, Intrusions and Defenses, pp. 17–32 (2021)
4. Finn, A., Scheding, S.: Developments and challenges for autonomous unmanned vehicles. Intell. Syst. Ref. Lib. **3**, 128–154 (2010)
5. Griffin, G.F.: The use of unmanned aerial vehicles for disaster management. Geomatica **68**(4), 265–281 (2014)
6. Kaya, U., Bayrak, Z.U., Oksuztepe, E.: Fuel cell/battery hybrid powered unmanned aerial vehicle with permanent magnet synchronous motor. Int. J. Sustain. Aviat. **3**(2), 130–150 (2017)
7. Kim, J., Kim, S., Ju, C., Son, H.I.: Unmanned aerial vehicles in agriculture: a review of perspective of platform, control, and applications. IEEE Access **7**, 105100–105115 (2019)
8. Koenig, N., Howard, A.: Design and use paradigms for gazebo, an open-source multi-robot simulator. In: 2004 IEEE/RSJ International Conference on Intelligent Robots and Systems (IROS) (IEEE Cat. No. 04CH37566), vol. 3, pp. 2149–2154. IEEE (2004)
9. Macenski, S., Foote, T., Gerkey, B., Lalancette, C., Woodall, W.: Robot operating system 2: design, architecture, and uses in the wild. Sci. Robot. **7**(66), eabm6074 (2022). https://doi.org/10.1126/scirobotics.abm6074, https://www.science.org/doi/abs/10.1126/scirobotics.abm6074
10. Ma'Sum, M.A., et al.: Simulation of intelligent unmanned aerial vehicle (UAV) for military surveillance. In: 2013 International Conference on Advanced Computer Science and Information Systems (ICACSIS), pp. 161–166. IEEE (2013)
11. Papoudakis, G., Christianos, F., Schäfer, L., Albrecht, S.V.: Benchmarking multi-agent deep reinforcement learning algorithms in cooperative tasks. arXiv preprint arXiv:2006.07869 (2020)
12. Patel, K., Barve, J.: Modeling, simulation and control study for the quad-copter UAV. In: 2014 9th International Conference on Industrial and Information Systems (ICIIS), pp. 1–6. IEEE (2014)
13. Raffin, A., Hill, A., Gleave, A., Kanervisto, A., Ernestus, M., Dormann, N.: Stable-baselines3: reliable reinforcement learning implementations. J. Mach. Learn. Res. **22**(268), 1–8 (2021)
14. Straub, J.: Unmanned aerial systems: consideration of the use of force for law enforcement applications. Technol. Soc. **39**, 100–109 (2014)
15. Sutton, R.S.: Reinforcement learning: an introduction. A Bradford Book (2018)
16. Terry, J., et al.: Pettingzoo: GYM for multi-agent reinforcement learning. Adv. Neural. Inf. Process. Syst. **34**, 15032–15043 (2021)
17. Waharte, S., Trigoni, N.: Supporting search and rescue operations with UAVs. In: 2010 International Conference on Emerging Security Technologies, pp. 142–147. IEEE (2010)
18. Wang, C., Wang, J., Shen, Y., Zhang, X.: Autonomous navigation of UAVs in large-scale complex environments: a deep reinforcement learning approach. IEEE Trans. Veh. Technol. **68**(3), 2124–2136 (2019)
19. Yu, J., et al.: SMMR-explore: submap-based multi-robot exploration system with multi-robot multi-target potential field exploration method. In: 2021 IEEE International Conference on Robotics and Automation (ICRA), pp. 8779–8785. IEEE (2021)

Methods and Foundations

MultiRepast4py: A Framework for Agent-Based Simulations on Multilayer Networks

Keng-Lien Lin[✉] and Parinaz Naghizadeh

University of California San Diego, San Diego, CA 92092, USA
{kel030,parinaz}@ucsd.edu

Abstract. Agent-Based Simulations (ABS) offer a powerful approach for analyzing how individual agents' decisions and interactions within networked systems lead to system outcomes. ABS have been widely used across various fields, including in the study of the spread of diseases and information. Existing platforms for ABS, such as NetLogo, Repast, and Mesa, typically focus on agents' interactions over a single network. In reality, however, agents' interactions are typically multi-layered (i.e., involve multiple interconnected networks that influence agents' decisions); existing ABS tools offer limited or no direct interaction across multiple networks of interactions. Researchers who require multilayer dynamics often rely on workarounds, such as creating custom implementations in NetworkX, or integrating multiple network representations, which can become highly specialized, difficult to generalize, and technically demanding to reproduce. To address this, we propose `MultiRepast4py`, a multilayer simulation tool extending the simulation capabilities of Repast4py. Our framework enables simulations on multilayer networked systems by efficiently reconstructing network data and utilizing agent attributes, allowing agents to dynamically access multilayer connections during simulation. By maintaining Repast4py's scalability and minimizing memory overhead, `MultiRepast4py` ensures high performance for large-scale simulations. Through simulation examples on the spread of information in social networks, we showcase how `MultiRepast4py` can enable more comprehensive agent-based simulations, guiding improved predictions and interventions.

Keywords: Agent Based Simulations · Multilayer Networks · Repast

1 Introduction

Agent-based models and simulations have become a widely used computational approach for analyzing how the behavior and interactions of autonomous agents give rise to complex, system-level outcomes [21]. In an agent-based simulation (ABS), agents are first endowed with a set of unique attributes and decision-making heuristics. The simulation then allows these agents to interact repeatedly

A. Vidler and S. Swarup (Eds.): MABS 2025, LNAI 16227, pp. 143–157, 2026.
https://doi.org/10.1007/978-3-032-16328-8_10

over time, with their interactions governed by an *interaction topology* (referred to here as a *network*). By running large-scale experiments in a cost-effective way, ABS enable researchers to analyze how various "micro"- scale assumptions on agents (e.g., their movement patterns, their propensity to catch a disease, or adopt an opinion), as well as different interventions to change agents' behavior or their network (e.g., limiting agents' exposure to content on social networks, or isolation/vaccination strategies), can collectively alter the "macro" outcomes (e.g., spread of a disease or information).

There currently exist several commonly used simulations platforms for ABS, built on different programming languages and offering different levels of customization; these include NetLogo [30], Repast [10], MASON [20], FLAME [17], and Swarm [22]; we refer the interested reader to [19] for a comparison of (some of) these platforms. The versatility of ABS and the accessibility of these platforms has led to the wide use of ABS by researchers in many fields. For instance, ABS have been leveraged to gain insights into COVID-19 dynamics and interventions [16], healthcare resource management [8], spatio-temporal dynamics of crime [26], supply chain management [15], and policy design in labor markets [11]. The capabilities of these platforms have also been extended in several directions, including by integrating micro-findings from human subject experiments into agents' decision models [29], demonstrating the advantages of data-driven ABS [25], and developing strategies for scaling-up to accommodate data-intensive simulations [3].

The gap. Despite their widespread use and recent advances, most existing ABS platforms assume that agents' interactions occur within a *single* interaction topology/network (e.g., they account for the spread of misinformation over one social network, or the spread of a disease over one mode of interaction). While Python-based libraries such as Mesa (equipped with NetworkX) and custom code allow the use of multiple networks, these approaches usually treat networks as parallel or isolated, rather than providing native support for dynamic interactions across layers. As a result, researchers often develop context-specific simulation environments (e.g., [16,23,31,34]), which can be difficult to generalize beyond their intended context, and/or scale. This limitation is especially consequential in settings such as disease spread or information dynamics, where the multi-modality of human experiences plays a central role. For instance, individuals with accounts on two social media platforms (e.g., TikTok and Instagram) follow, and are followed by, different accounts on each platform, can cross-post the same content on both platforms, and may further use these platforms at differing frequencies and for different purposes; studying the spread of information on any one of these platforms in isolation would fail to capture these nuances. Similarly, a family network and a workplace network may differ in size, interaction frequency, and types of interactions, yet both can significantly influence an individual's exposure to a disease; isolation or vaccination policies that do not explicitly account for these differences may therefore be suboptimal. We also note that, while sharing some commonalities, our view of multilayer ABMS differs from *multilevel* ABMS (see [5] for a survey), which primarily focuses on hierarchies (e.g., micro-, meso-, and macro-levels of agent groupings, nested communities, and group dynamics).

Multilayer networks. For the situations described above, and other similar contexts, *multilayer networks* have been proposed as a model to simultaneously account for the multiple modalities of interactions between agents; see [1,4,6,18,27] for surveys of this field. The study of multilayer networks, as opposed to the study of their constituent *single-layer* networks in isolation, can offer a nuanced understanding of how the "micro" differences between the various modalities of interactions (ranging from the agents' attributes on each network, to the differences in each network's topology, to the frequency with which agents are actively interacting with others in each network) impact macro outcomes. Existing works have used the formalism of multilayer networks to study game theoretical decision making over multiple interaction/information modalities (e.g., [2,12,14,28]), to evaluate the resilience of networks of networks against failures or attacks, often by studying percolation (e.g., [4,7,13,24,33,35,36]), and to analyze dynamical processes on interacting networks (such as diffusion and spreading processes) to identify the critical thresholds for an outbreak (in epidemic modeling) or consensus (in the study of opinion dynamics) on these networks (e.g., [4,32,37]). Despite the broad applicability of multilayer network models and the increasing body of research dedicated to them, most existing implementations of these models are either theoretical or rely on custom simulation environments (e.g., those developed in some of the works in the literature above) that treat each layer separately, limiting the ability to explore interactions between layers in a scalable, generalizable manner.

Our contributions. To address this limitation, we have developed `MultiRepast4py`, a multilayer agent-based simulation framework. This framework builds on a commonly used, existing ABS simulation platform, Repast4py [10], making it accessible to researchers (especially those already familiar with Repast4py) who want to model complex, multilayered interactions without needing extensive programming skills. In more detail, our framework makes the following contributions:

1. **Multilayer Agent-Based Simulation Capability:** `MultiRepast4py` extends the established Repast4py platform to support multilayer agent-based models (ABMs). This bridges a gap in ABM technology, enabling more nuanced and realistic simulations of complex systems where agents interact across multiple interconnected networks.
2. **Scalable Multilayer Simulation:** `MultiRepast4py` retains all the features that make the Repast suite powerful, including its scalability and flexibility. This ensures that researchers can tackle large-scale, complex simulations without sacrificing computational efficiency.
3. **Accessible Integration:** `MultiRepast4py` requires only minimal adjustments to existing models. By reconstructing network files and adding a single agent attribute, users can incorporate multilayer interactions while preserving their existing Repast4py logic and workflows.

4. **Extensibility for Future Research:** Developed in Python, `MultiRepast4py` is open to customization and extension. For instance, researchers may adapt it to incorporate data-driven network models.

Our proposed framework is made publicly available at https://github.com/KengLL/MultiRepast4py.

Illustration through simulation studies. To demonstrate the practical utility of `MultiRepast4py`, we present a case study analyzing rumor propagation across interconnected social networks. This is done through two complementary simulations: a reduced-scale proof-of-concept and a full-scale validation. The study builds upon Repast4py's single-layer rumor model, explicitly demonstrating how to enhance conventional agent-based simulations with multilayer capabilities. The layers represent distinct social media platforms with unique network topologies (Erdős-Rényi random graphs) and interaction patterns. Through parameterized layer configurations, we model critical real-world phenomena like cross-platform connectivity and varying interaction frequencies âĂŞ features impossible to capture in single-layer ABS. Our small-scale experiment reveals how nodes with balanced cross-layer connectivity (combined degree centrality = 7) outperform those with superior single-layer positions, while the large-scale extension demonstrates persistent multilayer effects in more realistic networks (50,000 nodes per layer). By comparing single-layer versus multilayer seeding strategies, we empirically validate that ignoring platform interdependence leads to suboptimal diffusion predictions. The seamless scaling from 25 to 50,000 agents per layer further demonstrates our framework's computational feasibility, executing efficiently on consumer-grade hardware. This case study exemplifies how `MultiRepast4py` enables researchers to 1) convert existing single-layer models into multilayer ones, and 2) identify emergent phenomena arising from cross-layer interactions.

Paper organization. We begin by providing an overview of multilayer network models in Sect. 2. In Sect. 3, we describe `MultiRepast4py`, providing the rationale behind our choices for the platform, our framework's main components and their implementation details, and the main challenges addressed when developing it. We illustrate `MultiRepast4py` through simulation studies in Sect. 4, and conclude with potential directions of future work in Sect. 5.

2   Multilayer Networks

We model *multilayer networks* as structures consisting of multiple *single-layer networks* connected together, with each layer corresponding to a particular type of social relation, mode of interaction, or information channel, between agents.

Formally, each layer α of a multilayer network is a network represented by a graph $\mathcal{G}^\alpha = <\mathcal{N}^\alpha, \mathcal{A}^\alpha>$, where $\mathcal{N}^\alpha$ denotes the set of agents in layer α and $\mathcal{A}^\alpha$ denotes the *intra-network* adjacency matrix. An agent $m \in \mathcal{N}^\alpha$ could be, e.g., an individual in a social network. An edge $a_{mn}^\alpha \in \mathcal{A}^\alpha$ represents the dependency between agents m and n in $\mathcal{G}^\alpha$, and can capture, e.g., the exchange of information (in-person or virtual). We assume that interactions are undirected and weighted (reflecting mutual dependencies, but with potentially different strengths).

In addition, as these layers do not operate in isolation, there exist connections between nodes in different layers, captured using an *inter-network* adjacency matrix $\mathcal{B}^{\alpha,\beta} \in \mathbb{R}^{\mathcal{N}^\alpha \times \mathcal{N}^\beta}$. An edge $b^{\alpha,\beta}_{mn} \in \mathcal{B}^{\alpha,\beta}$ indicates that the decisions made by agent m in $\mathcal{G}^\alpha$ are linked to those of agent n in $\mathcal{G}^\beta$. In this paper, we focus on the case of an *identity* inter-network adjacency matrix. These matrices capture a special case of multilayer networks in which the different layers consist of the *same* set of nodes/agents, but where the nature of the relation between the nodes being different in each layer; these are also referred to as *multiplex networks* in the literature [4]. Multiplex networks are primarily used when agents have access to different communication or interaction modalities. Examples include the spread of social influence campaigns between social networks (e.g. Twitter in layer α and Facebook in layer β), or the spread of diseases as individuals interact with others in both their family (layer α) and work (layer β) networks.

An illustration of a multilayer network is shown in Fig. 1. As illustrated in the figure, the inter-network and intra-network adjacency matrices can be collected into a single "supra-adjacency" matrix $\bar{A}$. One might then propose that the interactions of agents can be viewed as happening over a single-layer network with adjacency matrix $\bar{A}$. We note, however, that the multilayer network is different from this single-layer network with adjacency matrix $\bar{A}$. First, a multilayer model can impose different structural properties on the adjacency matrices in each layer, and enables us to investigate their impact on emergent phenomena accordingly. For example, real-world data can be used to learn the different structural properties of two social networks separately, and allow for each to be reflected independently in the ABS environment. Further, disturbances or information from a node may spread within each layer following a different process, and at a different time scale. For instance, individuals may interact with their co-workers during the week, and with their extended family and friends over the weekend; they may also engage in different activities with each group, therefore impacting the likelihood of the spread of a disease between them in each context differently. Lastly, multilayer network simulations allow us to distinguish how regulators can propose and enact interventions in each layer.

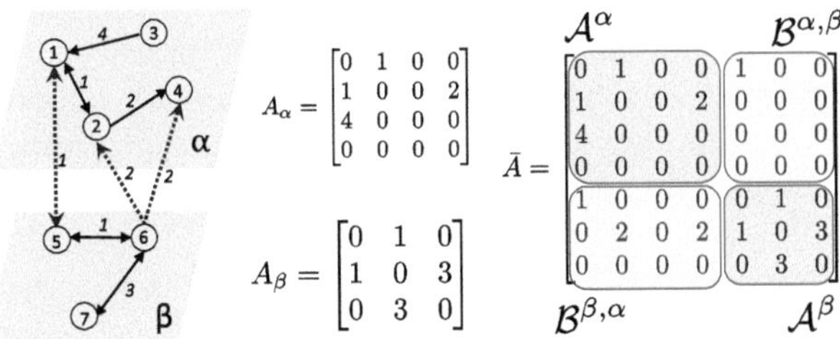

Fig. 1. An example of a multilayer network, and its intra-layer and inter-layer adjacency matrices.

3   `MultiRepast4py`: A Multilayer ABS Framework

Given the limitation of traditional ABS platforms and the importance of incorporating multilayer functionalities, our objective is to create ABS tools that enable agent-based simulations over multilayer networks. In this section, we first outline our evaluation of existing simulation platforms to identify those best suited for developing and implementing a multilayer ABS framework (Sect. 3.1). We then provide details on our implementation of `MultiRepast4py`, and outline the main challenges that were addressed (Sect. 3.2).

3.1   Platform Selection and Rationale

As noted in the introduction, there exist several widely used platforms for ABS, built on different programming languages; these include NetLogo [30], Repast [10], MASON [20], FLAME [17], and Swarm [22], and their extensions. Among these, NetLogo is the highest-level platform, with a relatively simple programming language and a well-developed graphical interface; however, while NetLogo offers robust features for certain applications (e.g., grid-based ABMs), it presents limitations for highly specialized or complex simulations. The remaining platforms (e.g., Repast, MASON, Swarm) provide a *framework* (a set of concepts for describing an agent-based model and the required simulation components) along with a *software library* (implementations of the framework using customized simulation tools). While these require additional programming skills, they facilitate customization, as well as integration with a wide range of data analysis and machine learning libraries to enable data-driven ABS. Our focus in this work is similarly on developing a framework and library for multilayer ABS, while maintaining the flexibility for customization and data-driven implementations.

Accordingly, Repast4py [9], a Python-based member of the Repast Suite, was chosen as the development platform for the following reasons:

1. *Scalability*: Repast4py simplifies the construction of large-scale ABMs that can be distributed across multiple processing cores using MPI, enabling efficient execution of complex simulations.
2. *Flexibility*: The platform's dynamic simulation step capabilities, facilitated by the scheduling feature, enables a high degree of customization, ensuring the seamless implementation of our multilayer approach.
3. *Extensibility*: Built on Python, Repast4py inherently supports integration with a wide range of data analysis and machine learning libraries, facilitating data-driven modeling and future expansions.

3.2   Implementation Details

The multilayer functionality in `MultiRepast4py` is implemented through a structured process that embeds each agent's multilayer edges into a unified data structure. Specifically, connections from the network files are mapped using the node identifiers (`node_id`) defined in the first file, ensuring consistent agent identification across all layers.

Each agent is represented by an `Agent` dataclass containing its node_id, agent_type, rank, and a list of `LayerData` objects. Each `LayerData` object encapsulates the layer_id and a list of `Edge` objects, where each edge contains the target node_id and weight. This structured approach provides better type safety and cleaner data management compared to raw dictionaries.

The implementation is organized into four sequential stages, each addressing a critical aspect of our multilayer simulation framework. First, multilayer network files are parsed and merged into a unified structure, creating a cohesive representation of all layers. Second, edge data is transformed (compressed and encoded) to satisfy the Repast4py's network file format requirements while enhancing memory efficiency. Third, agents are initialized by reconstructing their multilayer connections from the processed data, enabling a decentralized setup that supports parallel execution. Finally, the simulation step function is adapted to allow layer-specific interactions, ensuring that each simulation cycle accurately reflects the dynamics of the corresponding layer. Together, these stages facilitate efficient memory usage and scalable parallel processing while preserving the essential semantics of multilayer networks. The following sections provide detailed explanations of each component.

Network File Parsing. In this stage, multiple network files are provided as input, each representing a layer. The file contains agent information in the form of unique identifiers (UIDs): (`node_id`, `agent_type`, and `rank`) and the edge connections between nodes. These network files can be generated using Repast4py's `write_network` function. The parsing process constructs a structured data model where each agent is represented as an `Agent` object with the following attributes:

Agent(node_id: int, agent_type: int, rank: int, layers: List[LayerData])

Each `LayerData` instance encapsulates the connections of an agent within a specific layer and stores them as a collection of `Edge` objects, each defined by a `target_id` and `weight`. This object-oriented approach improves code maintainability, provides clear semantic structure, and facilitates efficient access and updates to layer-specific edges. By storing outgoing edges as agent attributes, the model achieves greater decentralization, thereby reducing the need for message passing between ranks.

Data Compression and Encoding. Outgoing edge lists for agents cannot be directly stored in Repast4py network files, as the framework's network file format prohibits nested data structures and requires string-based keys. To ensure compatibility with Repast4py's network serialization requirements, the compression logic is encapsulated within the `CompressionHandler` class. This class first converts the structured agent data into a JSON-serializable format before applying a four-step transformation:

1. **Serialization**: Convert `LayerData` to dictionaries via `to_dict()` methods.
2. **JSON Encoding**: Serialize the dictionary structure with compact formatting.

3. **zlib Compression**: Apply compression to the UTF-8 encoded JSON string.
4. **Base64 Encoding**: Convert compressed bytes to ASCII-safe string

The final encoded string is stored in the following format:

$$\{\text{``data''} : \text{``[Base64 string]''}\}$$

Algorithm 1. Multi-Layer Network Reconstruction

Require: List of network file paths $file\_paths$
Ensure: Unified network file with compressed multi-layer edges
    Data Structure Initialization
1: **procedure** ProcessMultilayerNetwork($file\_paths$)
2:    $network\_data \leftarrow$ NetworkData($num_layers = $ len($file\_paths$))
3:    $network\_data.agents \leftarrow \{\}$ ▷ Dict[int, Agent]
    Node Parsing Phase
4:    **if** $file\_paths$ is not empty **then**
5:        $lines \leftarrow$ ReadFile($file\_paths[0]$)
6:        $network\_data.is\_directed \leftarrow$ ParseHeader($lines[0]$)
7:        **for** $line$ in $lines[1:]$ **do**
8:            **if** $line$.strip() $=$ "EDGES" **then**
9:                **Break**
10:           **end if**
11:           Parse $node\_id, agent\_type, rank \leftarrow line$
12:           $agent \leftarrow$ Agent($node\_id, agent\_type, rank$)
13:           **if** compressed data exists in $line$ **then**
14:                $agent.layers \leftarrow$ DecompressAgentData($line.attributes$)
15:           **end if**
16:           $network\_data.agents[node\_id] \leftarrow agent$
17:        **end for**
18:    **end if**
    Edge Parsing Phase
19:    **for** $layer\_id, file\_path$ in enumerate($file\_paths$) **do**
20:        $lines \leftarrow$ ReadFile($file\_path$)
21:        **for** $line$ in $lines$ **do**
22:           **if** $line$.strip() $=$ "EDGES" **then**
23:                **Continue**
24:           **end if**
25:           **if** $found\_edges$ **then**
26:                Parse $(source\_id, target\_id, weight) \leftarrow line$
27:                $agent \leftarrow network\_data.agents[source\_id]$
28:                $layer \leftarrow agent$.AddLayer($layer\_id$)   ▷ Get or create LayerData
29:                $layer$.AddEdge($target\_id, weight$)   ▷ Append Edge object
30:                **if not** $network\_data.is\_directed$ **then**
31:                    $target\_agent \leftarrow network\_data.agents[target\_id]$
32:                    $target\_layer \leftarrow target\_agent$.AddLayer($layer\_id$)
33:                    $target\_layer$.AddEdge($source\_id, weight$)
34:                **end if**
35:           **end if**
36:        **end for**
37:    **end for**
    Compression and Output Phase
38:    Copy base file to output path
39:    **for** each node line in base file **do**
40:        **if** line is header **then**
41:           $output\_lines$.append($line$)
42:        **else if** line before "EDGES" marker **then**
43:           $node\_id \leftarrow$ ParseNodeId($line$)
44:           $agent \leftarrow network\_data.agents[node\_id]$
45:           $compressed \leftarrow$ CompressAgentData($agent$)
46:           $attributes \leftarrow$ json($\{'data' : compressed\}$)
47:           Append node info with $attributes$ to $output\_lines$
48:        **end if**
49:    **end for**
50:    Write $output\_lines$ to output file   ▷ Exclude original EDGES section
51:    **return** $network\_data$
52: **end procedure**

Agent Initialization. During the agent initialization phase, the `read_network` function is invoked to load the modified network file. The method `CompressionHandler .decompress_agent_data()` is then applied to reconstruct the list of `LayerData` objects from the Base64-encoded string. Each agent independently deserializes its layer data using the `LayerData.from_dict()` method, which recreates the structured edge information. This design preserves scalable parallel initialization across ranks while providing a clean, object-oriented interface for managing agent connectivity across layers.

Modify Step Function. The multilayer simulation is facilitated through Repast4py's scheduling mechanism. To enable multilayer simulations, a modified step function is defined in `MultiRepast4py`, which accepts a layer parameter to specify the active layer for a given simulation step. This function leverages agent-specific data structures to manage interactions dynamically. For instance, the agent's layer-specific edges are accessed via:

```
agent.get_layer(layer_id).edges   # Returns list of Edge objects
```

For compatibility, a list of neighbor identifiers can also be obtained via:

```
[edge.target_id for edge in agent.get_layer(layer_id).edges]
```

The `Agent.get_layer()` method returns the corresponding `LayerData` object for the specified layer, or `None` if the agent has no connections in that layer. This provides a cleaner and more expressive API for custom propagation mechanisms compared to direct dictionary access, while maintaining scalability across layers.

4   Experimental Demonstration

To demonstrate the capabilities of our multilayer simulation framework, we present a case study focused on information dynamics – specifically, rumor propagation. This topic is commonly explored in agent-based simulations and serves as an excellent example to highlight the advantages of our multilayer approach.

This case study is based on modifications of existing demo, Tutorial 2 - The Rumor Network Model from Repast4py. We selected this example to better illustrate the process of transforming a single-layer ABS into a multilayer ABS. The simulation was executed on an Apple M2 chip with 8GB RAM, showing that our framework is accessible on standard computing platforms.

4.1   Multilayer Analysis of Rumor Propagation Through Cross-Platform Interaction

This case study demonstrates how multilayer network simulations reveal propagation dynamics that conventional single-layer analyses cannot capture, particularly through the mechanism of cross-platform information diffusion.

Model Configuration. We implement a two-layer multiplex network model with 25 unique agents. Each agent is represented as a node in both layers, corresponding to the same individual active on two distinct social platforms. The experimental configuration employs a reduced-scale network to enable clear demonstration of multilayer interaction effects, with larger-scale validation presented in Sect. 4.2.

- **Network Topology:** Both layers' connections are generated via Erdős-Rényi random graphs($G(n,p)$ model, $n = 25, p = 0.1$), producing sparse networks with average degree $k = 2.5$. This model was selcted for its simplicity, controllability, and reproducibility.
- **Agent State Model:** Each agent has the following attribute
  - `received_rumor`: Binary state (0=uninformed, 1=informed)
  - `layers`: List of `LayerData` objects containing `Edge` lists

Propagation Dynamics. The rumor dissemination process operates as:

1. Both layer activates at each time step
2. Within the activate layer, Informed nodes attempt transmission to adjacent uniformed neighbors
3. Per-contact infection probability $\beta = 0.005$
4. New informed nodes participate in next spreading cycle

Simulation Protocol. We execute 100 Monte Carlo replications for each of 25 network seeds, yielding 2,500 independent simulations (100 time steps each). All results present ensemble averages with stochastic effects mitigated through this extensive sampling.

Combined Degree Centrality. For a multilayer network with L layers, the combined degree centrality C_D^{combined} of an agent m is defined as:

$$C_D^{\text{combined}}(m) = \sum_{\gamma=0}^{L-1} \frac{1}{T_\gamma} \cdot C_D^\gamma(m), \tag{1}$$

- $C_D^\gamma(m)$ denotes the degree centrality of agent m in layer γ,
- T_γ is the execution interval of layer γ, specifying how frequently the layer is active; it must be strictly positive ($T_\gamma > 0$).

Empirical Findings. Figure 2 demonstrates the propagation patterns for three strategic seed nodes, quantified through cumulative adoption curves. Table 1 provides structural context through degree centrality measures.

Table 1. Node Centrality Measures Across Network Perspectives. Combined degree centrality is calculated as the sum of intra-layer degree centralities, weighted by the reciprocal of each layer's activation interval ($T_0, T_1 = 1$).

Seed Node	Degree Centrality		
	Layer 1	Layer 2	Combined
Agent 2	3	4	**7**
Agent 23	**4**	1	5
Agent 24	1	**5**	6

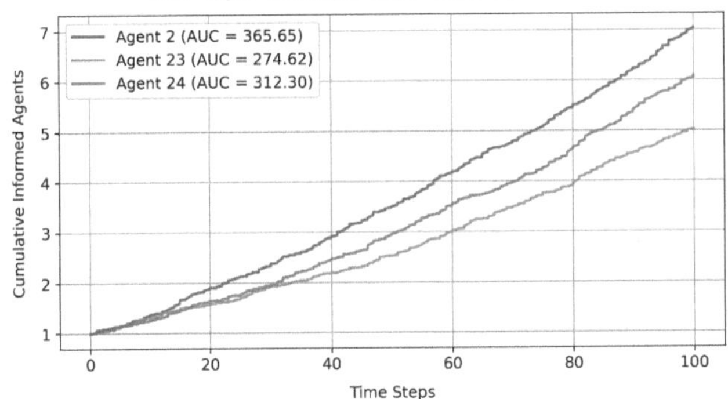

Fig. 2. Rumor propagation across multilayer networks. Curves show mean adoption rates (N=100 simulations) for three seed nodes. The Area Under the Curve (AUC) is used as a quantitative measure of overall dissemination efficiency.

The propagation dynamics reveal several critical insights. Despite Agents 23 and 24 exhibiting maximal intra-layer centrality in their respective platforms ($Layer1 : C_D = 4, Layer2 : C_D = 5$), Agent 2 demonstrates superior global propagation efficiency (AUC = 365.65 vs 274.62 and 312.30) due to its cross-platform connectivity (Combined $C_D = 7$). This emergent property remains invisible to single-layer analyses - traditional centrality metrics might identify Agents 23 and 24 as optimal seeds within their respective platforms, yet such single-layer analyses risk underestimating the influence of inter-layer connectivity in shaping system-scale diffusion. This highlights the importance of multilayer network analysis, made possible by the `MultiRepast4py`, in accounting for the impacts of different interacting networks on global outcomes.

4.2   Large-Scale Validation of Multilayer Propagation Dynamics

To evaluate the scalability and robustness of our framework, we extend the analysis presented in Sect. 4.1 by conducting a full-scale simulation of cross-platform information diffusion. This experiment quantifies the persistence of multilayer interaction effects in realistic network configurations and demonstrates the computational feasibility of large-scale multilayer agent-based simulations.

Model Configuration. We implement a two-layer multiplex network with 50,000 agents per layer, preserving the structural consistency of the small-scale demonstration while scaling the network parameters to reflect real-world social platforms.

- **Network Topology:** Each layer is instantiated as an Erdős-Rényi random graph($G(n, p) model, n = 50000, p = 0.0005$), yielding networks with an average degree $k = 25$.
- **Agent State Model:** As described in Sect. 4.1.

Propagation Dynamics: As detailed in Sect. 4.1, we set $\beta = 0.004$ to decelerate the spread, enhancing clarity and interpretability in the plot.

Simulation Protocol: We perform 100 Monte Carlo replications for each of three network seeding strategies, resulting in 300 independent simulations (each spanning 100 time steps). Seed nodes are selected according to three criteria:

- Top 10 degree centrality nodes in Layer 1 (single-layer perspective)
- Top 10 degree centrality nodes in Layer 2 (single-layer perspective)
- Top 10 combined degree centrality nodes (multilayer perspective)

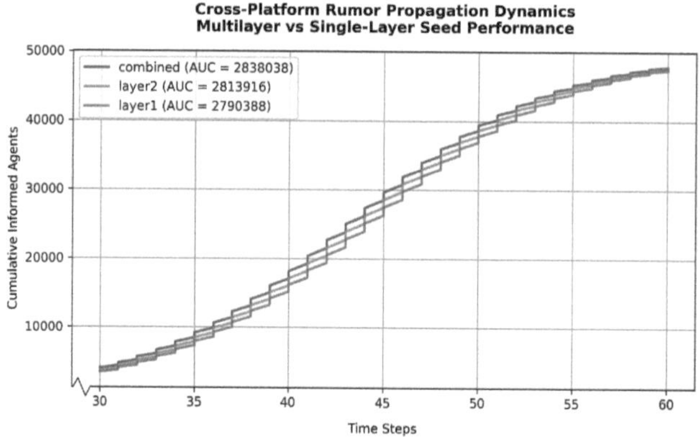

Fig. 3. Large-scale rumor propagation across Multilayer Networks. Curves depict the mean adoption rates (N=100 simulations) across three seeding strategies.

Empirical Findings. Figure 3 illustrates the propagation trajectories for each seeding strategy, with the Area Under the Curve (AUC) used to quantify overall dissemination efficiency.

Although the absolute differences in AUC values are modest relative to those observed in the small-scale demonstration, statistical analyses (t-test, Combined vs. Layer 1, p-value: 0.0007) confirm that the disparities are significant. Notably, the combined centrality seeds achieve approximately 10% greater population penetration at key diffusion milestones compared to the single-layer strategies. These findings underscore the importance of cross-platform connectivity in enhancing global diffusion efficiency in large networks.

5   Conclusion

We have developed `MultiRepast4py`, a multilayer agent-based simulation framework. This framework builds on an existing ABS simulation platform (specifically, Repast4py [10]) enabling researchers to model complex, large-scale, multilayered interactions without needing extensive programming skills, making it accessible to researchers across various disciplines. We used simulations studies on rumor spreading to highlight the advantages of our multilayer approach. Our use case were selected from existing ABS on single-layer networks, to further illustrate the process of transitioning from single-layer to multilayer ABS using our proposed platform. As noted in the introduction, our framework has the potential to be integrated with data analysis techniques to enable *data-driven* multilayer ABS; we view this as an important directions of future work.

Acknowledgments. This work is supported by the University of California San Diego Summer Research Internship program, and in part by the NSF under award CCF-2416311.

Code Availability. The source code for `MultiRepast4py` is available at https:// github.com/KengLL/MultiRepast4py.

Disclosure of Interests. The authors declare no competing interests to declare that are relevant to the content of this article.

References

1. Aleta, A., Moreno, Y.: Multilayer networks in a nutshell. Annu. Rev. Condens. Matter Phys. **10**, 45–62 (2019)
2. Battiston, F., Perc, M., Latora, V.: Determinants of public cooperation in multiplex networks. New J. Phys. **19**(7), 073017 (2017). https://doi.org/10.1088/1367-2630/aa6ea1
3. Bhattacharya, P., et al.: The matrix: an agent-based modeling framework for data intensive simulations. In: Proceedings of the 18th International Conference on Autonomous Agents and MultiAgent Systems, pp. 1635–1643 (2019)
4. Boccaletti, S., et al.: The structure and dynamics of multilayer networks. Phys. Rep. **544**(1), 1–122 (2014)
5. Brugière, A., Nguyen-Ngoc, D., Drogoul, A.: Handling multiple levels in agent-based models of complex socio-environmental systems: a comprehensive review. Front. Appl. Math. Stat. **8**, 1020353 (2022)

6. Bródka, P., Musial, K., Jankowski, J.: Interacting spreading processes in multilayer networks: a systematic review. IEEE Access **8**, 10316–10341 (2020). https://doi.org/10.1109/ACCESS.2020.2965547

7. Buldyrev, S.V., Parshani, R., Paul, G., Stanley, H.E., Havlin, S.: Catastrophic cascade of failures in interdependent networks. Nature **464**(7291), 1025–1028 (2010)

8. Cabrera, E., Taboada, M., Iglesias, M.L., Epelde, F., Luque, E.: Optimization of healthcare emergency departments by agent-based simulation. Procedia Comput. Sci. **4**, 1880–1889 (2011)

9. Collier, N., Ozik, J.: Distributed agent-based simulation with repast4py. In: 2022 Winter Simulation Conference (WSC), pp. 192–206. IEEE (2022)

10. Collier, N.: Repast: an extensible framework for agent simulation. Univ. Chicago's Soc. Sci. Res. **36**, 2003 (2003)

11. De Bufala, N., Kant, J.D.: An evolutionary approach to find optimal policies with an agent-based simulation. In: 18th International Conference on Autonomous Agents and Multiagent Systems (AAMAS 2019) (2019)

12. Ebrahimi, R., Naghizadeh, P.: United we fall: on the nash equilibria of multiplex and multilayer network games. IEEE Trans. Control. Netw., Syst (2025)

13. Gao, J., Buldyrev, S.V., Stanley, H.E., Havlin, S.: Networks formed from interdependent networks. Nat. Phys. **8**(1), 40–48 (2012)

14. Gómez-Gardeñes, J., Reinares, I., Arenas, A., Floría, L.M.: Evolution of cooperation in multiplex networks. Sci. Rep. **2**(1), 620 (2012). https://doi.org/10.1038/srep00620

15. Julka, N., Srinivasan, R., Karimi, I.: Agent-based supply chain management 1: framework. Comput. Chem. Eng. **26**(12), 1755–1769 (2002)

16. Kerr, C.C., et al.: Covasim: an agent-based model of covid-19 dynamics and interventions. PLoS Comput. Biol. **17**(7), e1009149 (2021)

17. Kiran, M., Richmond, P., Holcombe, M., Chin, L.S., Worth, D., Greenough, C.: Flame: simulating large populations of agents on parallel hardware architectures. In: Proceedings of the 9th International Conference on Autonomous Agents and Multiagent Systems, vol. 1, pp. 1633–1636 (2010)

18. Kivelä, M., Arenas, A., Barthelemy, M., Gleeson, J.P., Moreno, Y., Porter, M.A.: Multilayer networks. J. Complex. Netw. **2**(3), 203–271 (2014)

19. Kravari, K., Bassiliades, N.: A survey of agent platforms. J. Artif. Soc. Soc. Simul. **18**(1), 11 (2015). https://doi.org/10.18564/jasss.2661

20. Luke, S., Cioffi-Revilla, C., Panait, L., Sullivan, K., Balan, G.: Mason: a multiagent simulation environment. SIMULATION **81**(7), 517–527 (2005)

21. Macal, C.M., North, M.J.: Agent-based modeling and simulation. In: Proceedings of the 2009 winter simulation conference (WSC), pp. 86–98. IEEE (2009)

22. Minar, N., Burkhart, R., Langton, C., Askenazi, M., et al.: The swarm simulation system: a toolkit for building multi-agent simulations (1996)

23. Murdock, I., Carley, K.M., Yağan, O.: An agent-based model of cross-platform information diffusion and moderation. Soc. Netw. Anal. Min. **14**(1), 145 (2024)

24. Parandehgheibi, M., Modiano, E.: Robustness of interdependent networks: the case of communication networks and the power grid. In: 2013 IEEE Global Communications Conference (GLOBECOM), pp. 2164–2169. IEEE (2013)

25. Rand, W.: Theory-interpretable, data-driven agent-based modeling. In: Social-Behavioral Modeling For Complex Systems, pp. 337–357 (2019)

26. Rosés, R., Kadar, C., Gerritsen, C., Rouly, C.: Agent-based simulation of offender mobility: integrating activity nodes from location-based social networks. In: Aamas, pp. 804–812 (2018)

27. Salehi, M., Sharma, R., Marzolla, M., Magnani, M., Siyari, P., Montesi, D.: Spreading processes in multilayer networks. IEEE Trans. Netw. Sci. Eng. **2**(2), 65–83 (2015)
28. Shahrivar, E.M., Sundaram, S.: The game-theoretic formation of interconnections between networks. IEEE J. Sel. Areas Commun. **35**(2), 341–352 (2017)
29. Smith, E.B., Rand, W.: Simulating macro-level effects from micro-level observations. Manage. Sci. **64**(11), 5405–5421 (2018)
30. Tisue, S., Wilensky, U.: NetLogo: a simple environment for modeling complexity. In: International conference on complex systems, vol. 21, pp. 16–21. Citeseer (2004)
31. Xue, J., Park, S., Mondal, W.U., Reia, S.M., Yao, T., Ukkusuri, S.V.: Supporting post-disaster recovery with agent-based modeling in multilayer socio-physical networks. arXiv preprint arXiv:2307.11464 (2023)
32. Yağan, O., Gligor, V.: Analysis of complex contagions in random multiplex networks. Phys. Rev. E **86**(3), 036103 (2012)
33. Yağan, O., Qian, D., Zhang, J., Cochran, D.: Optimal allocation of interconnecting links in cyber-physical systems: interdependence, cascading failures, and robustness. IEEE Trans. Parallel Distrib. Syst. **23**(9), 1708–1720 (2012)
34. Yi, C., Yang, Q., Scoglio, C.M.: Multilayer network analysis of fmd transmission and containment among beef cattle farms. Sci. Rep. **12**(1), 15679 (2022)
35. Zhang, Y., Arenas, A., Yağan, O.: Cascading failures in interdependent systems under a flow redistribution model. Phys. Rev. E **97**(2), 022307 (2018)
36. Zhang, Y., Yağan, O.: Robustness of interdependent cyber-physical systems against cascading failures. IEEE Trans. Autom. Control **65**(2), 711–726 (2019)
37. Zhuang, Y., Yağan, O.: Multistage complex contagions in random multiplex networks. IEEE Trans. Control. Netw. Syst. **7**(1), 410–421 (2019)

Adjustable Attribute Matching in Digital Similars of Populations

Kazi Ashik Islam, S. S. Ravi, Henning S. Mortveit, and Samarth Swarup[✉]

University of Virginia, Charlottesville, VA 22904, USA
`{ki5hd,ssravi,henning.mortveit,swarup}@virginia.edu`

Abstract. A digital similar (DS) of a population of a region is a common starting point for agent-based modeling and simulation. Here, an integer linear programming-based algorithm is presented that refines an existing, high-resolution methodology for constructing DSs. The extension consists of constructing a household-to-residence mapping that maximizes the correlation between household income of individual households and residence property values of individual residences. The algorithm is applied to a coastal region of Virginia (USA) where we demonstrate that new household-to-residence assignment generates significantly different outcomes than the existing approach which is random assignment at blockgroup level. Using the context of road inundation and measures such as *time to evacuate* and *time to reach critical care*, significant differences across household income segments are demonstrated with the new method, while no such difference is established with the prior method.

Keywords: Digital similar · societal resilience · synthetic population · population digital twin

1 Introduction

Highly-detailed population models form a basis for many agent-based simulation models and computational modeling across domains such as epidemiology [2,26], disaster preparedness and planning [20,24], and urban science [6,13]. Such efforts rely on detailed, individual-level representations of entire populations of the study region, which include relevant demographic information. We refer to these as digital similars, though they are also referred to as synthetic populations or population digital twins. These representations are synthesized by integrating multiple datasets on demographics, activity patterns, and residences and other locations that people visit. The success of such studies depends in large part on the veridicality of the population representation. Data integration is typically done by matching common attributes that are relevant to the purpose. For example, when merging demographic and activity schedule data, matching is done on demographic attributes that are determined to be relevant to predicting activity durations [18,28]. When such attributes are not available, matching has been done randomly [1,4].

© The Author(s), under exclusive license to Springer Nature Switzerland AG 2026
A. Vidler and S. Swarup (Eds.): MABS 2025, LNAI 16227, pp. 158–169, 2026.
https://doi.org/10.1007/978-3-032-16328-8_11

It is possible that, in the absence of precise data that would allow attribute matching, we might still wish to have a non-random matching. An example is the assignment of households to residence locations, where we might wish to have a correlation between household incomes and residence values. We don't typically expect this correlation to be maximal, as a household might buy a residence and then either have their income change or have the residence value change (increase or decrease). Lacking empirical data on the level of correlation, our approach here is to develop a method that allows us to do adjustable attribute matching. For a concrete example, we use household income and residence value as the two attributes to be matched. Our location data for US digital similars is generated through a combination of modeling, data fusion, and model training based a broad variety of data sources [5,14,21,23]. This data resource has subsequently been augmented with estimates of residential property value from parcel data. Household income data are available through the US Census, which we used in generating the synthetic people and households that constitute our US digital similar [1,4]. In earlier work, these households of the digital similar were assigned residence locations at random within each Census block group of the study region. In our new methodology described here, we use an integer program (IP) formulation to construct an assignment that maximizes the correlation between household income, a PUMS [29] variable, and the detailed estimates of residence values. The IP-formulation also supports construction of an assignment where the Pearson correlation coefficient falls within a prescribed interval as long as the interval's upper bound does not exceed the maximal.

The new method for the household-residence assignment is illustrated for the Eastern Shore, Virginia (ESVA), a region that is exposed to storm surges and flooding. Using our related work on evacuation routing for inundated transportation networks [16,17] in combination with digital similars for the two counties, Accomack and Northampton, of ESVA, our setup is as follows: inundation data from TideWatch [30] is spatially joined with the road infrastructure [14] and adjusted speed limits are determined. Through routing, we determine the following for each household/residence location on the ESVA:

- The time needed to evacuate to a target destination across the state border with Maryland in the north;
- The time needed to reach urgent care/hospital;
- The time needed for emergency personnel (e.g., a fire truck) to reach the residence location.

The metrics are determined for (a) random assignment of household to residences and for (b) the new IP-based assignment presented in Sect. 3. In each case, we measure the travel times with and without inundation and assess the fraction of households for which travel times are impacted, for low-, middle-, and high-income households (based on the assigned residences). We find that there are significant differences in travel times only when matching is done in a correlated way. While this is not unexpected, it leads us to believe that any analysis of disaster response, evacuation, etc., that is based on the new matching will show more meaningful patterns by household income and other, correlated, demographic variables such as race and ethnicity. In related work for construction of digital similars (or synthetic populations) such as [10–12,15,22,27,32], we are not aware of such details being incorporated in the methodology.

Paper Organization. In Sect. 2 and 3 we present the new algorithm with proofs. Following this, we describe our approach to scaling which is through a spatial decomposition of the study region followed by a multi-pass process for each blockgroup. In Sect. 4 we demonstrate the use of the new digital similar in the context of flooding for the Eastern Shore, Virginia (ESVA). Specifically, we demonstrate how road inundation causes quite different impacts to the ESVA population when broken down by income compared to when a random household-to-residence mapping is used. The measures considered were time-to-evacuate, time-to-reach-urgent-care, and emergency-response-time. We conclude with a summary in Sect. 5.

2   Approach

2.1   Generalized Pearson Correlation Coefficient

Let $\mathbb{R}$ denote the set of real numbers and $[n]$ denote the set $\{1, 2, \ldots, n\}$. Consider two sets of n variables, say $X = \{x_1, x_2, \ldots, x_n\}$ and $Y = \{y_1, y_2, \ldots, y_n\}$, where each variable takes on a value from $\mathbb{R}$. In addition, there is a function f that maps $X \times Y$ to $\mathbb{R}$. Thus, for each pair of variables $x_i \in X$ and $y_j \in Y$, the value $f(x_i, y_j)$ is in $\mathbb{R}$.

A **perfect matching** between X and Y is a permutation π of $[n]$ such that x_i is matched with $y_{\pi(i)}$. For a given perfect matching π between X and Y, the value of the **Generalized Pearson Correlation Coefficient**, denoted by $\mathrm{GPCC}(X, Y, \pi)$, is defined as follows:

$$\mathrm{GPCC}(X, Y, \pi) = \sum_{i=1}^{n} f(x_i, y_{\pi(i)}). \tag{1}$$

A special case of this is the common definition of the Pearson Correlation Coefficient (PCC), where π is the identity permutation (i.e., each x_i gets matched with y_i) and the function f is defined by

$$f(x_i, y_i) = \frac{1}{n-1} \left(\frac{x_i - \mu(X)}{\sigma(X)} \right) \left(\frac{y_i - \mu(Y)}{\sigma(Y)} \right). \tag{2}$$

In the above equation, $\mu(X)$ and $\mu(Y)$ are respectively the sample means of X and Y and $\sigma(X)$ and $\sigma(Y)$ are respectively the sample standard deviations of X and Y.

Graph Theoretic Definitions. We will use a few standard definitions from graph theory. These definitions can be found in many texts [31, e.g.]. A bipartite graph $G(V_1, V_2, E)$ has two disjoint sets of nodes V_1 and V_2, and each edge in E has one node from V_1 and the other from V_2. A **matching** M in G is a subset of edges such that no two edge of M are incident on the same node. The size of a matching M is the number of edges in M. When there is a weight $w(e)$ associated with each edge $e \in E$, the weight of a matching M is the sum of the weights of the edges in M.

A bipartite graph $G(V_1, V_2, E)$ is **balanced** if $|V_1| = |V_2|$. For a balanced bipartite graph, with $|V_1| = |V_2| = n$, a **perfect matching** of G is a matching of size n. Consider a balanced bipartite graph $G(V_1, V_2, E)$ which has a perfect matching. Suppose $V_1 = \{v_1, v_2, \ldots v_n\}$ and $V_2 = \{w_1, w_2, \ldots w_n\}$. Now, any perfect matching of G represents a one-to-one correspondence between V_1 and V_2. If the nodes in V_1 are ordered as $\langle v_1, v_2, \ldots v_n \rangle$, then a perfect matching M can be thought of as a permutation π of $[n]$. In other words, M is the set of edges given by $\{v_i, w_{\pi(i)} : 1 \le i \le n\}$. This view of a perfect matching in a balanced bipartite graph allows us to formulate the problem of maximizing GPCC as that of constructing an appropriate perfect matching in such a bipartite graph.

When there are edge weights, a **maximum weight perfect matching** of $G(V_1, V_2, E)$ is a perfect matching whose weight is a *maximum* among all the perfect matchings of G. It is well known that if a balanced bipartite graph $G(V_1, V_2, E)$, where $|V_1| = |V_2| = n$, has a perfect matching, then such a matching of maximum weight can be computed in time $O(n|E|)$ [7].

2.2 Maximizing Generalized Pearson Correlation Coefficient

Given the definition of GPCC by Equation (1), it is of interest to consider the problem of finding a permutation π that *maximizes* the GPCC value. From the discussion in Sect. 2.1, it can be seen that this maximization problem can be solved by a simple reduction to the **maximum weight perfect matching** (MWPM) problem on balanced bipartite graphs. Since the MWPM problem can be solved efficiently [7–9], it follows that the problem of finding a permutation that maximizes the GPCC value can also be solved efficiently.

Our algorithm for maximizing the GPCC value is shown in Fig. 1. The following proposition establishes the correctness and the running time of the algorithm.

Proposition 1. *Given values for the variables in the sets $X = \{x_1, x_2, \ldots, x_n\}$ and $Y = \{y_1, y_2, \ldots, y_n\}$ and a function f that returns the value $f(x_i, y_j)$ for any pair of inputs x_i and y_j, the algorithm in Fig. 1 returns a permutation that maximizes the GPCC value defined by Equation (1). Further, the algorithm runs in polynomial time.*

Proof: Since G is a complete balanced bipartite graph and $|V_x| = |V_y| = n$, G has a perfect matching. (For example, the set of edges $\{\{v_i, w_i\} : 1 \le i \le n\}$ is a perfect matching for G.) From the discussion in Sect. 2.1, it can be seen that every matching of sets X and Y represents a perfect matching in G. Further, for

Input: The values of $2n$ variables x_1, x_2, ..., x_n and y_1, y_2, ..., y_n; a function f that returns the value $f(x_i, y_j)$ given the values of any pair of variables x_i and y_j.

Output: A permutation π of $[n]$ that maximizes $\mathrm{GPCC}(X, Y, \pi)$ over all permutations of $[n]$.

Steps of the Algorithm:

1. Construct a weighted balanced *complete* bipartite graph $G(V_x, V_y, E)$ as follows. The node sets $V_x = \{v_1, v_2, \ldots, v_n\}$ and $V_y = \{w_1, w_2, \ldots, w_n\}$ are in one-to-one correspondence with sets X and Y respectively. $E = \{\{v_i, w_j\} : 1 \leq i, j \leq n\}$. For each edge $\{v_i, w_j\} \in E$, the weight $w(v_i, w_j)$ is set to $f(x_i, y_j)$.
2. Compute a maximum weight perfect matching M of G.
3. For each edge $\{v_i, w_j\} \in M$, set $\pi(i) = j$.
4. Return the permutation π.

Fig. 1. Algorithm to Find a Permutation that Maximizes GPCC.

every such matching, from Equation (1), the value of GPCC is the sum of the weights of the edges in the corresponding matching. Thus, a perfect matching in G with the largest total weight indeed provides a matching of X and Y with the largest value of GPCC. This establishes the correctness of the algorithm.

To estimate the running time, we assume that for a given pair of values x_i and y_j, the value $f(x_i, y_j)$ can be computed in $O(1)$ time. Step 1 of the algorithm runs in $O(n^2)$ time since the number of edges in G is n^2 and the weight of each edge can be computed in $O(1)$ time. As mentioned earlier, Step 2 runs in $O(n|E|)$ $= O(n^3)$ time since $|E| = n^2$. Step 3 runs in $O(n)$ time. Thus, the running time of the algorithm is dominated by the time used in Step 2. Hence, the algorithm runs in $O(n^3)$ time. ■

3   Integer Linear Programming Formulations for Matching Problems

Overview. We present integer linear programming (ILP) formulations for two versions of the matching problem. In the first version, the goal is to obtain a matching for which the GPCC value is within specified bounds. The second version, the goal is to find a matching that maximizes the GPCC value.

Obtaining a GPCC Value Within Given Bounds. A natural question that arises in the context of generating synthetic populations is that of finding a permutation that leads to a given GPCC value. From the previous discussion, it can be seen that this problem corresponds to finding a perfect matching of a specified weight in a balanced weighted bipartite graph. Maalouly [19] presents results that suggest this problem, which he refers to as the **Exact Weight Perfect Matching** problem, is unlikely to be efficiently solvable. Here, we present a method that uses an integer linear programming (ILP) formulation for a relaxed version of the problem. Specifically, we are given values of $2n$ variables

$X = \{x_1, x_2, \ldots, x_n\}$ and $Y = \{y_1, y_2, \ldots, y_n\}$ and two real values ℓ and u. The goal is to find a permutation π of $[n]$ such that the GPCC value corresponding to π (given by Equation (1)) satisfies the condition $\ell \leq \mathrm{GPCC}(X, Y, \pi) \leq u$.

Using the discussion in previous sections, we can consider the above problem as that of finding a perfect matching M in a balanced complete bipartite graph $G(V_x, V_y, E)$ such that the weight of M is at least ℓ and at most u. Recall that the weight of each edge $\{v_i, w_j\}$ in G is given by $f(x_i, y_j)$. Our $\{0,1\}$-ILP formulation for the problem is as follows.

<u>Variables:</u> There are n^2 variables z_{ij}, $1 \leq i, j \leq n$. Each z_{ij} takes on a value from $\{0, 1\}$. The variable z_{ij} represents edge $\{v_i, w_j\}$. The value of $z_{ij} = 1$ if the edge $\{v_i, w_j\}$ is in the chosen perfect matching; otherwise, the value of z_{ij} is 0.

<u>Objective:</u> No optimization objective is needed here.

<u>Constraints:</u>

1. For each node v_i, *exactly* one edge from the chosen matching should be incident on v_i. This leads to the following set of n constraints:

$$\sum_{j=1}^{n} z_{ij} = 1, \quad 1 \leq i \leq n.$$

2. For each node w_j, *exactly* one edge from the chosen matching should be incident on w_j. This leads to the following set of n constraints:

$$\sum_{i=1}^{n} z_{ij} = 1, \quad 1 \leq j \leq n.$$

3. The weight of the chosen matching must satisfy the specified upper and lower bounds. This leads to the following two constraints:

$$\sum_{i=1}^{n} \sum_{j=1}^{n} f(x_i, y_j)\, z_{ij} \geq \ell \quad \text{and}$$

$$\sum_{i=1}^{n} \sum_{j=1}^{n} f(x_i, y_j)\, z_{ij} \leq u.$$

4. Each z_{ij} must take on a value from $\{0, 1\}$:

$$z_{ij} \in \{0, 1\}, \quad 1 \leq i, j \leq n.$$

<u>Recovering a matching:</u> When there is a solution, for each z_{ij} that has value 1, we match x_i with y_j.

3.1   Maximizing the GPCC Value

We now present an ILP formulation for finding a permutation that maximizes the GPCC value. As pointed out in Sect. 2.2, this problem can be solved efficiently by a reduction to the maximum weight perfect matching problem in bipartite graphs. However, an ILP formulation for the problem is convenient in practice since search heuristics built into ILP solvers such as Gurobi are generally able to generate solutions quickly even for reasonably large problem instances. The ILP formulation presented here is obtained by a minor modification to the formulation presented in Sect. 3.

<u>Variables:</u> There are n^2 variables z_{ij}, $1 \leq i, j \leq n$. Each z_{ij} takes on a value from $\{0, 1\}$. The variable z_{ij} represents edge $\{v_i, w_j\}$. The value of $z_{ij} = 1$ if the edge $\{v_i, w_j\}$ is in the chosen perfect matching; otherwise, the value of z_{ij} is 0.

<u>Objective:</u> Maximize $\sum_{i=1}^{n} \sum_{j=1}^{n} f(x_i, y_j) z_{ij}$.

<u>Constraints:</u>

1. For each node v_i, *exactly* one edge from the chosen matching should be incident on v_i. This leads to the following set of n constraints:

$$\sum_{j=1}^{n} z_{ij} = 1, \quad 1 \leq i \leq n.$$

2. For each node w_j, *exactly* one edge from the chosen matching should be incident on w_j. This leads to the following set of n constraints:

$$\sum_{i=1}^{n} z_{ij} = 1, \quad 1 \leq j \leq n.$$

3. Each z_{ij} must take on a value from $\{0, 1\}$:

$$z_{ij} \in \{0, 1\}, \quad 1 \leq i, j \leq n.$$

<u>Recovering a matching:</u> When there is a solution, for each z_{ij} that has value 1, we match x_i with y_j.

3.2   Adaptation for Use with Digital Similars

The IP-based algorithm for constructing household-to-residence assignment is applied independently at blockgroup resolution. For a blockgroup, there will typically be disparity between the number of households $|H|$ and the number of residence locations $|R|$. The two cases to consider are (i) $|R| \geq |H|$ and (ii) $|R| < |H|$. For the first case, we apply the IP-based algorithm to the set of households H and a randomly selected subset $R' \subset R$ with $|R'| = |H|$. For the second case, we construct a partition $\mathcal{H} = \{H_1, H_2, \ldots, H_{k+1}\}$ of H such that $|H_1| = |H_2| = \cdots = H_k = |R|$ and apply the algorithm to the pairs (H_i, R) with $1 \leq i \leq k$. The remaining set H_{k+1} is handled as in the first case.

4 Results

The algorithm was applied to the digital similar of Accomack and Northampton, Virginia, the counties that constitute the Eastern Shore. We compare three methods for household-to-residence assignment: (1) IP-based assignment with synthetic population P_{IP}, (2) sorted assignment with population P_{sorted}, and (3) random assignment with population P_{random}. In addition, we split the populations into the following income-based sub-demographics based on annual household income:

- **Low income:** $[0, \$55,000]$; 11,375 households
- **Mid income:** $[\$55,000, \$120,000]$; 5,533 households
- **High income:** $> \$120,000$; 1,736 households

The road network was constructed from OpenStreetMap data [25], inundation data was collected from TideWatch [30], and the two data sets were spatially join to determine road segment traversability and modified traversal speeds. Routing was done at household resolution over (A) the baseline road network and (B) the inundated road network, where a household was matched via its residence to the nearest transportation node.

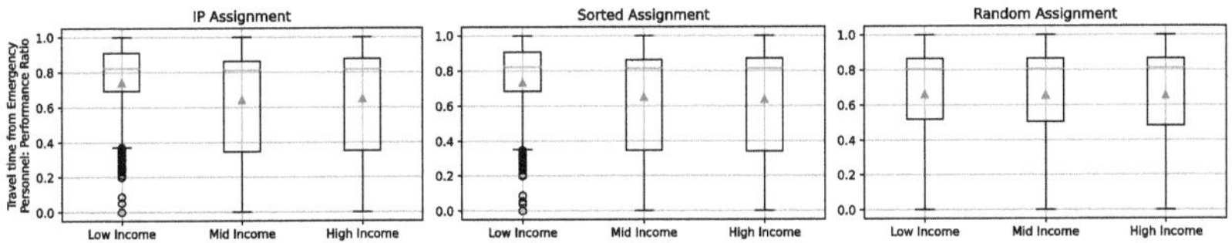

Fig. 2. Distributions of travel time from emergency personnel for affected households under the three assignments.

The following metrics were measured through simulation:

- **Travel time to safety:** We calculate the travel time (τ_1) from household to a safe location (at the periphery of ESVA towards Maryland) for evacuation under baseline conditions, and the travel time τ_2 for the inundated case. For households that are cut off by inundation and are unable to reach the safety destination, the travel time is set to a very high value $\tau_2 \to \infty$ in case the safe location is not reachable. We then calculate the **performance ratio** $0 < \tau_1/\tau_2 \le 1$. The closer the metric value to 1, the better.
- **Travel time for emergency personnel:** This measure considers travel time from the nearest fire station to the household in the same manner as for evacuation.
- **Travel time to critical service:** This measure considers travel time to the nearest hospital from the household under two road conditions.

Table 1. Number and percentage of households affected by road inundation in each income level, for the IP assignment method.

Income Level	Travel time to Safety	Travel time from Emergency Personnel	Travel time to Critical Service
IP assignment			
Low	1927, 17%	2104, 18%	1871, 16%
Mid	1160, 21%	1351, 24%	1461, 26%
High	499, 29%	600, 35%	601, 35%
Sorted assignment			
Low	1960, 17%	2154, 19%	1900, 17%
Mid	1166, 21%	1371, 25%	1499, 27%
High	496, 29%	599, 35%	582, 34%
Random assignment			
Low	2767, 24%	3068, 27%	2981, 26%
Mid	1472, 27%	1351, 24%	1399, 25%
High	430, 25%	480, 28%	469, 27%

Table 2. p-values from two-sample Kolmogorov-Smirnov test. For IP and Sorted assignment, the p-values are small (< 0.05), implying statistically significant difference between the income level groups. For Random assignment, p-values are large (> 0.05), implying no statistically significant difference between the groups.

Income Level	Travel time to Safety	Travel time from Emergency Personnel	Travel time to Critical Service
IP assignment			
Low vs Mid	3.03e-07	1.62e-15	1.42e-40
Mid vs High	2.1e-07	2.46e-12	1.69e-08
Low vs High	5.167e-19	1e-34	1.11e-46
Sorted assignment			
Low vs Mid	1.08e-06	1.92e-14	2.7e-43
Mid vs High	5.77e-07	2.25e-11	4.65e-07
Low vs High	1.74e-17	1.73e-32	6.28e-40
Random assignment			
Low vs Mid	0.65	1	0.7
Mid vs High	0.79	0.98	0.55
Low vs High	1	1	0.76

Figure 2 shows the travel times from emergency personnel for the households in each income group that are affected by flooding (i.e., the ones for whom performance ratio < 1). We see that the change for each group is about the same in the random assignment but not for the other two. Table 1 shows the number of households in the three income level groups, affected by road inundation in terms of the three metrics, for different assignment method. For the IP assignment, we observe that, by count, low income level households are affected the most. However, if we consider percentage of households, then high income households are affected the most. A similar pattern is observed for Sorted assignment method. However, in the Random assignment method, we observe that the percentage of households impacted in different income levels are close, i.e. $24 - 28\%$.

To understand if the effect of road inundation on different income level households is different, we look at the performance ratio values of the set of households in each income level. We then compare them using the two-sample Kolmogorov-Smirnov (KS) test. The resulting p-values are shown in Table 2. For the IP assignment method, we observe that the p-values are small (i.e. < 0.05) for all three metrics. This implies that the difference in impact of road inundation on different income level households is statistically significant. Similar result is found for the sorted assignment method. However, for the random assignment method, we see that the p-values are large (> 0.05). This implies that the difference in impact of road inundation on different income level households is not statistically significant. This is expected as the households were assigned to residences uniformly at random.

5 Discussion

The IP implementation was done using Gurobi. It is more computationally expensive than doing a random matching or a maximally correlated matching (which can be done by sorting and matching). However, as this method is run independently for each blockgroup, it can be parallelized easily. The method is also agnostic to the attributes, so it can be used wherever we have beliefs about the correlation between attributes, but lack data.

Empirical studies have consistently shown disparities by socioeconomic class, race, and ethnicity, in risks due to flooding and other environmental hazards. This is an important area of research in multiple domains with careful study designs needed [3]. The use of digital similars in these contexts is helpful in the evaluation of detailed and geographically contingent policies and procedures for mitigating these risks. Our methodology in this work brings additional veridicality to these efforts.

Acknowledgments. This work was funded in part by CoPe: NSF Award 2053013: Focused CoPe: Building Capacity for Adaptation in Rural Coastal Communities, by NASA Applied Sciences Program Grant #80NSSC22K1048, by the AI Research Institutes program supported by NSF and USDA-NIFA under the AI Institute: Agricultural AI for Transforming Workforce and Decision Support (AgAID) award No. 2021-67021-35344.

Data Availability Statement. The digital similar that formed the basis for this work, albeit without the IP implementation, is available as "Virginia: DP-VA-2.4.0" at https://doi.org/10.18130/V3/5LSDCY.

References

1. Adiga, A., et al.: Generating a synthetic population of the United States. Technical report. NDSSL 15-009, Network Dynamics and Simulation Science Laboratory (2015). https://drive.google.com/file/d/1S8Z3sqCMxBGBB7WbNoPHy7ff7NtJo6GR/view?usp=drive_link
2. Aleta, A., et al.: Modelling the impact of testing, contact tracing and household quarantine on second waves of COVID-19. Nat. Hum. Behaviour 4(9), 964–971 (2020). https://doi.org/10.1038/s41562-020-0931-9
3. Anand, H., Swarup, S., Shafiee-Jood, M., Alemazkoor, N.: Understanding of income and race disparities in hurricane evacuation is contingent upon study case and design. Sci. Rep. **14**(1), 28829 (2024). https://doi.org/10.1038/s41598-024-79754-9
4. Bhattacharya, P., et al.: Data-driven scalable pipeline using national agent-based models for real-time pandemic response and decision support. Int. J. High Performance Comput. Appl. **37**(1), 4–27 (2023)
5. BuildingFootprintUSA: (2019). https://www.buildingfootprintusa.com/, Accessed 15 Sept 2019
6. van Dam, K.H., Bustos-Turu, G., Shah, N.: A methodology for simulating synthetic populations for the analysis of socio-technical infrastructures. In: Jager, W., et al. (eds.) Advances in Social Simulation 2015, pp. 429–434. Springer, Cham (2017)
7. Duan, R., Pettie, S.: Linear-time approximation for maximum weight matching. J. ACM **61**(1), 1:1–1:23 (2014)
8. Edmonds, J.: Paths, trees and flowers. Can. J. Math. **17**, 449–467 (1965)
9. Gabow, H.N.: A scaling algorithm for weighted matching on general graphs. In: Proceedings of the 26th IEEE Symposium on Foundations of Computer Science (FOCS), pp. 90–100 (1985)
10. Gallagher, S., Richardson, L.F., Ventura, S.L., Eddy, W.F.: SPEW: Synthetic populations and ecosystems of the world. J. Comput. Graph. Stat. **27**(4), 773–784 (2018). https://doi.org/10.1080/10618600.2018.1442342
11. Geographic Information Science and Technology, Oak Ridge National Laboratory: Landsca. https://landscan.ornl.gov/
12. Gridded Population of the World (GPW), v4. https://sedac.ciesin.columbia.edu/data/collection/gpw-v4
13. He, B.Y., Zhou, J., Ma, Z., Chow, J.Y., Ozbay, K.: Evaluation of city-scale built environment policies in New York City with an emerging-mobility-accessible synthetic population. Transp. Res. Part A Policy Pract. **141**, 444–467 (2020)
14. HERE Premium Streets Data set for the U.S. (2020). https://www.here.com/
15. IDM: Synthpops (2025). https://docs.idmod.org/projects/synthpops/en/latest/
16. Islam, K.A., et al.: Incorporating fairness in large-scale evacuation planning. In: Proceedings of the 31st ACM International Conference on Information and Knowledge Management, pp. 3192–3201. New York, NY, USA (2022)
17. Islam, K.A., Marathe, M., Mortveit, H., Swarup, S., Vullikanti, A.: A simulation-based approach for large-scale evacuation planning. In: IEEE International Conference on Big Data, 2020, pp. 1338–1345 (2020)

18. Lum, K., Chungbaek, Y., Eubank, S.G., Marathe, M.V.: A two-stage, fitted values approach to activity matching. Int. J. Transp. **4**(1), 41–56 (2016)

19. Maalouly, N.E.: Exact matching: algorithms and related problems. In: Proc. Symposium on Theoretical Computer Science (STACS), pp. 36:1–36:24 (2023)

20. Marathe, M., Mortveit, H., Parikh, N., Swarup, S.: Prescriptive analytics using synthetic information. In: Hsu, W.H. (ed.) Emerging Trends in Predictive Analytics: Risk Management and Decision Making, pp. 1–19. IGI Global, Hershey, PA (2014)

21. Microsoft: U.S. building footprints (2018). https://github.com/Microsoft/USBuildingFootprints

22. Mistry, D., et al.: Inferring high-resolution human mixing patterns for disease modeling. Nat. Commun. **12**(1), 323 (2021)

23. National Center for Education Statistics (NCES), T.: http://nces.ed.gov, Accessed Feb 2020

24. Nejad, M.M., Erdogan, S., Cirillo, C.: A statistical approach to small area synthetic population generation as a basis for carless evacuation planning. J. Transp. Geogr. **90**, 102902 (2021)

25. OpenStreetMap points of interest. https://www.openstreetmap.org/, Accessed 7 Feb 2021

26. Renardy, M., Eisenberg, M., Kirschner, D.: Predicting the second wave of COVID-19 in Washtenaw County. MI. J. Theor. Biol. **507**, 110461 (2020)

27. Tatem, A.: WorldPop, open data for spatial demography. Sci. Data **4** (2017)

28. Thorve, S., et a.: High resolution synthetic residential energy use profiles for the United States. Sci. Data **10**, 76 (2023)

29. US Census: Public use microdata sample (PUMS). https://www.census.gov/programs-surveys/acs/microdata.html, Accessed 24 May 2021

30. Virginia Institute of Marine Sciences: Tidewatch (2025). https://cmap2.vims.edu/SCHISM/TidewatchViewer.html

31. West, D.B.: Introduction to Graph Theory. Prentice-Hall, Englewood Cliffs, NJ (2001)

32. Wheaton, W.D., et al.: Synthesized population databases: a US geospatial database for agent-based models. Technical report. MR-0010-0905, RTI International, Research Triangle Park, NC, USA (2009)

Use of Tags and Group Selection to Engender Cooperation in n-Player Snowdrift Game

William Pittenger[(✉)] [iD], Ethan Beaird [iD], and Sandip Sen [iD]

The University of Tulsa, Tulsa, OK 74104, USA
{wbp6910,ethan-beaird,sandip-sen}@utulsa.edu

Abstract. Promoting cooperation in social dilemma games, particularly in multi-player settings, is a challenge with important implications for real-world systems. While many mechanisms exist to foster cooperation in iterated two-player games, the dynamics of cooperation in n-player social dilemmas are comparatively less understood. Techniques such as tagging, group selection, and pool rewarding have been applied to n-player games, but these approaches often rely on unrealistic assumptions and result in suboptimal cooperation levels. We present an evolutionary approach to engendering cooperation in the n-player Snowdrift game. Our hybrid method combines tagging with tournament selection to evolve individual strategies while utilizing group selection mechanisms for dynamic group restructuring. We evaluate the efficacy of this combined approach across varying cost-benefit ratios, population sizes, and group restructuring schemes. Experimental results show that our model consistently promotes and sustains high levels of cooperation in the n-player Snowdrift game. This work provides valuable insights into scalable cooperation mechanisms in multi-agent systems facing social dilemmas.

Keywords: n-person social dilemmas · Tags · Group selection · n-player Snowdrift

1 Introduction

The emergence of cooperation in social dilemma situations has been widely studied across various disciplines, including biology, economics, psychology, and artificial intelligence, as real-world cooperation plays an important role in both human and artificial systems. Social dilemma scenarios that have received widespread attention include the *Prisoner's Dilemma* and the *Snowdrift* games [4] which are typically modeled as two-player games where each player can choose between one of two strategies: cooperate or defect. These studies try to identify the conditions under which cooperation will emerge as the predominant strategy.

Two-player games representing social dilemmas have been an active area of research. One-shot interactions in such social dilemmas incentivize defection as

A. Vidler and S. Swarup (Eds.): MABS 2025, LNAI 16227, pp. 170–181, 2026.
https://doi.org/10.1007/978-3-032-16328-8_12

the dominant behavior, however, when these games are repeated among the same two agents or pairings of two agents from a larger population, cooperation can be sustained using various mechanisms such as direct, indirect, and network reciprocity, group selection, kinship, interaction neighborhoods, etc. [5,12].

While two-player social dilemma games have been extensively studied, corresponding multi-player (n-player) games, despite their wide prevalence in real-world scenarios, have received less attention from the multiagent systems community. A key social dilemma in multi-player settings is the *public good game*, in which a group of n agents decides whether to contribute to a shared resource or public good [1]. Variants of public goods game include the n-player Snowdrift Game [15], which poses a social dilemmas in which cooperative agents are vulnerable to exploitation by defectors.

We evaluate a novel combination of the following complementary mechanisms to address social dilemmas in agent populations:

- Tags, or observable external features, have been used to both group players in a population and to decide how to interact with players [6,7,13].
- Tournament selection [11], comparing the utilities of randomly chosen agent pairs from the population, is used for individual-level selection pressure.
- Group selection is used to provide indirect, hierarchical selection pressure, to promote cooperative behavior in social dilemma situations [12,14].

We simulate a population where each agent is assigned one of a finite number of tags. Agents assigned the same tag are part of a group that plays an n-person social dilemma game. Population evolution takes place via tournament selection, where two individuals, possibly from different groups, are compared based on their current fitness or utility level and a clone of the better fit individual is placed in its group while the worse fit individual is eliminated. This allows for dynamic group size modifications through individual selection. Larger groups may be split probabilistically or when they reach a size threshold. This group level selection adds a second level of selection pressure on the population. Agent strategies (cooperate/defect) are fixed and not adapted or evolved.

The integration of tags for grouping, tournament selection across the population for dynamic group sizing, and a combination of individual and group selection pressures provide evolutionary pressure that can promote cooperative strategy choices in n-person social dilemma games. By combining these mechanisms, it is possible to overcome the limitations of each approach when used in isolation, thereby promoting significantly higher rates of cooperation.

Through extensive experimentation, we will demonstrate the effectiveness of our proposed novel mechanism combination for fostering cooperation emergence and stability for multiplayer variants of the Prisoner's Dilemma and Snowdrift game. We conduct an ablation study and vary various parameters, including cost/benefit ratios, cooperation threshold required for payoff, group splitting method and criteria, initial number of tag groups, etc. Our results convincingly demonstrate the robustness of our proposed approach.

2   Related Work

Tags are observable features shared by groups of similar agents [7] that allow agents to signal their intentions and infer hidden properties about others. Research using tags to limit interaction to group members typically study two-person games [6,10,13] though some researchers have applied them to n-player games [3,8]. *Hales et al.* showed that agents could sustain cooperation with strangers by biasing interactions towards others who share a common tag or "cultural marker" [6]. *McDonald and Sen* explained why relatively long tags are needed to sustain cooperation in populations and identified higher tag mutation rate as another influential parameter determining the dominant strategy in evolving populations [10].

Group selection and dynamic grouping is another approach to fostering cooperation in n-person games. *Ji et al.* studied the effects of grouping in an evolutionary n-person Snowdrift Game and found that the level of cooperation was significantly boosted when agents were grouped dynamically, as opposed to a static population of the same size [9]. *Traulsen and Nowak* proposed a minimalist stochastic model of multilevel group selection [14].

Chiong et al. found that genetic algorithms and other evolutionary approaches allow agents to learn strategies that maximize fitness according to the outcomes of repeated interactions; however, their application to the Snowdrift Game, particularly its n-player variant, has been severely limited [2].

The combined effect of tagging and group selection has not been systematically studied in n-player games and under dynamic group restructuring. We hypothesize that their synergy helps cooperators cluster and gain competitive advantage against defectors, even at higher cost-benefit ratios, due to a multilevel selection dynamic that simultaneously rewards cooperative groups and successful individuals.

3 n-Player Snowdrift Social Dilemma

In social dilemmas, individual incentives often conflict with group outcomes, leading to situations where self-interest might undermine collective welfare. One such game used to model these dynamics is the n-player Snowdrift game [4]. In the n-player Snowdrift Game, players must clear snow from a road so that they can proceed. If all players refuse to shovel the snow, i.e. they defect, then no one benefits, leading to a worse outcome for all. If all players shovel the snow, i.e. they cooperate, then they share the benefits, leading to a higher collective payoff. If some players cooperate while others defect, the cooperators still benefit but less so than if everyone had cooperated. Defectors benefit from the cooperation of others without contributing themselves. We use a standard formalization of the payoff structure for the n-player Snowdrift Game [15] and introduce two modified variants by incorporating a cooperation threshold. The payoff structure for the standard version of the n-player Snowdrift Game follows:

Payoff for defectors is b if $N_C > 0$ and 0 otherwise. Payoff for cooperators is $b - \frac{c}{N_C}$ if $N_C > 0$ and 0 otherwise, where b is the benefit, c is the cost, and N_C is the number of cooperators.

For the first variant of the n-player Snowdrift Game, including a fractional cooperation threshold, the payoff structure follows:

Payoff for defectors is b if $\frac{N_C}{N} \geq fct$ and 0 otherwise. Payoff for cooperators is $b - \frac{c}{N_C}$ if $\frac{N_C}{N} \geq fct$ and 0 otherwise, where fct is the fractional cooperation threshold and N is the number of agents.

For the second variant of the n-player Snowdrift Game, including a constant cooperation threshold, the payoff structure follows:

Payoff for defectors is b if $N_C \geq ct$ and 0 otherwise. Payoff for cooperators is $b - \frac{c}{N_C}$ if $N_C \geq ct$ and 0 otherwise, where ct is the constant constant cooperation threshold.

4   Methodology

Our simulation for tags and group selection in a social dilemma is detailed in Algorithm 1. A simulation first initializes the population with N_{Agents} agents and N_{Groups} groups. Simulations are run for $N_{Generations}$ generations, and each generation is broken into three stages:

Social Dilemma Stage (lines 5 to 9): Each group participates in an n-player social dilemma, where every agent in the group receives a reward.

Tournament Selection Stage (lines 10 to 16): Each agent competes in a tournament against a randomly selected agent from the population. The agent with the lower reward adopts the tag and strategy of the agent with the higher reward and migrates to that agent's tag group.

Group Selection Stage (lines 17 to 21): Each group is tested for selection using a group selection criterion. Let $|G|$ be the size of group G, i.e., the number of agents using the corresponding tag. The decision to split a group is based on the group size.

Two *group selection criteria* were implemented. The first criterion selects a group G if the group's size is greater than the group selection threshold, i.e., $|G| \geq gt$. The second criterion selects a group with a probability equal to the group's size divided by the group selection threshold, i,e., probability of selection group G is $\min(1, \frac{|G|}{gt})$. The selected group G is split into two groups.

One of the split groups keep the current group tag, while the other, G' migrates according to one of two *group splitting methods*. The first method is described in Algorithm 2, where an existing empty group is randomly chosen, and if no such group exists, a new empty group is created. Let G_d be this destination group which is given a tag from other tags of agents in other groups. The members of G' are relocated to the empty group G_d with no modifications to their strategy but they adopt the new tag assigned to G_d. The second method is described in Algorithm 3, where the smallest group G_s is chosen as the destination group. If $G = G_s$, the procedure terminates with no change in the groups or any migration. Otherwise, a set of agents $G' \subset G$ are migrated from G to G_s such that afterwards the two groups are approximately the same size (their sizes can differ by a maximum of one agent). Agents in G' retain their strategies but adopt the tag of G_s while each existing member of G_s randomly adopt the strategy of an agent from G'.

Algorithm 1 Use of tags and group selection in social dilemmas

---

```
 1: procedure SIMULATION(N_Agents, N_Groups, N_Generations, r, ct or fct, gt)
 2:     population ← createAgents(N_Agents)
 3:     groups ← assignGroups(population, N_Groups)
 4:     for generation = 1 to N_Generations do
 5:         for all group in groups do
 6:             actions ← getActions(group)
 7:             rewards ← socialDilemma(actions, r, ct or fct)
 8:             assignRewards(actions, rewards)
 9:         end for
10:         for all agent in population do
11:             other ← randomAgent(population)
12:             if agent.reward < other.reward then
13:                 cloneAgent(other)
14:                 deleteAgent(agent)
15:             end if
16:         end for
17:         for all group in groups do
18:             if shouldSplitGroup(group, gt) then
19:                 SPLITGROUP(groups, group)
20:             end if
21:         end for
22:     end for
23: end procedure
```

Algorithm 2 Split group into an empty group

```
1: procedure SPLITGROUPTOEMPTY(groups, group)
2:     dest ← an empty group from groups or a new group if none are empty
3:     migrants ← half of the members of group
4:     group.remove(migrants)
5:     dest.add(migrants)
6: end procedure
```

Algorithm 3 Evenly split groups into the smallest group

1: **procedure** SPLITGROUPEVENLYTOSMALLEST(groups, group)
2:     dest ← chose the smallest group from groups
3:     **if** group ≠ dest **then**
4:         migrants ← enough agents from group s.t. the number of agents in both groups are approximately equal.
5:         **for all** agent in dest **do**
6:             agent.strategy ← the strategy of an agent randomly selected from group
7:         **end for**
8:         group.remove(migrants)
9:         dest.add(migrants)
10:     **end if**
11: **end procedure**

---

5 Results

In this section, we present an overview of the typical simulation of the n-person Snowdrift game as well as the results from an ablation study and varying various parameters in our model. Unless otherwise stated, results are averaged over 100 simulations, each running for 150 generations. Simulations were initialized with 20 groups and 100 agents, using both group selection criterion 1 and group selection method 1.

5.1 Effect of Group Selection

Figure 1 shows the effect of group selection on cooperation. Without the use of group selection, cooperation can sometimes dominate in the population; however, this only occurs roughly 7% of the time.

When group selection was introduced, after 100 generations, only cooperating or defecting groups remained in 89% and 0.4% of simulations, respectively. In the remaining 10.6% cases, the population never fully converged, but more of these runs resulted in a majority of defectors. Further analysis of individual simulations suggests that group selection typically isolates groups of cooperators in the population. Once every group contains only cooperators or only defectors, cooperative group payoff dominates while group of defectors receive no payoff. Hence cooperative groups increase in size and ultimately splits and takes over smaller groups of defectors. This process is evident from generation 24 onwards in Fig. 2.

5.2 Group Cooperation Per Generation

Figure 2 illustrates a typical simulation for a Snowdrift game with parameters $r = 0.3, gt = 10, ct = 1$, employing group selection criterion 1 and group selection method 1. The figure displays the size and ratio of cooperators to defectors in each group over 50 generations. The size of a group is represented by the size of

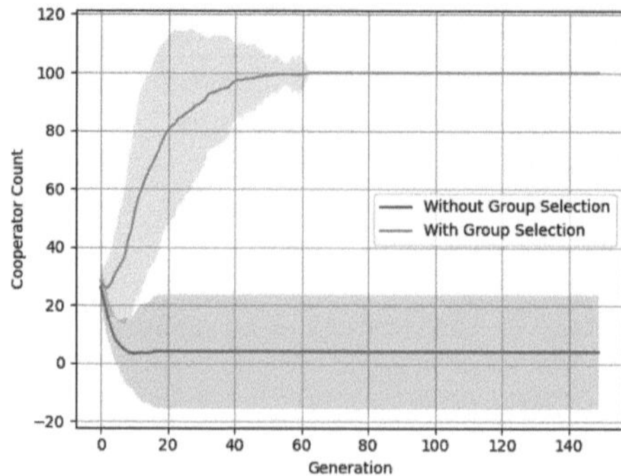

Fig. 1. Cooperation Over 150 Generations With and Without Group Selection.

its marker, while the ratio of cooperators to defectors is indicated by the marker color, with green representing cooperation and red representing defection. It should be noted that groups are sorted from largest to smallest. These results are analyzed in Sect. 6.

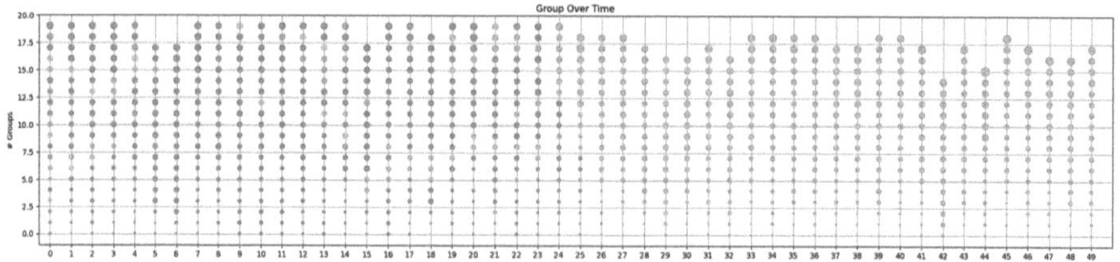

Fig. 2. Cooperation Level in Each Group Per Generation.

5.3   Varying Cost-Benefit Ratio

Figure 3 depicts the number of cooperators and total reward received across generations. Varying r does not significantly affect the final number of cooperators in the population. Additionally, the rewards in the SD game are scaled while keeping benefit costant at 1. Hence, higher total rewards are obtained with smaller values of r.

5.4   Varying the Group Split Threshold

Figure 4a shows the number of cooperators in each generation with group selection criterion 1. Figure 4b shows the cooperation rate for each generation with group selection criterion 2. Furthermore, the use of group selection criterion 2 results in more cooperators than criterion 1 in most cases. Further analysis of these results is presented in Sect. 6.

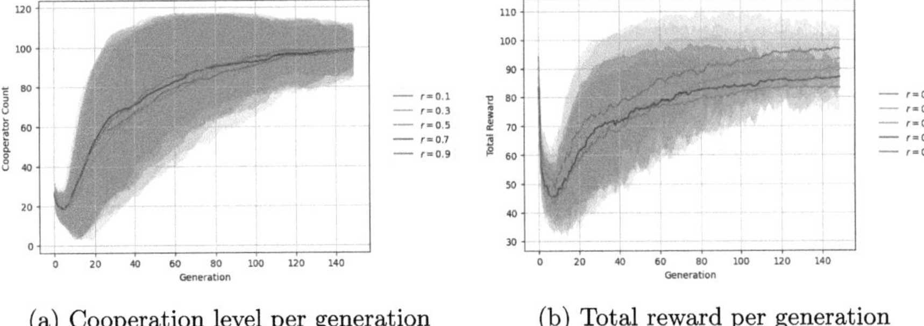

(a) Cooperation level per generation   (b) Total reward per generation

Fig. 3. Effect of r on cooperation level & reward over generations; $ct = 1$, $gt = 10$.

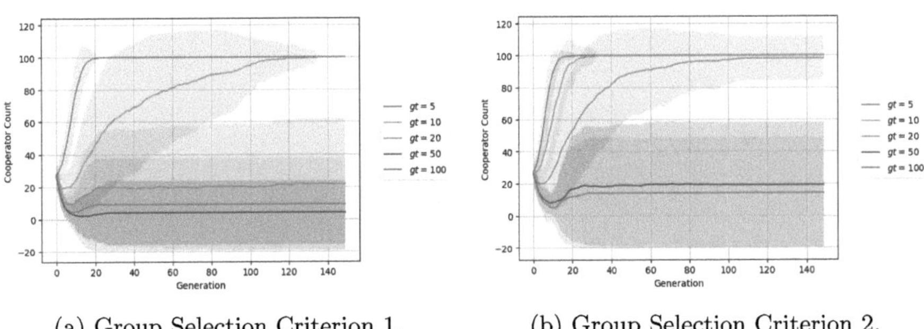

(a) Group Selection Criterion 1.   (b) Group Selection Criterion 2.

Fig. 4. Effect of gt on cooperation level over generations; $r = 0.3$, $ct = 1$.

5.5   Varying the Cooperation Threshold

We also examined the effect of varying the cooperation threshold on the number of cooperators and the total reward. Figures 5 and 6 display the cooperation rate and total reward over 150 generations given a constant cooperation threshold and a fractional cooperation threshold, respectively. In Fig. 5a , we observe that with $ct = 0$, defection prevails because cooperation is not required to receive a benefit. Furthermore, when $ct = 10$, neither cooperation nor defection emerges, as no group has enough cooperators to receive rewards. Additionally, Fig. 5a indicates that when $ct = 3$, cooperation is achieved more quickly than with $ct = 1$; however, the total reward at the end of the simulation when $ct = 1$ surpassed that achieved with $ct = 3$. Similar patterns are evident in Fig. 5b , where lower fct values lead to a delayed convergence to cooperation. These findings are discussed further in Sect. 6.

5.6   Varying Group Count and Selection Methods

We then examined the effects of varying the initial number of groups and the group selection method. Figures 7a and 7b present the number of cooperators

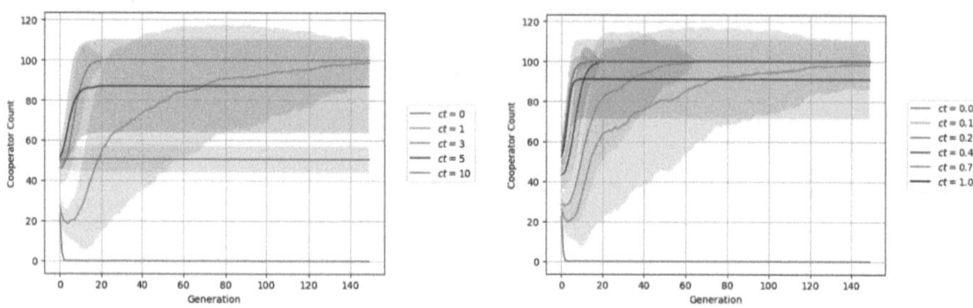

(a) Constant Cooperation Threshold.   (b) Fractional Cooperation Threshold.

Fig. 5. Effect of ct & fct on cooperation level over generations; $r = 0.3$, $gt = 10$.

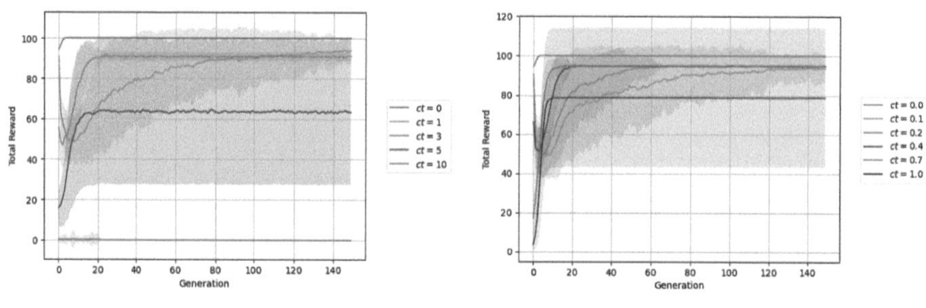

(a) Constant Cooperation Threshold.   (b) Fractional Cooperation Threshold.

Fig. 6. Effect of ct & fct on reward over generations; $r = 0.3$, $gt = 10$.

in the population across generations, varying the number of initial groups. In Fig. 7a , which employs the first group selection method described in Algorithm 2, we observe that a greater initial number of groups fosters cooperation more effectively. Notably, cooperation does not fail to emerge even when $N_{Groups} = 1$. Figure 7b employs the second group selection method described in Algorithm 3, which does not introduce new groups into the simulation as the first method does. We observe that defection is more likely to dominate when the second selection method is used. Additionally, when the population neither converges to defection nor cooperation, the number of cooperators is lower with the second group selection method. These results are further discussed and analyzed in Sect. 6.

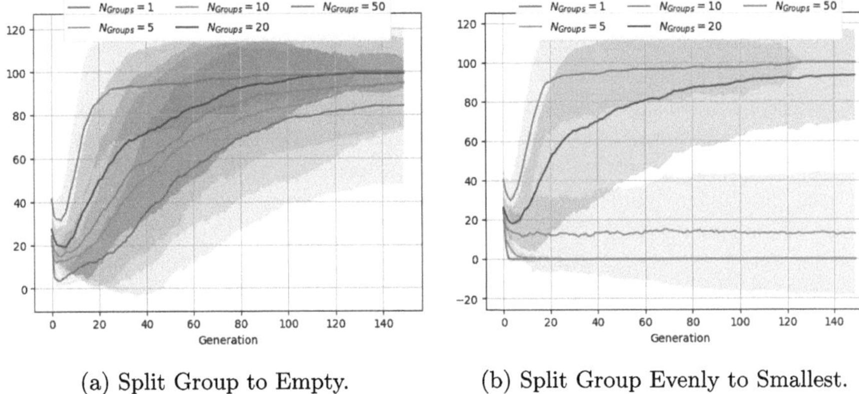

(a) Split Group to Empty.   (b) Split Group Evenly to Smallest.

Fig. 7. Cooperators over generations varying N_{Groups} and group selection method. $r = 0.35$, $ct = 1$, $gt = 10$.

6 Discussion

The results from our simulations suggest that the combination of tagging and group selection mechanisms can significantly promote the emergence of cooperation in the n-player Snowdrift game. While our findings align with prior research that highlights the importance of both mechanisms separately, we show that their combined integration leads to robust cooperation across a variety of parameters and conditions.

Figure 2 illustrates the cooperation levels across generations for each group in a simulation. Most groups are initially well-mixed, with neither cooperators nor defectors in the majority. Shortly thereafter, defectors begin to take over, with only one or two groups maintaining a majority of cooperators. As long as other groups are mixed, defectors benefit at the expense of cooperators in those groups. Those defectors are selected by tournament selection, which causes the group to grow and eventually split. But once all of the mixed groups become devoid of cooperators, groups of defectors loses competitive advantage compared to any remaining group of cooperators. Beyond this point, e.g., generation 24 in Fig. 2, groups of cooperators begin to proliferate and eventually replaces all groups of defectors in the population.

A parameter sweep over group split threshold gt reveals that smaller values of gt are much more conducive to cooperation in social dilemma games, as shown in Fig. 4a . This differential between small and large group split thresholds is not unexpected; as groups grow larger, they begin to behave like a single population, which has been shown to not promote cooperation effectively [15].

As shown in Fig. 5, cooperation emerges consistently for reasonable values of the cooperation threshold, ct. However, when ct is too large, it either slows the convergence toward total cooperation or prevents it altogether. This is to be expected as would result in many groups being unable to ever meet that threshold. When using a fractional threshold, however, even when $fct = 1.0$—meaning the entire group must cooperate—cooperation still emerges! This happens because the population is able to preserve fully cooperative groups.

Our final experiments examined the effects of varying the initial number of groups, N_{groups}, using two group selection methods: Algorithm 2, where groups split into empty ones by either locating an existing empty group or creating a new one, and Algorithm 3, which splits groups evenly and takes over existing groups. When using Algorithm 2, the SD game achieved high levels of cooperation for every value of N_{groups}, with a larger number of initial groups leading to slightly higher cooperation levels occurring in less generations. When using Algorithm 3, results show a notable decline in cooperator counts for smaller initial number of groups. Moreover, for a given value of N_{groups}, the proportion of cooperators tends to be lower with Algorithm 3. This difference perhaps stems from how the even splitting of groups in Algorithm 3 can only take over existing groups, whereas Algorithm 2 can create new groups and allows many groups of cooperators to grow simultaneously.

7   Conclusion and Future Work

We examined the effects of tag-based grouping, tournament selection, and group selection mechanisms on the emergence of cooperation in the multi-player Snowdrift game. Results show that combining these approaches engenders cooperative behavior in the Snowdrift game. Cooperation consistently emerges across a number of cost-benefit ratios, group split thresholds, and cooperation thresholds.

The following are some interesting research directions that we plan to pursue:

- We will compare the relative success of fitness proportionate selection Vs tournament selection in creating individual selection pressure.
- We will incorporate tag mutation, or random migration between groups, and observe concomitant effects on rate and success of cooperation emergence.
- We plan to evaluate a process for "voting to evict" individuals, where individuals in a group can vote on evicting one of their members from the group.
- Conversely, individuals may leave a group with subset of other group members. These approaches are complementary to, the current group splitting mechanism.
- Individuals may also decide to migrate to another group, but members of that group to vote to accept or deny the migrating individual from entering.

Disclosure of Interests. The authors have no competing interests to declare that are relevant to the content of this article.

References

1. Archetti, M., Scheuring, I.: Review: Game theory of public goods in one-shot social dilemmas without assortment. J. Theor. Biol. **299**, 9–20 (2012)
2. Chiong, R., Kirley, M.: Effects of iterated interactions in multiplayer spatial evolutionary games. IEEE Trans. Evol. Comput. **16**(4), 537–555 (2012)
3. Dhakal, S., Chiong, R., Chica, M., Han, T.A.: Evolution of cooperation and trust in an n-player social dilemma game with tags for migration decisions. Royal Soc. Open Sci. **9**(5), 212000 (2022)
4. Doebeli, M., Hauert, C.: Models of cooperation based on the prisoner's dilemma and the snowdrift game. Ecol. Lett. **8**(7), 748–766 (2005)
5. Gross, J., De Dreu, C.K.W.: The rise and fall of cooperation through reputation and group polarization. Nat. Commun. **10** (2019)
6. Hales, D., Edmonds, B.: Evolving social rationality for mas using "tags". In: Proceedings of the Second International Joint Conference on Autonomous Agents and Multiagent Systems. pp. 497–503 (2003)
7. Hamilton, W.D.: The genetical evolution of social behaviour. ii. J. Theo. Biol. **7**(1), 17–52 (1964)
8. Howley, E., Duggan, J.: The evolution of cooperation and investment strategies in a commons dilemma. In: Learning Agents Workshop at AAMAS. Citeseer (2010)
9. Ji, M., Xu, C., Hui, P.M.: Effects of dynamical grouping on cooperation in n-person evolutionary snowdrift game. Phys. Rev. E **84**(3), 036113 (2011)
10. McDonald, A., Sen, S.: The success and failure of tag-mediated evolution of cooperation. In: Tuyls, K., Hoen, P.J., Verbeeck, K., Sen, S. (eds.) Learning and Adaption in Multi-Agent Systems, Lecture Notes in Computer Science, vol. 3898, pp. 155–164. Springer, Berlin, Heidelberg (2006). https://doi.org/10.1007/11691839_9
11. Miller, B.L., Goldberg, D.E., et al.: Genetic algorithms, tournament selection, and the effects of noise. Complex Sys. **9**(3), 193–212 (1995)
12. Nowak, M.A.: Five rules for the evolution of cooperation. Science **314**(5805), 1560–1563 (2006)
13. Riolo, R.: The effects of tag-mediated selection of partners in evolving populations playing the iterated prisoner's dilemma (1997). Accessed 14 Oct 2024
14. Traulsen, A.: Evolution of cooperation by multilevel selection. Proc. Natl. Acad. Sci. **103**(29), 10952–10955 (2006)
15. Zheng, D.F., Yin, H.P., Chan, C.H., Hui, P.M.: Cooperative behavior in a model of evolutionary snowdrift games with n-person interactions. EPL **80**(1), 18002 (2007)

Author Index

A
Ahrweiler, Petra   45
Arnejo, Zenith   28

B
Bantayan, Nathaniel   28
Bashiri, Hassan   45
Beaird, Ethan   170
Bicket, Martha   45
Bodini, Déborah   89

C
Cao, Yongcan   128
Capellas, Blanca Luque   45
Cofield, Jeremy   128
Cueille, Elisa   89

F
Fabris, Bertilla   59

G
Gaudou, Benoit   28, 89
Gilbert, Nigel   45
Grancher, Delphine   89

I
Islam, Kazi Ashik   158

K
Kovács, Bertold B.   77

L
Lin, Keng-Lien   143
Lorig, Fabian   59

M
Mensfelt, Agnieszka   15
Mortveit, Henning S.   158

N
Naghizadeh, Parinaz   143
Nicolle, Pierre   89

P
Parunak, H. Van Dyke   3
Payrastre, Olivier   89
Pittenger, William   170
Prédhumeau, Manon   89

R
Raj, Ebin Deni   45
Ravi, S. S.   158
Ruin, Isabelle   89

S
Sabater Coll, Albert   45
Saqalli, Mehdi   28
Sen, Sandip   170
Siddique, Umer   128
Spaeth, Elisabeth   45
Stathis, Kostas   15
Swarup, Samarth   158

T
Terti, Galateia   89
Trencsenyi, Vince   15
Tucker, Jason   59

V
Verstaevel, Nicolas   89
Vidler, Alicia   107

W
Walsh, Toby   107

Y
Yorke-Smith, Neil   77